Basic CPT/HCPCS Coding

2004 Edition

Gail I. Smith, MA, RHIA, CCS-P

AHiMA
American Health Information
Management Association®

CPT five-digit codes, nomenclature, and other data are copyright 2003, American Medical Association. All Rights Reserved. No fee schedules, basic unit, relative values, or related listings are included in CPT.

The AMA assumes no liability for the data contained herein.

First edition 1987, revised annually

ISBN 1-58426-137-4
AHIMA Product No. AC200604 (without answer key)
AHIMA Product No. AC200604K (with answer key)
Production No. IPC 5700-1103

Ann Zeisset, RHIT, CCS, CCS-P, Reviewer
Katherine Kerpan, Project Editor
Dana G. Carman, Production Editor

American Health Information Management Association
233 North Michigan Avenue, Suite 2150
Chicago, Illinois 60601-5800

http://www.ahima.org

Contents

About the Author

Gail I. Smith, MA, RHIA, CCS-P, is program chair of the health information management program at Cincinnati State Technical and Community College in Cincinnati, Ohio. She has been an HIM professional and educator for more than thirty years. Prior to joining the faculty at Cincinnati State, she was director of health information management in a multihospital healthcare system.

Ms. Smith also is a coding consultant and a frequent presenter at conferences throughout the United States. An active member of the American Health Information Management Association, she has served on several of its committees and task forces. Currently, she is a member of the panel of reviewers for the Council on Accreditation and serves on its board of directors.

Ms. Smith received a bachelor of science degree in health information management from The Ohio State University in Columbus and a master of arts degree in education from The College of Mt. St. Joseph in Cincinnati.

Preface

This edition of *Basic CPT/HCPCS Coding* has been written for students who have no prior CPT coding knowledge or experience. The material is not specific to any particular practice setting but, rather, applies to both hospital-based and physician-based coding. The exercises provide hands-on coding experience for some of the more common ambulatory procedures and services. Because many healthcare facilities and providers use a systematic method for assigning CPT codes to frequently encountered diagnostic tests, the exercises for those chapters are minimal.

The coding process involves a combination of skills that are developed throughout this workbook. In addition to those skills, students must apply knowledge of medical terminology, body systems, disease processes, and operative procedures. The author has established the following objectives to assist students as they use this book:

- To provide a basic introduction to CPT coding format and conventions

- To demonstrate different ways to locate CPT codes using the index

- To illustrate how to apply coding guidelines to ensure accurate code assignment

- To identify the documentation necessary for code assignment

Chapter 1, Introduction to CPT and HCPCS, discusses the purpose and different levels of HCPCS codes and addresses diagnostic coding and Medicare requirements for claims submission.

Chapter 2, Procedural Terminology in Current Use, introduces the applications and conventions of CPT coding.

Chapter 3, Modifiers, provides an overview of the use of CPT and HCPCS Level II modifiers.

Chapter 4, Surgery, reviews coding guidelines associated with surgical procedures commonly performed in the ambulatory setting.

Chapter 5, Radiology, discusses hospital and physician billing and radiology code reporting.

Chapter 6, Pathology and Laboratory, addresses the intricacies related to the code assignment of common radiological, pathological, and laboratory tests and procedures.

Chapter 7, Evaluation and Management Services, provides a concise explanation of this section of CPT and offers directed exercises designed to address the complexities of assigning evaluation and management (E/M) codes.

Chapter 8, Medicine, provides a general overview of common procedures and services found in the medicine chapter of the CPT codebook.

Chapter 9, Anesthesia, introduces the codes used by physicians who provide or supervise anesthesia services.

Chapter 10, HCPCS Levels II and III, reviews the format and usage of HCPCS National Codes and modifiers.

Chapter 11, Reimbursement in the Ambulatory Setting, addresses ambulatory reimbursement, which is built on correct CPT code assignment. A skills practice at the end of this chapter asks students to review sections of a CMS-1500 form to determine the accuracy of code assignment. This practice reinforces the students' understanding of previously discussed coding principles and guidelines.

This 2004 edition of the publication has been expanded and updated in the following manner:

- Chapter 7, Evaluation and Management Services, has been moved from its position in previous editions to better match existing instructional use of this publication.

- A new Web resources section has been added to the end of the book so that users are alerted to online sites offering additional guidance, various coding, medical, and health topics.

- A new glossary of terms has been added.

- Existing exercises have been revised and many additional exercises have been added throughout the publication.

- Based on user feedback, a number of text sections have been revised or enhanced to increase clarity and reader understanding.

This book must be used with the current edition of *Current Procedural Terminology (CPT 2004)* (code changes effective January 1, 2004), published by the American Medical Association. The HCPCS Level II codes included in this publication are current as of October 1, 2003. In addition, a file containing the most current versions of the HCPCS Level II codes can be found under the "Utilities/Miscellaneous" heading at the following CMS Web site: www.cms.gov/providers/pufdownload/.

Students beginning a CPT course of study should have several additional references to assist with the task of code assignment. Suggested references and recommended readings that may be helpful to students are provided at the back of this workbook.

Chapter 7 of this publication reflects the Evaluation and Management Documentation Guidelines developed jointly in 1997 by the AMA and the Centers for Medicare and Medicaid Services (CMS), formerly known as the Health Care Financing Administration (HCFA). For additional information on these guidelines or to check for additional revisions, visit the CMS Web page at www.cms.gov.

The Web sites listed in this book were current and valid as of the date of publication. However, Web page addresses and the information on them may change or disappear at any time and for any number of reasons. The user is encouraged to perform his or her own general Web searches to locate any site addresses listed here that are no longer valid.

Notes to educators:

The HCPCS Level II codes included in this publication are current as of October 1, 2003. A file containing the most current versions of the HCPCS Level II codes can be found under the "Utilities/Miscellaneous" heading at the following CMS Web site: www.cms.gov/providers/pufdownload/.

Instructor materials for this book include chapter plans, chapter slides, and other useful resources. The instructor materials are available in online format through the Assembly on Education (AOE) Community of Practice (CoP). Instructors who are AHIMA members can sign up for this private community by clicking on the help icon within the CoP home page and requesting additional information on becoming an AOE CoP member. An instructor who is not an AHIMA member or an AHIMA member who is not an instructor may contact the publisher at publications@ahima.org. The instructor materials are not available to students enrolled in college or university programs.

Acknowledgments

AHIMA wishes to acknowledge Rita A. Scichilone, MHSA, RHIA, CCS, CCS-P, CHC; the late Rita Finnegan, RHIA, CCS; and Toula Nicholas, RHIT, CCS, CCS-P, who served as authors of previous editions of *CPT/HCPCS Basic Coding,* as well as the many internal and external reviewers who have contributed throughout the years to this publication.

In addition, AHIMA wishes to thank the following individuals who provided extensive suggestions for improving the 2004 edition of this publication:

- Jill Buathier, RHIA, CPHQ, Chair, Health Information Technology Program, Owens Community College, Toledo, Ohio

- Kelly C. Dale, RHIA, Instructor, Medical Office Careers, St. Paul College, St. Paul, Minnesota

- Therese M. Jorwic, RHIA, CCS, Assistant Professor, Health Information Management Program, University of Illinois at Chicago; Senior Consultant, MC Strategies, Atlanta, Georgia

- Lou Ann Schraffenberger, RHIA, CCS, CCS-P, Manager of Clinical Data/Clinical Information Services, Advocate Health Care/Oak Brook Support Center, Oak Brook, Illinois

Chapter 1

Introduction to CPT and HCPCS

Accurate coding is the cornerstone of information management in today's expanding menu of outpatient services provided in healthcare settings. The coding systems required for data processing and physician reimbursement in these settings are described in two books: *Current Procedural Terminology (CPT),* published by the American Medical Association (AMA), and *Healthcare Common Procedure Coding System (HCPCS),* published by the Centers for Medicare and Medicaid Services (CMS). The CMS is the division of the U.S. Department of Health and Human Services that is responsible for the Medicare program. The information conveyed by CPT/HCPCS codes is used for multiple purposes, including:

- Reimbursement
- Trending
- Planning
- Benchmarking
- Measurement of care quality

Health record documentation continues to play a pivotal role in the accurate and complete collection of health services data. The documentation records pertinent facts, findings, and observations about an individual's health history, including past and current illnesses, examinations, tests, treatments, and outcomes. By chronologically documenting the patient's care, the health record becomes an important element in the provision of high-quality healthcare and serves as the source document for code assignment.

The following general principles of health record documentation, developed jointly by the AMA and the CMS, apply to all types of medical and surgical services:

- The medical record should be complete and legible.
- The documentation of each patient encounter should include:

    —Reason for the encounter and relevant history, physical examination findings, and prior diagnostic test results

    —Assessment, clinical impression, or diagnosis

    —Plan for care

    —Date and legible identity of observer

- If not documented, the rationale for ordering diagnostic and other ancillary services should be easily inferred.

- Past and present diagnoses should be accessible to the treating and/or consulting physician.

- Appropriate health risk factors should be identified.

- The patient's progress, response to and changes in treatment, and revision of diagnosis should be documented.

- The CPT and ICD-9-CM codes reported on health insurance claim forms or billing statements should be supported by documentation in the health record.

Additional documentation guidelines pertinent to evaluation and management (E/M) services are discussed in chapter 7 of this book. Various links pertinent to information discussed in this chapter are listed in the Web Resources at the back of this book.

Development of HCPCS

In 1983, the CMS developed HCPCS to report physician and nonphysician services provided to Medicare and Medicaid patients. The primary purpose of the HCPCS coding system is to meet the operational needs of Medicare and Medicaid reimbursement programs. The codes enable providers and suppliers to accurately communicate the services they provide, allow carriers to establish controls to prevent escalation of program payments, and permit uniform application of CMS coverage and reimbursement policies.

Examples of HCPCS Level II codes include the following:

- A4550   Surgical trays
- E1625   Water softening system, for hemodialysis
- J0475   Injection, baclofen, 10 mg
- L3260   Ambulatory surgical boot, each

Since 1985, the federal government has required physicians to use HCPCS codes to report services provided to Medicare patients, and in October 1986, the CMS required physicians to use HCPCS codes to report services provided to Medicaid patients.

Moreover, with implementation of the Omnibus Reconciliation Act of 1986 (OBRA 86), hospitals were required to use HCPCS codes when reporting ambulatory surgery, radiology, and other diagnostic services.

Composition of HCPCS

HCPCS includes three separate levels of codes:

1. Level I: Current Procedural Terminology (CPT)

2. Level II: National Codes

3. Level III: Local Codes (CMS is in the process of eliminating certain unofficial Local Codes.)

Copyrighted and published by the AMA, Level I of HCPCS (CPT) codes are five-digit codes used by physicians to report services such as hospital visits, surgeries, radiological procedures, and supervisory and other services. Hospitals also use CPT codes to report hospital-based outpatient services, such as laboratory and radiological procedures and ambulatory surgeries, to Medicare and other third-party payers. CPT codes represent approximately 80 percent of the HCPCS codes submitted for reimbursement. CPT codes are updated annually, with additions, revisions, and deletions becoming effective each January. A new CPT codebook is published every year. To ensure accurate coding, the new edition should be purchased every year.

Known as the National Codes, Level II HCPCS codes were developed by the CMS to report services not found in CPT, such as injectable drugs, ambulance services, prosthetic devices, and selected provider services. Like CPT codes, Level II HCPCS codes are updated annually in January. The HCPCS Level II codes included in this publication are current as of October 1, 2003. A listing of these five-digit, alphanumeric codes may be purchased from the U.S. Government Printing Office or any local Medicare carrier. Several publishing firms offer the National Codes as books, which are user-friendly because of enhancements such as indexing and cross-referencing. In addition, a file containing the most current versions of the HCPCS Level II codes can be found under the "Utilities/Miscellaneous" heading at the following CMS Web site: www.cms.gov/providers/pufdownload/. HCPCS level II codes are discussed further in chapter 10.

Level III HCPCS codes are referred to as Local Codes. Each local Medicare and/or Medicaid carrier develops its own version of the Local Codes, which then are available for use in that carrier's particular geographic area. Like the Level II codes, these five-digit codes are alphanumeric and available in computer-generated lists from the individual carrier. Revisions or updates were published in that carrier's manuals and newsletters. Some nongovernment health plans have adopted codes that resemble HCPCS codes with an alphanumeric number that begins with W, X, Y, or Z. The Health Insurance Portability and Accountability Act of 1996 (HIPAA) requires that there be nationally standardized procedure coding. To comply with this act, the CMS will eliminate the use of HCPCS Level III local procedure and modifier codes on December 31, 2003.

Diagnostic Coding

Whereas HCPCS codes describe physician and nonphysician services, codes from the *International Classification of Diseases, Ninth Revision, Clinical Modification (ICD-9-CM)*, identify the symptoms, conditions, diagnoses, diseases, or other reasons why a patient may seek care. Claim forms for all outpatient services must contain at least one ICD-9-CM code.

However, caution must be exercised to ensure complete and accurate code reporting. ICD-9-CM codes must be reported at the highest level of specificity, based on the documentation in the health record. Medicare and most other third-party payers reject claims that include incomplete ICD-9-CM codes.

Example:

250.00	Diabetes mellitus without mention of complication, Type II or unspecified type, not stated as uncontrolled	**Correct**
250.0	Diabetes mellitus without mention of complication, Type II or unspecified type, not stated as uncontrolled	**Incorrect**
250	Diabetes mellitus without mention of complication, Type II or unspecified type, not stated as uncontrolled	**Incorrect**

Inpatient ICD-9 Dx & Px

Outpatient ICD9- Dx CPT· Px

Official ICD-9-CM Coding Guidelines for Outpatient Services was developed in 1990 and revised in 1995 and 2002. Coders must thoroughly understand and follow these guidelines to submit accurate and complete ICD-9-CM codes. Official ICD-9-CM coding advice is published by the American Hospital Association (AHA) in its monthly publication, *Coding Clinic.*

ICD-9-CM codes are evaluated annually, and appropriate revisions are implemented on October 1 of each year. To ensure the submission of complete and accurate claims, all ICD-9-CM codebooks must be purchased or updated yearly (for example, by replacing individual loose-leaf pages in codebooks maintained in binders). In addition, all coding software, such as encoders, must be updated.

For a more detailed discussion of the basics of ICD-9-CM coding and for exercises designed to help learn the system, consult *Basic ICD-9-CM Coding,* by Lou Ann Schraffenberger, MBA, RHIA, CCS, CCS-P, which is published by the American Health Information Management Association (AHIMA).

In the near future, the ICD-10-CM coding system is expected to replace the ICD-9-CM system in the United States. ICD-10, which is a revised classification system for morbidity and mortality coding, is already in use in other countries. Coding professionals must stay attuned to regulatory changes that affect coding systems.

Medicare Requirements

The Social Security Act contains the federal laws governing Medicare. These laws require carriers to capture the following coded data on Medicare patients:

- Claims submitted by hospitals for inpatient services: ICD-9-CM diagnosis and procedure codes

- Claims submitted by hospitals for ambulatory patients, including laboratory and radiology services: ICD-9-CM diagnosis codes and HCPCS procedure codes

- Claims submitted by hospitals, physicians, or other organizations for physician or other allied health professional services: ICD-9-CM diagnosis codes and (regardless of location of service) HCPCS procedure codes

Claims Submission

The CMS-1500 form shown in figure 1.1 is the standard billing document used when physician claims are submitted on paper for Medicare Part B, as well as when they are submitted to many private health insurance companies and Medicaid agencies. All CMS forms also may be accessed on the Web by following the links and instructions at www.cms.hhs.gov/providers/edi/edi5.asp.

Up to four diagnosis codes may be reported in field location 21 of this form; information on the service or procedure provided is reported in field location 24. Up to six HCPCS codes may be reported in column D of field location 24; in column E, the diagnosis codes are linked with the related HCPCS codes by placing a number (1, 2, 3, or 4) to show which diagnosis code is related to the procedure.

Coders must be sure that any linking of the ICD-9-CM diagnosis code with the HCPCS procedure code is logical and appropriate.

Figure 1.1. Sample CMS-1500 form

PLEASE
DO NOT
STAPLE
IN THIS
AREA

CARRIER

| | PICA | | HEALTH INSURANCE CLAIM FORM | PICA | |

HEALTH INSURANCE CLAIM FORM

		PICA

1. MEDICARE ☐ (Medicare #)   MEDICAID ☐ (Medicaid #)   CHAMPUS ☐ (Sponsor's SSN)   CHAMPVA ☐ (VA File #)   GROUP HEALTH PLAN ☐ (SSN or ID)   FECA BLK LUNG ☐ (SSN)   OTHER ☐ (ID) | 1a. INSURED'S I.D. NUMBER   (FOR PROGRAM IN ITEM 1)

2. PATIENT'S NAME (Last Name, First Name, Middle Initial) | 3. PATIENT'S BIRTH DATE MM | DD | YY   SEX   M ☐   F ☐ | 4. INSURED'S NAME (Last Name, First Name, Middle Initial)

5. PATIENT'S ADDRESS (No., Street) | 6. PATIENT RELATIONSHIP TO INSURED   Self ☐   Spouse ☐   Child ☐   Other ☐ | 7. INSURED'S ADDRESS (No., Street)

CITY | STATE | 8. PATIENT STATUS   Single ☐   Married ☐   Other ☐ | CITY | STATE

ZIP CODE   TELEPHONE (Include Area Code) ( ) | Employed ☐   Full-Time Student ☐   Part-Time Student ☐ | ZIP CODE   TELEPHONE (INCLUDE AREA CODE) ( )

9. OTHER INSURED'S NAME (Last Name, First Name, Middle Initial) | 10. IS PATIENT'S CONDITION RELATED TO: | 11. INSURED'S POLICY GROUP OR FECA NUMBER

a. OTHER INSURED'S POLICY OR GROUP NUMBER | a. EMPLOYMENT? (CURRENT OR PREVIOUS) ☐ YES ☐ NO | a. INSURED'S DATE OF BIRTH MM | DD | YY   SEX   M ☐   F ☐

b. OTHER INSURED'S DATE OF BIRTH MM | DD | YY   SEX   M ☐   F ☐ | b. AUTO ACCIDENT?   PLACE (State) ☐ YES ☐ NO | b. EMPLOYER'S NAME OR SCHOOL NAME

c. EMPLOYER'S NAME OR SCHOOL NAME | c. OTHER ACCIDENT? ☐ YES ☐ NO | c. INSURANCE PLAN NAME OR PROGRAM NAME

d. INSURANCE PLAN NAME OR PROGRAM NAME | 10d. RESERVED FOR LOCAL USE | d. IS THERE ANOTHER HEALTH BENEFIT PLAN? ☐ YES ☐ NO *If yes, return to and complete item 9 a-d.*

READ BACK OF FORM BEFORE COMPLETING & SIGNING THIS FORM.
12. PATIENT'S OR AUTHORIZED PERSON'S SIGNATURE I authorize the release of any medical or other information necessary to process this claim. I also request payment of government benefits either to myself or to the party who accepts assignment below.

SIGNED _____ DATE _____

13. INSURED'S OR AUTHORIZED PERSON'S SIGNATURE I authorize payment of medical benefits to the undersigned physician or supplier for services described below.

SIGNED _____

PATIENT AND INSURED INFORMATION

14. DATE OF CURRENT: MM | DD | YY   ◄ ILLNESS (First symptom) OR INJURY (Accident) OR PREGNANCY(LMP) | 15. IF PATIENT HAS HAD SAME OR SIMILAR ILLNESS. GIVE FIRST DATE MM | DD | YY | 16. DATES PATIENT UNABLE TO WORK IN CURRENT OCCUPATION MM | DD | YY   FROM   TO MM | DD | YY

17. NAME OF REFERRING PHYSICIAN OR OTHER SOURCE | 17a. I.D. NUMBER OF REFERRING PHYSICIAN | 18. HOSPITALIZATION DATES RELATED TO CURRENT SERVICES MM | DD | YY   FROM   TO MM | DD | YY

19. RESERVED FOR LOCAL USE | | 20. OUTSIDE LAB? ☐ YES ☐ NO $ CHARGES

21. DIAGNOSIS OR NATURE OF ILLNESS OR INJURY. (RELATE ITEMS 1,2,3 OR 4 TO ITEM 24E BY LINE) ↓
1. |___.__   3. |___.__
2. |___.__   4. |___.__ | 22. MEDICAID RESUBMISSION CODE   ORIGINAL REF. NO.

23. PRIOR AUTHORIZATION NUMBER

24.	A DATE(S) OF SERVICE From MM DD YY To MM DD YY	B Place of Service	C Type of Service	D PROCEDURES, SERVICES, OR SUPPLIES (Explain Unusual Circumstances) CPT/HCPCS	MODIFIER	E DIAGNOSIS CODE	F $ CHARGES	G DAYS OR UNITS	H EPSDT Family Plan	I EMG	J COB	K RESERVED FOR LOCAL USE
1												
2												
3												
4												
5												
6												

PHYSICIAN OR SUPPLIER INFORMATION

25. FEDERAL TAX I.D. NUMBER   SSN ☐ EIN ☐ | 26. PATIENT'S ACCOUNT NO. | 27. ACCEPT ASSIGNMENT? (For govt. claims, see back) ☐ YES ☐ NO | 28. TOTAL CHARGE $ | 29. AMOUNT PAID $ | 30. BALANCE DUE $

31. SIGNATURE OF PHYSICIAN OR SUPPLIER INCLUDING DEGREES OR CREDENTIALS (I certify that the statements on the reverse apply to this bill and are made a part thereof.)

SIGNED _____ DATE _____ | 32. NAME AND ADDRESS OF FACILITY WHERE SERVICES WERE RENDERED (If other than home or office) | 33. PHYSICIAN'S, SUPPLIER'S BILLING NAME, ADDRESS, ZIP CODE & PHONE #

PIN# _____ GRP# _____

(APPROVED BY AMA COUNCIL ON MEDICAL SERVICE 8/88)   *PLEASE PRINT OR TYPE*   APPROVED OMB-0938-0008 FORM CMS-1500 (12-90), FORM RRB-1500, APPROVED OMB-1215-0055 FORM OWCP-1500,   APPROVED OMB-0720-0001 (CHAMPUS)

Example: Patient's chief complaint is lower leg pain. The physician orders a lower leg X ray and an EKG. The lower leg pain is linked with the X ray, but there is no logical symptom or diagnosis to link with the EKG. Review of the health record may reveal an existing condition, such as premature ventricular contractions, or a symptom, such as tachycardia. Documentation must support the procedure or service provided; otherwise, the claim will be denied.

Third-party payers often have specific diagnosis requirements, depending on the service, procedure, or test provided, that indicate medical necessity. These requirements are issued as Local Medical Review Policies (LMRPs). A list of policies can be found on the Web at http://www.cms.hhs.gov/mcd (Medicare Coverage Database). For an example of an LMRP, the following policy was located on the Web site for the Ohio fiscal intermediary (Adminastar Federal):

Example: CPT code 55873 for Cryosurgery of the Prostate Gland is covered by Medicare only if the diagnosis code of 185 for malignant neoplasm of the prostate appears on the claim form.

The CMS-1450 form, better known as UB-92 (figure 1.2), is used primarily by hospitals (for both outpatient and inpatient services) and ambulatory surgery centers (ASCs) to submit claims to Medicare for Part A services and to other insurance companies.

Up to nine diagnosis codes can be reported in field locations 67 through 75 and six ICD-9-CM procedure codes in field locations 80 and 81. HCPCS codes (for outpatient services including surgery) are reported in field location 44. Required modifiers are appended to the HCPCS code in this field location. Up to two modifiers may be used to provide additional information about the HCPCS codes on the claim form for Medicare patients. Field locator 76 is for admitting diagnosis and 77 is for E-code reporting.

Figure 1.2. Sample UB-92 (CMS-1450) form

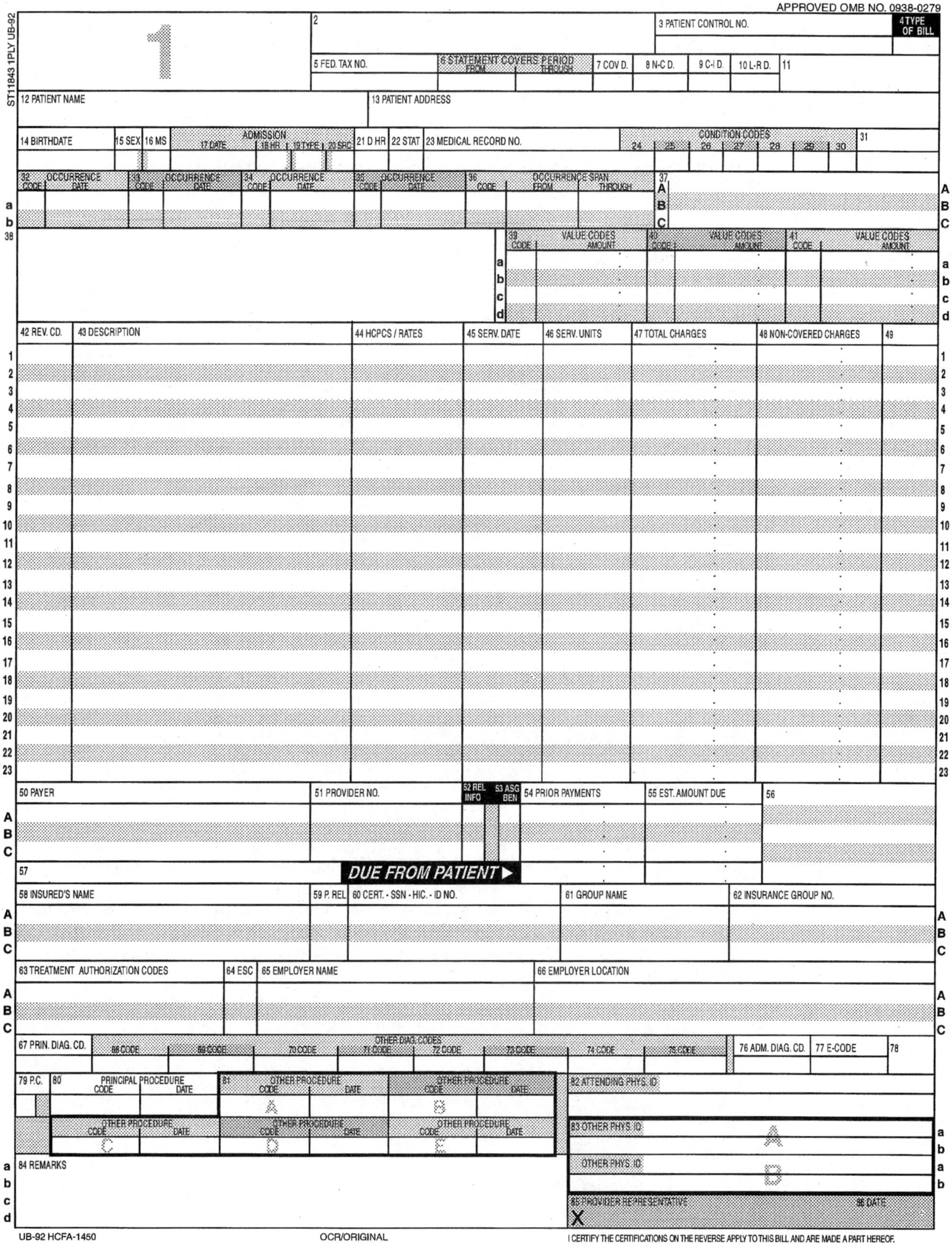
APPROVED OMB NO. 0938-0279

ST11843 1PLY UB-92

1

2

3 PATIENT CONTROL NO.

4 TYPE OF BILL

5 FED. TAX NO.

6 STATEMENT COVERS PERIOD FROM THROUGH

7 COV D. 8 N-C D. 9 C-I D. 10 L-R D. 11

12 PATIENT NAME

13 PATIENT ADDRESS

14 BIRTHDATE 15 SEX 16 MS ADMISSION 17 DATE 18 HR 19 TYPE 20 SRC 21 D HR 22 STAT 23 MEDICAL RECORD NO.

CONDITION CODES 24 25 26 27 28 29 30 31

32 OCCURRENCE CODE DATE 33 OCCURRENCE CODE DATE 34 OCCURRENCE CODE DATE 35 OCCURRENCE CODE DATE 36 OCCURRENCE SPAN CODE FROM THROUGH 37 A B C

38

39 VALUE CODES CODE AMOUNT 40 VALUE CODES CODE AMOUNT 41 VALUE CODES CODE AMOUNT

42 REV. CD. 43 DESCRIPTION 44 HCPCS / RATES 45 SERV. DATE 46 SERV. UNITS 47 TOTAL CHARGES 48 NON-COVERED CHARGES 49

1–23

50 PAYER 51 PROVIDER NO. 52 REL INFO 53 ASG BEN 54 PRIOR PAYMENTS 55 EST. AMOUNT DUE 56

57 DUE FROM PATIENT ▶

58 INSURED'S NAME 59 P. REL 60 CERT. - SSN - HIC. - ID NO. 61 GROUP NAME 62 INSURANCE GROUP NO.

63 TREATMENT AUTHORIZATION CODES 64 ESC 65 EMPLOYER NAME 66 EMPLOYER LOCATION

67 PRIN. DIAG. CD. OTHER DIAG. CODES 68 CODE 69 CODE 70 CODE 71 CODE 72 CODE 73 CODE 74 CODE 75 CODE 76 ADM. DIAG. CD. 77 E-CODE 78

79 P.C. 80 PRINCIPAL PROCEDURE CODE DATE 81 OTHER PROCEDURE CODE DATE A OTHER PROCEDURE CODE DATE B 82 ATTENDING PHYS. ID

OTHER PROCEDURE CODE DATE C OTHER PROCEDURE CODE DATE D OTHER PROCEDURE CODE DATE E 83 OTHER PHYS. ID A OTHER PHYS. ID B

84 REMARKS

85 PROVIDER REPRESENTATIVE X 86 DATE

UB-92 HCFA-1450 OCR/ORIGINAL

I CERTIFY THE CERTIFICATIONS ON THE REVERSE APPLY TO THIS BILL AND ARE MADE A PART HEREOF.

Exercise 1.1

Review each question and write the appropriate answer in the space provided.

1. What organizations are responsible for updating CPT codes and HCPCS Level II codes?

   _____

2. How many diagnosis codes may be submitted on the CMS-1500 form?

   _____

3. Which coding system(s) is/are used for claims submitted by physicians?

   _____

4. Dr. Smith saw a Medicare patient with a diagnosis of rectal abscess in Central Hospital. She performs an incision and drainage in the outpatient surgery department.

   A. Identify the coding system(s) Dr. Smith would use to bill for her services.

      Diagnosis: _____

      Procedure: _____

   B. Identify the coding system(s) Central Hospital would use to bill for its services.

      Diagnosis: _____

      Procedure: _____

   C. What billing form will Central Hospital submit to Medicare for payment?

      _____

5. Which coding system describes the reason for the visit or encounter?

   _____

6. A patient was seen in the physician's office for excision of a 0.5 cm facial nevus (HCPCS Level I code 11440). The ICD-9-CM diagnosis code for the benign lesion is 216.3. During this encounter, the physician also evaluates the patient's hyperglycemia (ICD-9-CM code 790.6) and chronic simple anemia (ICD-9-CM code 281.9). A three-specimen glucose tolerance test (HCPCS Level I code 82951) is performed. Using the CMS-1500 form provided, link the appropriate ICD-9-CM codes found in block 21 with HCPCS Level I codes found in block 24D. In column 24E, place the number 1, 2, or 3 to show which diagnosis code is related to the procedure.

Exercise 1.1 (cont.)

21. DIAGNOSIS OR NATURE OF ILLNESS OR INJURY, (RELATE ITEMS 1,2,3 OR 4 TO ITEM 24E BY LINE)

1. |216.3 (benign lesion)　　　　　3. |790.6 hyperglycemia

2. |281.9 chronic anemia　　　　　4. |

24.	A					B	C	D		E
	\multicolumn{6}{c|}{DATE(S) OF SERVICE}	Place of Service	Type of Service	\multicolumn{2}{c|}{PROCEDURES, SERVICES, OR SUPPLIES (Explain Unusual Circumstances)}	DIAGNOSIS CODE
	\multicolumn{3}{c|}{From}	\multicolumn{3}{c|}{To}			CPT/HCPCS	MODIFIER	
	MM	DD	YY	MM	DD	YY					
1	01-19-03								excision facial nevus 11440		
2	01-19-03								gluc tol test 82951		
3											
4											
5											
6											

Chapter 2

Procedural Terminology in Current Use

The American Medical Association (AMA) developed *Current Procedural Terminology (CPT)* to provide a uniform language that could be used to accurately designate medical, surgical, and diagnostic services. The CPT coding system is an effective means of facilitating communication among physicians, patients, and third-party payers nationwide. Published in 1966, the first edition of the CPT codebook consisted primarily of surgical procedures and limited codes for medicine, radiology, and laboratory procedures and services. The second edition, published in 1970, expanded the four-digit codes to five digits. And the last two editions, published in the late 1970s, reflected advances in medical technology and introduced a mechanism for updating the CPT codebook annually to keep it in step with changes in the medical field.

The AMA's CPT Editorial Panel, consisting of fifteen physicians and representatives from the Health Insurance Association of America, the CMS, Blue Cross and Blue Shield, AHIMA, and the AHA, is responsible for the annual revision and modification of the codebook. The panel is assisted in this task by the CPT Advisory Committee, which is composed of physicians nominated by the National Medical Specialty Societies, and by the AMA Health Care Professionals Advisory Committee, which is composed of other healthcare professionals.

Links to the AMA and the CMS Web sites pertinent to the discussion in this chapter are listed in the Web Resources at the back of this book.

Inclusion of Procedures and Services

To be included in the CPT codebook, a procedure or service must meet the following conditions:

1. It must be commonly performed by many physicians across the country.
2. It must be consistent with contemporary medical practice.

Consequently, a procedure's inclusion in, or exclusion from, the CPT codebook does not imply that the AMA does or does not endorse it. Nor does it mean that the procedure is or is not covered for reimbursement by insurance plans. For example, although codes exist in CPT to describe cosmetic surgery, most insurance carriers do not provide reimbursement for such procedures. Thus, patients would pay for such services out of pocket. Reimbursement rules and guidelines are not always consistent with CPT coding rules and guidelines. Just as insurance policies for healthcare services vary, so do the reporting requirements involving codes.

The listing of procedures or services and their codes by subsections does not restrict use of these codes to certain specialty groups. For example, when describing a service that has been rendered, a surgeon may use codes from any section, not just those from the surgery section. Similarly, a family practice physician may use a code from the surgery section to describe office procedures or maternity care.

Each major section in the CPT codebook is divided into categories or subsections, subcategories, headings, and procedures/services, as follows:

Surgery	Section
Integumentary system	Subsection/Category
Skin, subcutaneous, and accessory structures	Subcategory
Incision and drainage	Heading
Incision and drainage of pilonidal cyst, simple	Procedure

The categories, subcategories, and headings may identify any of the following:

- Services

- Procedures or therapies

- Examinations or tests

- Body systems

- Anatomic sites

Table 2.1 provides an example of each subdivision (when applicable) by section.

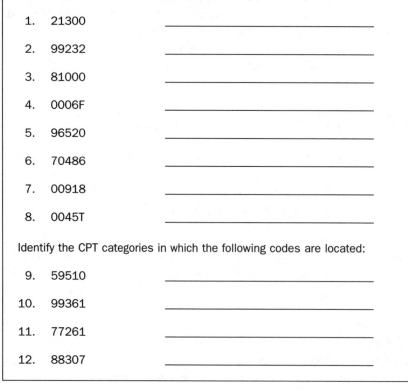

Exercise 2.1

Identify the section of CPT where the following codes are located.

1. 21300 _____

2. 99232 _____

3. 81000 _____

4. 0006F _____

5. 96520 _____

6. 70486 _____

7. 00918 _____

8. 0045T _____

Identify the CPT categories in which the following codes are located:

9. 59510 _____

10. 99361 _____

11. 77261 _____

12. 88307 _____

Table 2.1. Examples of CPT subdivisions

Section	Category/Subsection	Subcategory	Heading	Procedure/Service
E/M Services	Hospital Inpatient Services (99221–99239)	Initial Hospital Care (99221–99223)	New or Established Patient (99221–99223)	99223 Initial hospital care
Anesthesia	Head (00100–00222)	—	—	00104 Anesthesia for electroconvulsive therapy
Surgery	Respiratory System (30000–32999)	Nose (30000–30999)	Incision (30000–30020)	30020 Drainage abscess or hematoma, nasal septum
Radiology	Diagnostic Radiology (Diagnostic Imaging) (70010–76499)	Aorta and Arteries (75600–75790)	—	75600 Aortography, thoracic, without serialography, radiological supervision, and interpretation
Pathology and Laboratory	Anatomic Pathology (88000–88099)	Postmortem Exam (88000–88099)	—	88020 Necropsy (autopsy), gross and microscopic; without CNS
Medicine	Psychiatry (90801–90899)	Psychiatric Therapeutic Procedures (90804–90899)	Other Psychotherapy (90845–90857)	90845 Psychoanalysis
Category II Codes	—	—	—	0001F Blood pressure, measured
Category III Codes	—	—	—	0003T Cervicography

Conventions and Characteristics of CPT

The following sections discuss many of the conventions and characteristics of the CPT codebook. These include:

- The semicolon

- The bullet and triangle

- Facing triangles

- The plus sign

- Exemptions to modifier –51, Multiple Procedures

Note that the CPT book has a legend at the bottom of each page.

Semicolon

The format of the CPT codebook is designed to provide descriptions of procedures that can stand alone without additional explanation. To conserve space, many descriptions refer to a common portion of the procedure listed in a preceding entry rather than repeating the procedure in its entirety. When this occurs, the incomplete procedural description or descriptions are indented under the main entry, and the common portion of the main entry is followed by a semicolon (;). This signifies that the main entry applies to, and is part of, all indented entries that follow with their codes. The indented entries can yield different kinds of information, as illustrated in the following examples:

1. The indented information may provide diagnostic data.

49520	Repair recurrent inguinal hernia, any age; reducible
49521	incarcerated or strangulated

The common portion of the description for code 49520 (the part before the semicolon) should be considered part of code 49521. Therefore, the full description of code 49521 reads: Repair recurrent inguinal hernia, any age; incarcerated or strangulated.

2. The indented entries may describe alternate anatomical sites.

27705	Osteotomy; tibia
27707	fibula
27709	tibia and fibula
27712	multiple, with realignment on intramedullary rod (eg, Sofield-type procedure)

The full description of code 27707 reads: Osteotomy; fibula.

3. The indented entries may designate specific procedures.

44150   Colectomy, total, abdominal, without proctectomy; with ileostomy or
                  ileoproctostomy
44151   with continent ileostomy
44152   with rectal mucosectomy, ileoanal anastomosis, with or without loop
                  ileostomy
44153   with rectal mucosectomy, ileoanal anastomosis, creation of ileal reservoir
                  (S or J), with or without loop ileostomy

The full description of code 44153 reads: Colectomy, total, abdominal, without proc-tectomy; with rectal mucosectomy, ileoanal anastomosis, creation of ileal reservoir (S or J), with or without loop ileostomy.

4. The indented entries also may describe extensive procedures requiring the assignment of two codes. CPT often designates more extensive procedures by using the code for a stand-alone procedure and the code for an indented procedure to fully describe the extent of the surgery. When both codes are appropriate, the code for the indented description is preceded by the plus symbol (+) for add-on code.

15200   Full thickness graft, free, including direct closure of donor site, trunk;
               20 sq cm or less

+ 15201   each additional 20 sq cm (List separately in addition to code for
               primary procedure.)

When a 40 sq cm graft is performed on a patient, both codes 15200 and 15201 are assigned. The performance of a 60 sq cm graft requires the following codes to be reported: 15200, 15201, and 15201.

Bullet and Triangle

CPT uses two symbols (• and ▲) to identify changes to the current codebook. A bullet (•) before a code identifies that code as a new addition, and a triangle (▲) before a code identifies a revision to the narrative description accompanying that code. Appendix B of the CPT codebook contains a comprehensive list of all revisions, including deletions and additions in code order.

Following is an example of a new code found in *CPT 2004*:

• 21685   Hyoid myotomy and suspension

Following is an example of a code that has been changed in *CPT 2004*:

▲20240   Biopsy, bone, open; superficial (eg, ilium, sternum,
             spinous process, ribs trochanter of femur)

Facing Triangles

The facing triangles (▶◀) symbol is used to indicate the beginning and ending of new and/or revised text within the guidelines and instruction notes. The coder should carefully review the information identified within facing triangles to ensure correct code assignment. An example of new text found in *CPT 2004* can be found in the note that appears before code 20000:

> ▶(For computer-assisted musculoskeletal surgical navigational orthopedic procedures, report 0054T–0056T)◀

Plus Sign (+)

If a procedure is commonly carried out with another procedure, it may be designated as an add-on code and therefore should not be used alone. CPT identifies add-on codes with the symbol +.
For example:

> 11000 Debridement of extensive eczematous or infected skin; up to 10% of body surface
> +11001 each additional 10% of body surface (List separately in addition to code for primary procedure.)

The + symbol indicates that 11001 is an add-on code and must be used with code 11000. It may not be reported alone.

Notes have been added to reinforce the correct use of add-on codes. For example, after code 11001, the following directional note appears:

> (Use 11001 in conjunction with code 11000)

Appendix D of *CPT 2004* contains a complete list of add-on codes.

Exemptions to Modifier –51

The symbol ⊘ indicates codes that may not be appended with modifier –51, Multiple Procedures. For example, code 32000, Thoracentesis, puncture of pleural cavity for aspiration, initial or subsequent, may not be used with modifier –51. Appendix E of *CPT 2004* contains a complete list of codes that are exempt from the use of modifier –51. For a more detailed discussion of modifiers, see chapter 3.

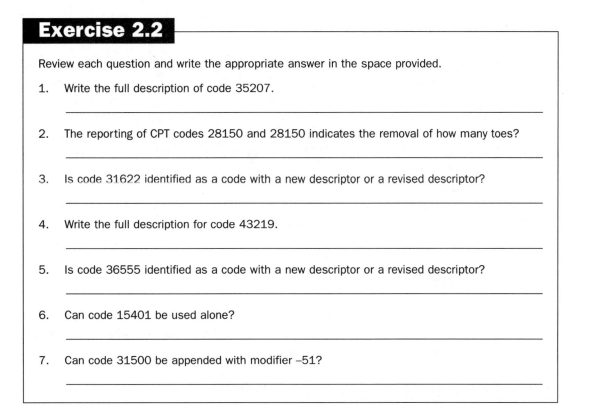

Exercise 2.2

Review each question and write the appropriate answer in the space provided.

1. Write the full description of code 35207.

   _____

2. The reporting of CPT codes 28150 and 28150 indicates the removal of how many toes?

   _____

3. Is code 31622 identified as a code with a new descriptor or a revised descriptor?

   _____

4. Write the full description for code 43219.

   _____

5. Is code 36555 identified as a code with a new descriptor or a revised descriptor?

   _____

6. Can code 15401 be used alone?

   _____

7. Can code 31500 be appended with modifier –51?

   _____

Category I, II, and III Codes

In 2000, the AMA completed the CPT-5 project, which was an initiative to make improvements in the structure and processes of CPT. As a result, three categories of CPT codes were established:

- Category I codes: The traditional, five-digit numeric codes that identify procedures and services.

     Example: 10021   Fine needle aspiration; without imaging guidance

- Category II codes: These alphanumeric codes represent performance measurements for tracking purposes. The use of tracking codes for performance measurement will help in data collection and minimize administrative burden. The five-digit alphanumeric code can be identified with the letter F at the end of the code. The uses of these codes are optional. The Category II tracking codes are reviewed as part of healthcare quality tracking by the AMA, the Joint Commission on Accreditation of Healthcare Organizations (JCAHO), the National Committee for Quality Assurance (NCQA), among other groups.

     Example: 0002F   Tobacco use, smoking, assessed

- Category III codes: This section follows the Category II codes located behind the medicine section of the CPT codebook. These temporary codes are used for emerging technology services and procedures. They are assigned an alphanumeric identifier (for example, 0017T). Category III codes were developed to allow researchers to track emerging technology services. When approved by the CPT Editorial Panel, newly added Category III CPT codes will be made available on a semiannual (twice yearly) basis on the AMA Web site. A Category III code will be archived after five years if it has not been placed in the Category I section or unless it is demonstrated that it is still needed. Payment for Category III coded services and procedures depends on individual payer policy.

Unlisted Procedures

Because of rapid advances in medical research and technology, a service or procedure may be performed that does not yet have an available CPT code. In these rare instances, an unlisted code should be reported and accompanied by a written report describing the procedure/service. The operative report is usually sufficient when reporting an unlisted surgical code. The introduction to each section of the CPT codebook includes a complete list of the unlisted service/procedure codes available for that section. Unlisted codes for various subsections can be found in the alphabetic index of the CPT codebook under the main heading of "Unlisted Services and Procedures."

Note: Before assigning an unlisted code, the National (HCPCS Level II) and CPT Category III (Emerging Technology) codes should be reviewed to determine whether the CMS or the Medicare carrier has developed a specific code for the procedure/service in question.

Location of Notes

Coders using the CPT codebook must focus special attention on the notes located at various levels within the text. Notes may appear at the beginning of a heading, within parentheses before or after a code, or within parentheses included as part of the code.

Notes at the Beginning of a Heading

Notes found at the beginning of a heading provide information such as:

- Integral components of a service or procedure

  Example: The note under the heading "Endoscopy" (31231–31294) states that a surgical sinus endoscopy always includes a sinusotomy (when appropriate) and a diagnostic endoscopy.

- Definitions of terms and/or codes

  Example: Under the heading "Shaving of Epidermal or Dermal Lesions" (11300–11313), a note defines the procedure of shaving as "the sharp removal by transverse incision or horizontal slicing to remove epidermal and dermal lesions without a full-thickness dermal excision."

- Directions to assign additional codes

  Example: Under the heading "Combined Arterial-Venous Grafting for Coronary Bypass" (33517–33530), the note reminds the coder that two codes are required to identify coronary artery bypass grafting using both arterial and venous grafts.

Notes before or after Codes

Notes appearing before or after codes include information such as:

- Alternative codes

  Example: The note appearing after code 11772 directs the coder to use 10080 or 10081 for an incision of a pilonidal cyst.

- Deleted codes

    Example: The note appearing after code 36522 advises the coder that 36530 has been deleted. To report the procedure previously identified by code 36530, the coder should assign code 36563.

- Add-on codes

    Example: The note appearing after code 19001 instructs the coder not to use code 19001 alone. It must be used with code 19000.

- Other instructional information

    Example: The note appearing before code 35480 instructs the coder to use modifier –51 or –52 when the procedures are performed as part of another operation.

Notes within the Text

Notes may appear within the text for an individual code to provide further explanation.

> **Example:** Within code 10040, the coder is provided with the example of acne surgery.

Alphabetic Index

Located at the back of the CPT codebook, the alphabetic index is organized by the main terms that appear in bold print. Main terms, or entries, may include the following information:

- Procedure, service, or examination: Coccygectomy, mastopexy, preventive medicine, physical therapy, nuclear medicine, and organ- or disease-oriented panel

- Organ or other anatomic site: Bladder, blood vessels, ethmoid, ganglion, muscle, and sweat glands

- Condition or diagnosis: Abrasion, hematoma, heel spur, meningioma, mumps, omphalocele, and septal defect

- Synonym, eponym, or abbreviation: Ewart procedure, FAST, LHR, Pereyra procedure, Pomeroy's operation, TLC screen, and HLA typing

Often following main entries, subterms provide additional information that must be reviewed before selecting a code, such as:

Laryngoscopy	
Diagnostic	31505
Direct	31515–31571
Exploration	31505, 31520–31526, 31575
Fiberoptic	31575–31579
with Stroboscopy	31579
Indirect	31505–31513
Newborn	31520
Operative	31530–31561

To assist in appropriate code selection, CPT employs cross-references. Appearing most often with eponyms, synonyms, and abbreviations, the term see and the text that follows it refer the coder to another main term. For example:

```
AHG
See Clotting Factor
```

See can also direct the coder to another main term, but only if all the information being sought did not follow the first main term, as in:

```
Cognitive Function Tests . . . . 96115
        See Neurology, Diagnostic
```

These examples illustrate the importance of referring to the additional main entries as directed by the cross-references to ensure the highest level of specificity in code selection.

The alphabetic index offers at least one code for review under each entry, although in some cases more than one code or a range of codes is provided. However, whatever the circumstance, each code and its description must be reviewed carefully to ensure accurate assignment and appropriate payment. To illustrate:

```
Mastectomy
Gynecomastia . . . . . . . . . . . . . . . . . . . . . . 19140
Modified Radical . . . . . . . . . . . . . . . . . . . . 19240
Partial. . . . . . . . . . . . . . . . . . . . . . 19160–19162
Radical. . . . . . . . . . . . . . . . . . . . 19200–19220
Simple, Complete. . . . . . . . . . . . . . . . . . 19180
Subcutaneous . . . . . . . . . . . . . . . . . . . . . 19182
```

When coding a partial mastectomy, a coder must review the descriptions of all codes in the 19160–19162 range before assigning a final code.

The first step in locating a code in the alphabetic index is to find the procedure or service performed, such as jejunostomy or peritoneocentesis. If the service or procedure is not listed, the coder should locate the organ or anatomic site involved; the condition or diagnosis; or the synonym or eponym, such as phalanx, Epstein-Barr virus, or Dandy operation. The subterms should be reviewed and any cross-references followed. Each code listed in the index should be noted and each description reviewed until a match is established.

Note: Having familiarity with the CPT codebook will expedite the coding process. For example, a comprehensive knowledge of the codebook would show that correct codes often are found under several main terms.

Consider these procedures: hallux valgus correction and Mayo bunionectomy. Review of the alphabetic index will yield the following entries and codes:

Bunion Repair 28296–28299
Mayo Procedure 28292

Mayo Procedure. 28292

Repair
Hallux Valgus 28290–28299

Repair
Toe
     Bunion. 28290–28299

Repair
Bunion. 28290–28299

It should be noted that the terms "Hallux valgus" and "Correction, hallux valgus" do not appear in the alphabetic index.

General Rules for CPT Coding

Here are some general rules to consider when applying CPT codes:

- Analyze the note or procedural statement provided by the physician or other healthcare provider and/or included in the health record.

- Determine the procedure, test, or service to be coded.

- Locate the main term in the index by checking under the procedure, anatomic site, condition, synonym, eponym, service, or abbreviation, as necessary.

- Review and select the subterms indented below the main term.

- Note the code number(s) found opposite the selected main term or subterm:

  —If a single code number is provided, locate the code in the body of the CPT codebook. Verify the code and its description against the procedural statement to make sure they match.

  —If two or more codes separated by a comma are shown, locate each code in the body of the CPT codebook. Read the description of each code before selecting the appropriate one to match the procedural statement.

  —If a range of codes is shown, locate that range in the body of the CPT codebook. Review the description of each entry before selecting a code. The code description should always match the procedural statement.

- If applicable, follow cross-references.

- Never code directly from the index.

- Read all notes that apply to the code selected. They can appear at the beginning of a section or subsection, directly under, or within the code description.

- Select the appropriate modifier, when applicable, to complete the code description. Modifiers may not always apply to hospital reporting of outpatient hospital procedures. Individual health plans may have specific guidelines for the use of modifiers and for the acceptance of Level II modifiers. For accurate reporting, the coding professional must be familiar with the specific reporting requirements for the circumstances.

- Continue coding all components of the procedure/service according to the directions in the CPT codebook.

Exercise 2.3

Assign the appropriate CPT code and provide the corresponding index entry.

1. Green operation

    Code _____

    Index entry: _____

2. Fine needle aspiration of cyst of thyroid, without imaging guidance

    Code _____

    Index entry: _____

3. Femoral-popliteal bypass graft with vein

    Code _____

    Index entry: _____

4. Repair of reducible recurrent femoral hernia

    Code _____

    Index entry: _____

5. Incision and drainage of infected bursa, left hip

    Code _____

    Index entry: _____

6. Anesthesia provided for application of shoulder cast (assign only the code for the anesthesia services)

    Code _____

    Index entry: _____

7. Direct diagnostic laryngoscopy for 45-year-old

    Code _____

    Index entry: _____

Exercise 2.3 (cont.)

8. MRI of lumbar spine with contrast material

    Code _____

    Index entry: _____

9. Paring of a single corn of the right foot

    Code _____

    Index entry: _____

10. HIV-1 antibody testing

    Code _____

    Index entry: _____

11. Biopsy of posterior one-third of tongue

    Code _____

    Index entry: _____

12. Esophagogastroduodenoscopy (EGD) with biopsy

    Code _____

    Index entry: _____

13. Arthroscopic medial meniscectomy

    Code _____

    Index entry: _____

14. All-night recording EEG

    Code _____

    Index entry: _____

15. Removal of metal shaving from cornea without use of slit lamp

    Code _____

    Index entry: _____

16. Endometrial cryoablation with ultrasound guidance

    Code _____

    Index entry: _____

17. Beta-blocker therapy prescribed

    Code _____

    Index entry: _____

Abstracting Documentation

This workbook provides two types of exercises: one-line procedure coding and operative narratives. The one-line procedures offer students the opportunity to use the index to locate the coding selection and apply the guidelines introduced in the chapter. Coding from operative notes found in office records, operative reports, and/or emergency department notes allows students to practice the skill of abstracting needed information to assign a code successfully. When reviewing the documentation in an operative report, students are encouraged to scan the report for:

- Procedures performed (Look for action types of words: excision, incision, aspiration, endoscopy, and so forth.)

- Associated diagnoses

After looking in the index and, subsequently, in the main body portion of the CPT codebook to locate coding selections, it will be necessary to note the types of information that may influence the choice of codes and then to read the operative report again for information that will help determine the correct answer.

Exercise 2.4

Read the following operative report. Then perform the steps in the coding process as listed below:

Operative Report

Preoperative Diagnosis:	History of colon cancer	→ Reason for encounter
Postoperative Diagnosis:	Rectosigmoid polyp	
Procedure:	Colonoscopy and polypectomy	→ Procedure performed

Indications: The patient has had three previous resections of three different primary carcinomas of the colon. His last resection of carcinoma was in 1998. He has been doing well in general.

Premedications: Demerol 50 mg IV and Versed 2.5 mg IV

Procedure: The CF100-L video colonoscope was passed without difficulty from the anus up through the anastomosis, which appears to be in the distal transverse colon. The instrument was advanced into the distal small bowel and then slowly withdrawn with good view obtained throughout. A small 3 mm polyp near the rectosigmoid junction was removed with hot biopsy forceps and retrieved. Otherwise, the patient has a satisfactory postoperative appearance of the colon. It is shortened due to previous resections, but there is no other evidence of neoplasm. The instrument was completely withdrawn without other findings.

1. Scan the documentation and indicate the procedure performed.

   _____

2. Search the index for "Colonoscopy, Removal, Polyp" and record the coding selection range.

   _____

3. Review the coding descriptions and determine what additional documentation is needed before you can accurately select a code.

   _____

4. Read the operative report *again* to determine the method of removal utilized.

   _____

5. Choose the code that reflects this documentation.

   _____

Exercise 2.5

In this exercise, you must also reference the pathological diagnosis to assist with the code assignment. Read the operative report and the pathological diagnosis. Then perform the steps in the coding process as listed below.

Operative Report

Preoperative Diagnosis:	Subepidermal nodular lesion of the forearm
Operation:	Excision of 2.0 cm lesion of the forearm
Procedure:	Under local anesthesia, the 2.0 cm lesion was removed with 0.5 cm margins. The lesion was submitted to pathology. Bleeding is controlled with electro-cautery, and the wound is closed with five vertical mattress sutures of 5-0 nylon. Polysporin and dressing are applied to the wound.
Pathological Diagnosis:	Well-organized basal cell carcinoma

1. Scan the documentation and record the main procedure to be located in the alphabetic index.

    _____

2. Search the index for the main terms/subterms and record the code selections.

    _____

3. Review the code descriptions to determine what additional documentation is needed before you can accurately select a code.

    _____

4. Read the operative report and pathological diagnosis *again* to determine the additional documentation to clarify the selection.

    _____

5. Choose the code that reflects this documentation.

    _____

In summary, for the above case, you need to abstract the following documentation from the operative report:

• Size of lesion and margins

• Morphology (benign, malignant)

• Location

• Method of removal

Exercise 2.6

Read the following operative report to abstract information that is needed for a correct code assignment.

Operative Report

Preoperative Diagnosis: Umbilical hernia

Postoperative Diagnosis: Same

Indications: This is a 38-year-old male who presents with an umbilical hernia. He has been experiencing flu-like symptoms, which he describes as crampy abdominal pain. Risks versus benefits including bleeding, infection and the high recurrence rate because of his obesity were discussed. The patient states he understands and elects to proceed.

Procedure: After adequate general endotracheal anesthesia had been induced, the patient was placed in the supine position and prepped and draped in the usual sterile manner. A curvilinear incision was made just inferior to the umbilicus. This was extended down through adipose tissue to the level of the rectus fascia. The herniosac was amputated and sent to pathology. The fascia was then reapproximated transversely using interrupted 0 prolene sutures. The skin was reapproximated using 4-0 nylon. Sponge and needle counts were accurate. The patient tolerated the procedure well and left the operating room in stable condition.

1. What procedure was performed?

    _____

2. Search the index for the main term(s) and record the code selections.

    _____

3. Review the code descriptions to determine what additional documentation is needed before you can accurately select a code.

    _____

4. Abstract the needed information and select the correct code.

    _____

5. Should you also assign a CPT code for the suturing of the wound at the conclusion of the procedure?

    _____

Identification of Operative Procedures for Coding

New coders often have difficulty determining whether a procedure is an integral part of the main operative procedure or a separately identifiable procedure. For example, when a patient has a breast mass removed, a code for the wound closure would not be assigned because it is an integral part of the main procedure. The ability to discriminate between reportable and non-reportable procedures is a skill that must be developed and one that significantly affects accurate code selection. Coders need to have surgical references to help them understand procedures and techniques. The references section of this book provides a list of helpful resources. In addition to understanding surgical techniques, coders must know when to assign additional codes and will find instructions on doing so in the CPT guidelines. Various types of notes and descriptions located throughout CPT guidelines are illustrated below.

> 52601   Transurethral electrosurgical resection of prostate, including control of postoperative bleeding, complete (Vasectomy, meatotomy, cystourethroscopy, urethral calibration and/or dilation, and internal urethrotomy are included.)

Many CPT codes combine the main procedure with minor procedures that do not warrant additional codes. In these cases, the code description contains a note specifying the secondary procedures that are to be included in the primary code. In the preceding example, if the surgeon performs a transurethral electrosurgical resection of prostate (TURP) with vasectomy, the correct code assignment is 52601. Because the code description states that vasectomy is included in the code for the TURP procedure, the vasectomy is not assigned a separate code.

> 58150   Total abdominal hysterectomy (corpus and cervix), with or without removal of tube(s), with or without removal of ovary(s)

If the surgeon performs a total abdominal hysterectomy with salpingo-oophorectomy, the only code submitted would be 58150. The code description explains that no additional code would be submitted for the salpingo-oophorectomy.

Some notes in the CPT codebook offer guidance on multiple code assignment for an entire section.

➡ For example, look at the note before code 14000 in the "Adjacent Tissue Transfer or Rearrangement" portion of the integumentary system subsection of the surgery section. The second paragraph states:

> Excision *(including lesion)* and/or repair by adjacent tissue transfer or rearrangement

According to this note, when a surgeon removes a skin lesion and the defect is repaired with an adjacent tissue transfer, only the tissue transfer should be coded. The excision of lesion is not identified with an additional code.

Some notes provide instructions for use of add-on codes. For example, code 69990, Operating microscope, is reported only as an additional code. In some procedures, physicians utilize an operating microscope during the surgical episode. CPT provides specific instructions in the note before code 69990 to help the coder determine whether this add-on code is to be used with a particular primary procedure code. Instruction is often given in the form of a note under a specific code.

➡ Read the note under CPT code 63078 that states "(Do not report code 69990 in addition to codes 63075–63078)."

Coding References

Both the American Medical Association and the Centers for Medicare and Medicaid Services are resources for CPT codes guidelines.

American Medical Association *(CPT Assistant)*

The AMA is the primary, authoritative reference for CPT guidelines and changes. On a monthly basis, the AMA publishes CPT Assistant as a communication tool for correct application of CPT codes. Included in the publication is a question-and-answer section replying to coders' questions. The AMA also provides a subscription service for assistance with coding questions. Most large healthcare facilities have an online version of *CPT Assistant* for reference. The following exercises (2.7 and 2.8) require access to *CPT Assistant.*

Exercise 2.7

In a previous exercise (2.4), you were asked to analyze documentation and assign the correct code for a colonoscopy with polypectomy procedure. For correct CPT assignment, you needed to know what method was used to remove the polyp. In that particular operative report, the surgeon used hot biopsy forceps. Assume that the surgeon removed the polyp using a cold biopsy forceps. What would be the correct coding assignment for this procedure? What edition of *CPT Assistant* was referenced?

Centers for Medicare and Medicaid Services

In some situations, the federal government provides interpretative guidance for use of CPT codes and modifiers. Most Medicare and Medicaid manuals are available on CMS's Web site. These guidelines are published in the form of transmittals, manuals, and so on. For the following exercise, a reference was published in *CPT Assistant* and CMS Reginal PRO letter No. 91-18, Regional Office VI, Dallas (according to 3M Software).

Exercise 2.8

In a previous exercise (2.5), the surgeon excised a lesion of the forearm. Assume that the physician took a biopsy of the lesion before it was excised. Do you code both the biopsy and the excision or just the excision? What *CPT Assistant* was referenced to answer this question?

Exercise 2.9 Chapter Review

1. What symbol indicates that a procedure is new this year?

   _____

2. Reference CPT codes 11100 and 11101. If the surgeon performed a biopsy of two different skin lesions, what would be the correct code assignment?

   _____

3. Which category of CPT codes is reserved for emerging technology?

   _____

4. Reference CPT codes 42310 and 42320. If the surgeon performed drainage of an external submaxillary abscess, what would be the correct code assignment?

   _____

5. Reference CPT code range of 40840-40844. If the surgeon performed a bilateral, posterior vestibuloplasty, what would be the correct code assignment?

   _____

Chapter 3

Modifiers

Modifiers may be reported along with a CPT code to indicate that a particular event modified the service/procedure, but with no change to its basic definition. Modifiers may indicate any of the following situations:

- A service/procedure has both a professional component and a technical component.

- A service/procedure was performed by more than one physician and/or in more than one location.

- A service/procedure has been increased or reduced in scope.

- A service was performed only partially.

- An adjunctive service was performed.

- A bilateral procedure was performed.

- A service/procedure was performed more than once.

- An unusual event occurred during the service/procedure.

There is a distinct advantage to conveying as much information as possible to the third-party payer to ensure appropriate payment when billing for professional physician services or services provided by an ambulatory surgery or service center. Use of a modifier, in selected cases, allows the healthcare provider to explain special circumstances that surround the charge for the service and may affect claim payment. Use of an appropriate modifier also can prevent a claim from being denied.

Appendix A of the CPT codebook includes a complete list of currently accepted modifiers and their descriptions. Coders should examine modifier descriptions carefully for conditions that may limit use of a modifier to a specific section of CPT. For example, modifier –25 is limited by definition to evaluation and management codes and would not be appended to a code from the surgery section. Modifier –78 (Return to Operating Room for a Related Procedure During the Postoperative Period) would only be appended to a CPT surgical code.

Links to the Centers for Medicare and Medicaid Services Web site pertinent to the discussion in this chapter are in the Web Resources at the back of this book.

Use of Modifiers

In an effort to report all pertinent information on a particular case, modifiers have been acceptable for use by physicians and other Part B Medicare professional service providers for many years. With the adoption of the ambulatory patient classification prospective payment system (APC PPS) for hospital outpatient services in 2000, hospital outpatient services now also are required to report selected modifiers for Medicare patient services. Several modifiers were added to CPT that are designated for hospital use only.

Physician Use of Modifiers

Physicians report modifiers appended to the CPT code as follows:

> **Example:** 99271–32
>
> Patient saw Dr. Jones for a confirmatory consultation per the request of his insurance company.

In the reporting of the bilateral modifier –50, some third-party payers have requested that the surgical procedure be listed twice, with the two-digit modifier attached to the second listing of the code. According to the AMA, this is not the appropriate reporting format for bilateral procedures. The CMS requires a one-line method of reporting.

> **Example:** 49500
>
> 49500–50   Required reporting by some payers
>
> 49500–50   AMA-directed method of reporting

In addition to the CPT modifiers, the National Codes (Level II of HCPCS) include many modifiers for more concise reporting of procedures. These two-digit alphanumeric modifiers can identify:

- The specific finger or toe involved
- A visit for a second or third opinion
- A service provided by someone other than a physician
- Right- or left-side involvement

The CPT codebook lists the required HCPCS modifiers for outpatient services in appendix A. Additional HCPCS modifiers may be found in the national HCPCS codebook.

> **Example:** –RT   Right side
>
> –TA   Left foot, great toe
>
> –AH   Clinical psychologist
>
> –F9   Right hand, fifth digit
>
> –QW   CLIA-waived test

Hospital Use of Modifiers

The following CPT modifiers are available for use by hospitals for outpatient Medicare services and should be reported as two digits appended to the appropriate CPT code in field location 44 of the CMS-1450 form (UB-92) (See figure 1.2 on page 7.):

-25 Significant, Separately Identifiable Evaluation and Management Service by the Same Physician on the Same Day of a Procedure or Other Service

-27 Multiple Outpatient Hospital E/M Encounters

-50 Bilateral Procedure

-52 Reduced Services

-58 Staged or Related Procedure or Service by the Same Physician During the Postoperative Period

-59 Distinct Procedural Service

-73 Discontinued Outpatient Hospital/Ambulatory Surgery Center (ASC) Procedure Prior to the Administration of Anesthesia

-74 Discontinued Outpatient Hospital/Ambulatory Surgery Center (ASC) Procedure after Administration of Anesthesia

-76 Repeat Procedure by Same Physician

-77 Repeat Procedure by Another Physician

-78 Return to Operating Room for a Related Procedure During the Postoperative Procedure

-79 Unrelated Procedure or Service by the Same Physician During the Postoperative Period

-91 Repeat Clinical Diagnostic Laboratory Test

Example: 49505–50 Repair initial inguinal hernia, age 5 years or over; reducible

By adding modifier –50, the coder has identified a left-sided and right-sided hernia repair (bilateral).

In addition, the following Level II modifiers are acceptable for use by hospitals:

-LT Left Side
-RT Right Side
-E1 Upper Left, Eyelid
-E2 Lower Left, Eyelid
-E3 Upper Right, Eyelid
-E4 Lower Right, Eyelid
-FA Left Hand, Thumb
-F1 Left Hand, Second Digit
-F2 Left Hand, Third Digit
-F3 Left Hand, Fourth Digit
-F4 Left Hand, Fifth Digit
-F5 Right Hand, Thumb
-F6 Right Hand, Second Digit
-F7 Right Hand, Third Digit
-F8 Right Hand, Fourth Digit
-F9 Right Hand, Fifth Digit
-TA Left Foot, Great Toe
-T1 Left Foot, Second Digit
-T2 Left Foot, Third Digit
-T3 Left Foot, Fourth Digit
-T4 Left Foot, Fifth Digit
-T5 Right Foot, Great Toe
-T6 Right Foot, Second Digit
-T7 Right Foot, Third Digit
-T8 Right Foot, Fourth Digit
-T9 Right Foot, Fifth Digit
-LC Left Circumflex Coronary Artery
-LD Left Anterior Descending Coronary Artery
-RC Right Coronary Artery
-CA Procedure payable only in the inpatient setting when performed emergently on an outpatient who dies prior to admission

–GA	Waiver of liability statement on file
–GG	Peformance and payment of a screening mammogram and diagnostic mammogram on the same patient, same day
–GH	Diagnostic mammogram converted from screening mammogram on same day
–GY	Item or service statutorily excluded or does not meet the definition of any Medicare benefit
–GZ	Item or service expected to be denied as not reasonable and necessary
–QM	Ambulance Service Provided under Arrangement by a Provider of Services
–QN	Ambulance Service Furnished Directly by a Provider of Services

Medicare Transmittals

Periodically, Medicare issues its own guidelines or clarification memos pertaining to coding issues. Whenever the CMS sees the need to alter or provide additional clarification for use of CPT codes or modifiers for Medicare reimbursement, it issues one of these memorandums. Several transmittals related to the use of modifiers have been issued, including:

- Transmittal 726, January 1998 (Use of Modifiers in Reporting Hospital Outpatient Services)

- Transmittal A-99-41, September 1999 (Clarification of Modifier Usage in Reporting Outpatient Hospital Services)

- Transmittal A-00-07, February 2000 (Addition of Modifiers –25, –58, –78, and –79 to the List of Modifiers Approved for Hospital Outpatient Use and Correction to Program Memorandum A-99-41)

- Transmittal A-00-40, July 2000 (Further Information on the Use of Modifier –25 in Reporting Hospital Outpatient Services)

- Transmittal A-00-73, October 2000 (Clarification of Modifier Usage in Reporting Out-patient Hospital Services)

- Transmittal A-02-129, January 2003 (Update of the Hospital Outpatient Prospective Payment System)

For the most updated transmittal information, refer to the CMS Web site at www.cms.gov.

Modifier Usage with Surgery Codes

The selected modifiers described below are available for use with surgery codes. Other modifiers are described in related sections of this book. Note that a complete list of CPT modifiers and modifiers approved for ambulatory surgery center (ASC) hospital outpatient use may be found in appendix A of CPT.

–22 **Unusual Procedural Services** *(for physician use only):* Modifier –22 may be reported to identify that the service provided was greater than that usually required for a particular procedure. It may be necessary to submit supportive documentation to the third-party payer to justify use of modifier –22.

> **Example:** Because of the patient's extreme obesity, a physician required an additional 30 minutes to perform a cholecystectomy. He should report 47600–22.

−47 **Anesthesia by Surgeon** *(for physician use only):* Modifier −47 may be reported to indicate that the surgeon provided regional or general (not local) anesthesia for a surgical procedure. This modifier should not be reported with the anesthesia codes (00100–01999).

> **Example:** Obstetrician performs emergency Cesarean delivery for an out-of-town patient visiting relatives. He also administers a pudendal block (regional anesthesia). Moreover, he will provide postpartum care for the patient until she is able to return home. The physician should report 59515–47 and 64430.

−50 **Bilateral Procedure** *(for hospital and physician use):* Modifier −50 may be reported to identify bilateral procedures that are performed during the same operative episode.

Exception: If the description specifies the procedure as bilateral, modifier −50 should not be reported.

> **Example:** Physician performs a complex anterior packing of both nares for a nose-bleed. Both physicians and hospitals providing this service for Medicare patients should report 30903–50.

−51 **Multiple Procedures** *(for physician use only):* Modifier −51 may be reported to identify that multiple procedures were performed on the same day or during the same operative episode. The first procedure listed should identify the major or most resource-intensive procedure, which usually is paid at 100 percent of the allowed reimbursement. Subsequent or secondary procedures should be appended by modifier −51, and payment should be reduced according to the terms of the health plan. Policies on payment of multiple procedures vary depending on the third-party payer, so a complete understanding of the individual payer's policies is required to ensure appropriate reimbursement. This is a physician-only modifier and is not used in the hospital setting.

> **Example:** Physician performed an excision of a chalazion and a dacryolith from the lacrimal passage. She should report 67800 and 68530–51.

Some procedures in the CPT codebook are not intended to stand alone, so they are reported as add-on codes to describe a more extensive procedure. Modifier −51 should not be appended to these codes.

> **Example:** Percutaneous transluminal coronary angioplasty is performed on two coronary arteries. The physician should report 92982 and 92984. Modifier −51 should not be reported in this situation because code 92984 is considered a stand-alone code and thus must be reported with code 92982.

−52 **Reduced Services** *(for hospital and physician use):* Modifier −52 may be reported to indicate that a service/procedure is partially reduced in scope or eliminated at the discretion of the physician.

Although this modifier serves the purpose of identifying a reduction in the procedure/service, many physicians also use it to report a reduction in the charge for a particular procedure because the complete procedure was not performed. However, the CMS directs hospitals to use modifier −73 instead of −52 when a procedure is partially reduced or eliminated at the physician's election before anesthesia is induced. This would apply when the patient has been prepared and taken to the room for surgery, but the surgery is not carried out due to specified circumstances. In 1999, modifier −73 was added to differentiate the definitions between physicians and hospitals for this situation.

> **Example:** Patient was taken to the operating room (OR) for excisional debridement of a decubitus ulcer. However, before anesthesia was administered, the physician was called for emergency surgery of a trauma patient, and the

ulcer surgery was postponed until a later date. In this case, the hospital would report the appropriate code for the excisional debridement, along with modifier –73 to indicate that, at the discretion of the physician, the surgery was not performed. The physician would not report a procedure code because no professional services were rendered.

–53 **Discontinued Procedure** *(for physician use only):* Modifier –53 is appropriate in circumstances where the physician elects to terminate or discontinue a surgical or diagnostic procedure, usually because of a risk to the patient's well-being. However, this modifier should not be used to report the elective cancellation of a procedure prior to the patient's surgical preparation or prior to the induction of anesthesia. Also, the appropriate ICD-9-CM code should be assigned to identify the reason for the procedure's termination or discontinuation.

For hospital reporting, the CMS guidelines state that modifier –74, not –53, should be used when a procedure must be discontinued at the physician's election after the induction of anesthesia or after the procedure is under way. Elective cancellation of a procedure by the patient is not reported in this way.

> **Example:** Patient was admitted for a cystourethroscopy with bladder biopsy. Twenty minutes into the procedure, the patient developed some arrhythmia and the surgery was stopped. The physician should report 52204–53. The hospital should report 52204–74.

–54 **Surgical Care Only** *(for physician use only):* Modifier –54 may be reported to indicate that one physician performed the surgical procedure and another provided the pre- and postoperative care.

> **Example:** Dr. Reynolds is asked to perform an extracapsular cataract extraction for his partner, Dr. Owens, who is detained out of town. Dr. Owens provided the preoperative care and will provide postoperative care for his patient. Dr. Reynolds should report 66940–54.

–55 **Postoperative Management Only** *(for physician use only):* Modifier –55 may be reported to identify that the physician provided only postoperative care services for a particular procedure.

> **Example:** Patient sustains a fracture of the distal femur while skiing in Colorado. The physician in Colorado performed a closed treatment of the fracture with manipulation. However, the patient's postoperative care will be provided by his hometown physician, Dr. Rogers. Dr. Rogers should report 27510–55.

–56 **Preoperative Management Only** *(for physician use only):* Modifier –56 may be reported to indicate that the physician provided only preoperative care services for a particular procedure.

> **Example:** Dr. Smith provides preoperative care services for his patient, who will be transferred later the same day to another hospital to undergo a lower lobectomy of the right lung. The physician should report 32480–56.

–58 **Staged or Related Procedure or Service by the Same Physician During the Postoperative Period** *(for hospital and physician use):* Modifier –58 may be reported to indicate that a staged or related procedure performed by the same physician is provided during the postoperative period. This procedure may have been planned (staged) prospectively at the time of the original procedure, it may be more extensive than the original procedure, or it may be for therapy following a diagnostic surgical procedure.

> **Example:** Physician performed the first stage of a hypospadias repair one month ago. The patient now returns for the second-stage repair, which includes a urethroplasty with a free skin graft obtained from a site other than genitalia. The physician should report the following for the second-stage procedure: 54316–58.

–59   **Distinct Procedural Service** *(for hospital and physician use):* Modifier –59 may be used to identify that a procedure/service was distinct or independent from other services provided on the same day. Furthermore, modifier –59 is useful when circumstances require that certain procedures/services be reported together, even though they usually are not. Use of this modifier often signifies a different session or patient encounter, a different procedure or surgery, a different site or organ system, a separate incision/excision, or a separate lesion or injury not ordinarily encountered or performed on the same day by the same physician. Modifier –59 should not be reported if another modifier can more appropriately describe the circumstance.

       Example: Procedures 23030 (Incision and drainage of shoulder area; deep abscess or hematoma) and 20103 (Exploration of penetrating wound; extremity) are performed on the same patient during the same operative session. Ordinarily, if these codes were reported together without a modifier, code 20103 would be denied as integral to code 23030. Because incision and drainage of the shoulder is the definitive procedure, any exploration of the area (code 20103) preceding this would be considered an inherent part of the more comprehensive service. If the exploration procedure were performed on the other limb, modifier –59 explains that the codes are distinct from each other and both services are eligible for reimbursement from the health plan.

–62   **Two Surgeons** *(for physician use only):* Modifier –62 may be reported to identify that two surgeons were required to perform a particular procedure. Each surgeon should report his or her distinct operative work by adding the modifier to the procedure code and any associated add-on code(s) for that procedure as long as both surgeons continue to work together as primary surgeons. To expedite payment, the operative note dictated by each physician should be sent to the third-party payer.

-63   **Procedure Performed on Infants Less than 4 kg** *(for physician use only):* Modifier –63 may be appended to codes in the 20000–69999 series when a procedure or service is performed on a neonate or infant with a body weight of up to 4 kg. Use of this modifier indicates that the procedure involved significantly increased complexity of physician work, which is commonly associated with these patients. Modifier -63 should not be appended to any CPT code listed in the evaluation and management services, anesthesia, radiology, pathology and laboratory, or medicine sections.

–66   **Surgical Team** *(for physician use only):* Modifier –66 may be reported to identify a complex procedure performed by a team of physicians and other highly skilled personnel.

       Example: Patient is admitted for a liver transplant. All the physicians involved in performing this complex procedure should report 47135–66.

–73   **Discontinued Outpatient Procedure Prior to Anesthesia Administration** *(for hospital use only):* Modifier -73 was approved for hospital use on and after January 1, 1999. If a surgical patient is taken to the operating room (or cystoscopy suite, gastrointestinal lab, and so on) and is prepared for surgery, but the surgery is cancelled before anesthesia is administered, the intended procedure code, along with modifier –73, is assigned. This modifier is not to be reported for an elective cancellation of a procedure. The medical record documentation should reflect the circumstances surrounding the cancellation.

       Example: Patient is scheduled for a knee arthroscopy for a lateral meniscus repair. The patient is taken to the OR and prepped, but it was noted that before anesthesia was administered, the patient was experiencing severe hypotension. The procedure was cancelled. The correct code assignment would be 29882–73.

–74 **Discontinued Outpatient Procedure after Anesthesia Administration** *(for hospital use only):* Modifier –74 is reported when a patient's surgery is cancelled after administration of anesthesia or after the procedure was begun (for example, after an incision was made or after an endoscope was inserted). The procedure in progress at the time of cancellation should be reported, not all intended procedures.

> **Example:** Patient is scheduled for a knee arthroscopy for a lateral meniscus repair. The patient is taken to OR, prepped, and anesthesia is administered. Ten minutes into the procedure, the patient develops cardiac arrhythmia and the surgery is cancelled. The correct code assignment would be 29882–74.

–76 **Repeat Procedure by Same Physician** *(for hospital and physician use):* Modifier –76 may be reported to identify a procedure that was repeated by the physician who performed the original procedure. Some third-party payers may require supportive documentation. Hospitals also may report this modifier.

> **Example:** Patient is admitted with significant pleural effusion and congestive heart failure, and the physician performs a thoracentesis. Later in the day, the lungs again fill up with fluid and the same physician performs a second thoracentesis. The physician or hospital should report the following: 32000 (first thoracentesis); 32000–76 (second thoracentesis identified as a repeat procedure with modifier –76).

–77 **Repeat Procedure by Another Physician** *(for hospital and physician use):* Modifier –77 may be reported to identify a procedure that was repeated by a physician other than the one who performed the original procedure. As with modifier –76, some third-party payers may require supportive documentation. Hospitals also may report this modifier as appropriate.

> **Example:** Dr. Reynolds performs a percutaneous transluminal balloon angioplasty of the renal artery. Later in the day, a diagnostic evaluation determines that the artery has occluded again. Because Dr. Reynolds cannot be reached, Dr. Smith repeats the earlier procedure. Dr. Reynolds should report 35471 to identify the first angioplasty performed, and Dr. Smith should report 35471–77 to identify the repeat angioplasty.

–78 **Return to the Operating Room for a Related Procedure During the Postoperative Period** *(for hospital and physician use):* Modifier –78 may be used to report a related procedure performed during the postoperative period of the initial procedure.

> **Example:** Patient has a fracture of the tibia and fibula that has not healed properly. The physician who repairs the malunion should report 27720–78. Reporting modifier –78 indicates to the third-party payer that the second procedure was performed during the postoperative period of the first procedure and is related to it in some way.

Note: Procedures repeated on the same day as the original procedure should be reported with modifier –76.

–79 **Unrelated Procedure or Service by the Same Physician During the Postoperative Period** *(for hospital and physician use):* Modifier –79 may be used to report an unrelated procedure performed during the postoperative period of the initial procedure.

Note: Procedures repeated the same day as the original procedure should be reported with modifier –76.

> **Example:** Patient had a hernia repair two weeks ago. He now returns to the hospital complaining of chills, fever, and right quadrant abdominal pain. Suspecting appendicitis, the physician admits the patient for an emergency

appendectomy. To describe the appendectomy admission, the physician should report 44950–79. The appendectomy is unrelated to the initial procedure performed (hernia repair), so modifier –79 is reported to indicate that the procedure was performed during the postoperative period but is unrelated to the initial surgery.

–80 **Assistant Surgeon** *(for physician use only):* Modifier –80 may be reported to indicate that the physician provided surgical assistant services for a particular procedure. The surgeon who assists another physician reports the code for the procedure that was performed along with modifier –80. The operating surgeon should not report modifier –80.

Note: An assistant surgeon typically is present throughout the entire surgical procedure.

Example: Dr. Reynolds performs a total abdominal hysterectomy with removal of fallopian tubes and ovaries. Dr. Jones provides surgical assistance. Dr. Reynolds should report 58150, and Dr. Jones should report 58150–80.

–81 **Minimum Assistant Surgeon** *(for physician use only):* Modifier –81 may be reported to indicate that a physician provided minimal surgical assistance when another surgeon's presence typically is not required throughout the entire procedure. The physician who provided minimal assistance reports the code for the procedure performed, along with modifier –81. As in the case of modifier –80, the operating surgeon should not report modifier –81.

–82 **Assistant Surgeon (when qualified resident surgeon not available)** *(for physician use only):* Modifier –82 may be reported when a physician provides surgical assistance to another surgeon and a resident surgeon is unavailable. This situation occurs primarily in teaching facilities where resident surgeons typically assume the role of assistant surgeon. When a qualified resident surgeon is unavailable, another physician may serve as an assistant surgeon and report the appropriate procedure code along with modifier –82. As in the case of modifiers –80 and –81, the operating surgeon should not report modifier –82.

–99 **Multiple Modifiers** *(for physician use only):* Modifier –99 may be reported to alert third-party payers that more than one modifier is being submitted on a claim. Many health plans have limitations on the number of modifiers recognized.

Exercise 3.1 Chapter Review

Refer to appendix A of the CPT codebook to identify the modifiers for procedures 1 through 5.

1. The modifier that indicates that a physician provided only postoperative care. _____

2. The modifier used when a different physician repeated a procedure on the same date. _____

3. The modifier used when more than one procedure is performed on a patient during the same operative episode. _____

4. The modifier appended to a code to identify that two surgeons were required to perform the procedure. _____

5. The modifier used when a procedure was begun but had to be discontinued because of deterioration in the patient's condition (coding is for physician services, not hospital). _____

For procedures 6 through 11, assign the correct CPT code(s) and the appropriate modifier (CPT and HCPCS National).

6. A patient undergoes carpal tunnel releases on both the left and right wrists. _____

7. The physician performed a partial avulsion of the nail plate of the left thumb. _____

8. A patient was taken to the outpatient surgery suite for an excisional debridement of the skin that extended into the muscle. The patient was prepped, but before anesthesia was administered, the physician was called for an emergency surgery of a trauma patient and the outpatient surgery was cancelled. (Assign code[s] to be reported by the hospital.) _____

9. A patient who had previously had the left leg amputated was seen in the hospital for a Doppler scan arterial study of the right leg. What CPT code assignment should be submitted on the UB-92? _____

10. With the use of imaging, the patient had a percutaneous needle core biopsy of the left breast. _____

11. The surgeon performed an open reduction with internal fixation for the right, fifth metatarsal fracture. _____
   foot

1 -80
2 -79
3 -54
4 -76
5 -50
6 -32
7 -24

Chapter 4

Surgery

To assign codes accurately from the surgery section, physicians and coders must work together to ensure that the documentation in the health record supports the code(s) selected. In the hospital setting, as in the office setting, the operative or procedure report serves as the source document when identifying the type of procedure that has been performed.

The surgery section provides codes for procedures performed by physicians of any specialty type (general surgeons, ophthalmologists, cardiovascular surgeons, neurosurgeons, and so on). It is further divided into the following subsections:

Subsection	Code Range
General	10021–10022
Integumentary System	10040–19499
Musculoskeletal System	20000–29999
Respiratory System	30000–32999
Cardiovascular System	33010–37799
Hemic and Lymphatic Systems	38100–38999
Mediastinum and Diaphragm	39000–39599
Digestive System	40490–49999
Urinary System	50010–53899
Male Genital System	54000–55899
Intersex Surgery	55970–55980
Female Genital System	56405–58999
Maternity Care and Delivery	59000–59899
Endocrine System	60000–60699
Nervous System	61000–64999
Eye and Ocular Adnexa	65091–68899
Auditory System	69000–69979
Operating Microscope	69990

This chapter reviews the guidelines and conventions specific to surgical coding and introduces specific subsections.

Links to various Web sites pertinent to the discussion in this chapter are located in the Web Resources at the back of this book.

Surgical Package

Most surgical procedures in this section include the following services:

- The actual surgical procedure

- Local infiltration, metacarpal/metatarsal/digital block or topical anesthesia

- Subsequent to the decision for surgery, one related E/M encounter on the date of or immediately prior to the date of the procedure (including history and physical)

- Immediate postoperative care, including dictating operative notes and talking with the family and other physicians

- Writing orders

- Evaluating the patient in the postanesthesia recovery area

- Typical postoperative follow-up care

This concept is often referred to as a surgical package or a global surgery concept, and it is covered by a single fee. Thus, if a physician performs a surgical procedure on March 5 and sees the patient in the office two weeks later for normal follow-up care (for example, removal of sutures), both visits are reported for payment purposes with one code (the code for the procedure) and then submitted as a single claim. For documentation purposes or data capture, the postoperative follow-up visit code (99024) may be reported.

    Example: Four weeks ago, Dr. Smith repaired a closed tibial shaft fracture without manipulation. Today, the patient has returned to Dr. Smith's office to have his cast removed. Dr. Smith may bill only for the repair of the fracture, which includes the normal, uncomplicated follow-up care, including cast removal. Thus, only code 27750 is reported on his claim. The subsequent visit for removal of the cast is not billed separately; however, for tracking purposes only, code 99024 may be assigned for that encounter.

When follow-up visits involve the treatment of complications resulting from the surgical procedure (for example, wound infection at operative site), the appropriate E/M level of service code may be reported, along with the appropriate ICD-9-CM code, to describe the complication.

    Example: Two weeks ago, Dr. Smith performed a cholycystectomy. Today, the patient returns with complaints of redness, inflammation, and oozing from the wound site. Dr. Smith determines that the patient has developed an infection at the operative wound site and treats it appropriately. For the second office visit, Dr. Smith should report the appropriate E/M level of service code and assign ICD-9-CM code 998.59 to describe the wound infection.

Medicare guidelines for reimbursement for services involving complications are slightly different from CPT. These guidelines can be referenced in the *Medicare Providers Manual* published by the Centers for Medicare and Medicaid Services (CMS).

The definition of the surgical package or global surgery does not apply in the hospital out-patient setting. Hospitals may report postoperative visits that occur on subsequent days by using standard billing procedures, such as assigning the appropriate ICD-9-CM diagnosis code to describe the reason for the visit.

Example: Patient returns to the outpatient department of Central Hospital for a change of surgical dressing. The hospital assigns ICD-9-CM code V58.3 (Attention to surgical dressings) to identify the reason for the visit. The E/M code appropriate to the circumstance (new or established) reflects the service rendered.

The surgical package definition may vary depending on individual third-party payer requirements. The Medicare global surgery definition for major surgeries includes:

- The actual surgical procedure

- Preoperative services provided one day prior to surgery or the day of surgery, except when modifier –57 or modifier –25 applies

- Postoperative services provided within 90 days of the surgical procedure, except when modifier –24 applies

- Insignificant surgical procedures not performed in the OR, including: dressing changes, removal of operative packs, and care of the operative incision site; removal of sutures, staples, wires, lines, tubes, drains, casts, and splints; insertion, irrigation, and removal of urinary catheters; routine peripheral intravenous lines; nasogastric tubes and rectal tubes; care of tracheostomy tubes

The Medicare global surgery definition for minor and endoscopic surgeries includes:

- The actual surgical procedure

- Preoperative services provided one day prior to surgery or the day of surgery, except when modifier –57 or modifier –25 applies

- Postoperative services provided within 0 to 10 days of the surgical procedure, except when modifier –24 applies

Follow-up Care for Diagnostic and Therapeutic Procedures

Follow-up care for diagnostic or therapeutic procedures includes only that care related to recovery from the diagnostic procedure itself or care that is usually part of the surgical service. When follow-up care involves the initiation of treatment for the condition that has been diagnosed or for a complication, the treatment should be coded and reported separately. Complication, exacerbation, or recurrence, or the presence of other diseases or injuries requiring additional services should be reported with the appropriate code for that procedure.

Separate Procedure

The CPT codebook defines a separate procedure as one that, when performed in conjunction with another service, is considered an integral part of the major service; therefore, it should not be coded separately. In normal circumstances, it is fraudulent to report the codes separately and charge separate fees for each procedure.

However, the separate procedure may be coded when it is performed independently and not in conjunction with the so-called larger or major procedure. A modifier, such as modifier –59 (Distinct Services), may be added to explain special circumstances where the separate procedure was not performed integral to the larger procedure. For example, assume that the following procedures were performed on a patient:

Example: 58720 Salpingo-oophorectomy, complete or partial, unilateral or bilateral (separate procedure)

58150 Total abdominal hysterectomy (corpus and cervix), with or without removal of tube(s), with or without removal of ovary(s)

58180 Supracervical abdominal hysterectomy (subtotal hysterectomy), with or without removal of tube(s), with or without removal of ovary(s)

Assignment of code 58720 would be appropriate in circumstances where only a salpingo-oophorectomy was performed. If the salpingo-oophorectomy was done as part of a larger procedure, as described in code 58150 or 58180, an additional code of 58720 is inappropriate and would be considered unbundling of services.

In another example, assume the physician performed a flexible bronchoscopy with cell washings (CPT code 31622) and a transbronchial lung biopsy (CPT code 31628). In this example, only CPT code 31628 is reported. CPT code 31622 is a "separate procedure" code and would not be assigned with 31628.

National Correct Coding Initiative (NCCI) or Correct Coding Initiative (CCI)

A list of coding edits was developed by the CMS in an effort to promote correct coding nationwide and to prevent unbundling. The edits help the CMS to detect inappropriate codes submitted on claims and are based on CPT coding guidelines, current standards of medical/surgical coding practice, and advice from specialty societies. There are two major types of coding edits: the comprehensive/component edit and the mutually exclusive edit.

Comprehensive/Component Edit

The comprehensive/component edit pertains to HCPCS codes that should not be used together. Note the following table as an example of a National Correct Coding Initiative (NCCI) listing. Under the NCCI, if bills contain a procedure in both the comprehensive code column and the component code column for the same patient on the same date of service, only the comprehensive code column code is covered (provided that code is on the list as an approved procedure for reimbursement).

Comprehensive Code	Component Code
20912	12014, 13152

In the preceding example, code 20912 describes a cartilage graft of nasal septum. During the procedure, the surgeon may mention that a wound repair (12014, 13152) was performed, but it is considered part of the more involved procedure (20912) and should not be coded. If the coder assigned the additional wound repair codes, it would be considered unbundling.

Mutually Exclusive Edit

The mutually exclusive edit applies to improbable or impossible combinations of codes. For example, code 69601, Revision mastoidectomy; resulting in complete mastoidectomy, would never be performed with code 69604, Revision mastoidectomy; resulting in tympanoplasty.

CCI edits are included in most encoding software packages. The software vendors are responsible for maintaining up-to-date edits to support the coding/billing function.

Integumentary System Subsection

The integumentary system subsection includes codes for procedures performed on the following body parts:

- Skin and subcutaneous structures, including excision of skin lesions, wound closure, skin grafting, burn treatment, Mohs chemosurgery, incision and drainage, and debridement

- Nails, including debridement, excision, and reconstruction of nail bed

- Breast, including needle, incisional, and excisional biopsies, and all types of mastectomies

Figure 4.1 shows the skin and its components.

This subsection includes many definitions that are located at various levels within the subsection. Although some are discussed in this chapter, a careful review of each definition is necessary before codes are assigned.

Figure 4.1.   The skin and its components

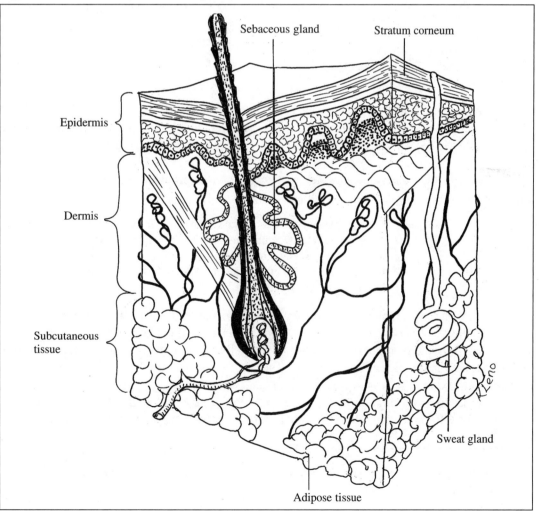

Excision of Lesions

Two separate code ranges can be found in this subsection to describe the excised site of benign (11400–11471) and malignant (11600–11646) lesions. Both series of codes are further subdivided, first by body parts and then by lesion size. To accurately code excision of lesions, the coder must be able to answer the following questions:

1. Is the lesion malignant or benign? Careful review of the operative report and, more important, the pathology report is required to determine the lesion type. Coding from superbills or encounter forms, which do not reveal pathology results, often leads to inappropriate code assignment.

2. What is the site or body part involving the lesion? The operative report should be reviewed for this information.

3. What is the size of the excised area (in centimeters, including margins *if applicable*)?

    Note: The total size of the excised area is needed for accurate coding. Usually, this information is provided in the operative report. It is very important that surgeons be educated and trained to provide lesion size information. The pathology report typically provides the specimen size rather than the lesion or excised size. Because the specimen tends to shrink, this is not an accurate measurement according to the intent of the code assignment. Inches should be converted to centimeters, when necessary.

    1 mm = 0.1 cm
    10 mm = 1.0 cm
    1 inch = approximately 2.54 cm
    1 cm = 0.4 inch

4. What type of wound closure was performed? Both series of codes (11400–11471 and 11600–11646) include simple closure. Separate codes should be reported when the excision requires more than simple closure, such as an intermediate repair.

When more than one dimension for an excised area is provided, the size is equal to the largest dimension of the excision, including margins.

> **Example:** The physician excised a benign lesion of the hand that was reported as 3.0 cm × 1.0 cm. Documentation in the operative report states that 0.5 cm margins were excised around the lesion. For coding purposes, the size of the excision was 3.0 cm + 0.5 cm + 0.5 cm = 4.0 cm in total. The correct code assignment would be 11424.

When excision of a malignant or benign lesion involves repair by adjacent tissue transfer—such as Z-plasty, W-plasty, V-Y plasty, rotation, advancement, or double pedicle flap—codes 14000–14350 should be reported. It should be noted that these codes include both the excision and the tissue transfer or rearrangement. A separate code should not be reported for the lesion excision.

The preceding information describes excision of a skin lesion involving full-thickness removal. The CPT codebook identifies other methods of skin lesion removal in the following code series:

- Shaving (11300–11313) is the sharp removal by a horizontal slicing to remove epidermal and dermal lesions.

- Destruction (17000–17286) is the eradication, ablation, or obliteration of benign, pre-malignant, or malignant lesions by any method including electrocautery, electrodesiccation, cryosurgery, laser, or chemical treatment.

Note: Report each excised lesion with the correct CPT code. Multiple lesion excisions are not added together.

Exercise 4.1

Assign surgical CPT code(s) to the following procedures, along with the index entries used to find the codes.

Note: For all the exercises in the remainder of chapter 4, assign CPT surgical codes only (no E/M codes) and append modifiers, if applicable.

1. Physician excises two benign skin lesions. The excised areas are: 2.0 cm from arm, 1.0 cm from neck.

   Code(s) _____

   Index entries: _____

2. Laser removal of four benign skin lesions from the back.

   Code(s) _____

   Index entries: _____

3. Physician excises a lesion from the chin. The excised dimension is 1.5 cm. Pathology report reveals malignant melanoma.

   Code(s) _____

   Index entries: _____

4. In the physician's office, the patient has seven skin tags removed.

   Code(s) _____

   Index entries: _____

5. Physician excised a 3 cm × 2 cm × 1.5 cm area from the back. The pathology report shows a lipoma in the subcutaneous layer of skin.

   Code(s) _____

   Index entries: _____

6. Physician excised a 2.0 cm squamous cell carcinoma from the forehead. The total excision, including margins, was 3.5 cm in diameter.

   Code(s) _____

   Index entries: _____

7. Excision of malignant melanoma of the forehead (1.0 cm) and nose (0.5).

   Code(s) _____

   Index entries: _____

Exercise 4.2

Operative Report

Preoperative Diagnosis: Sebaceous cyst, left face

Postoperative Diagnosis: Same

Operation: Excision of left-face sebaceous cyst

Anesthesia: Local with IV sedation

Indications for Procedure: The patient is a 69-year-old female who has a sebaceous cyst on the left side of her face that has started to get larger. She presents now for excision of the cyst.

Description of Procedure: The patient was brought to the OR and placed on the operating table in the supine position. She was given 50 mg of Demerol and 1 mg of Versed IV. The left face was prepped and draped in the usual sterile fashion. The area overlying the cyst was anesthetized with 1% lidocaine with epinephrine. An elliptical incision was made of the cyst in the direction of the facial wrinkles. The cyst itself was 1 cm in diameter. The underlying cyst was dissected away from the surrounding tissues, taking care to remove the entire cyst, with an excised area of 2.0 cm × .5 cm. Hemostasis was obtained using electrocautery. The wound was then closed with 3-0 Vicryl. It was then dressed with Masticel and Steri-Strips. The patient tolerated the procedure well and was taken to the recovery room in stable condition.

Pathology Report

Clinical Diagnosis: Cyst of the face

Specimen: Ellipse of skin measuring 2 × 0.5 × 0.2 cm

Pathological Diagnosis: Epidermal inclusion cyst with rupture, marked acute and chronic inflammation

1. Code(s): _____

   What index entries were used to find the code(s)?

   _____

   _____

Exercise 4.3

Operative Report

Preoperative Diagnosis: Epidermoid nevus of scalp

Postoperative Diagnosis: Same

Procedure: Shave excision of 4.0 cm benign scalp lesion

Indications for Procedure: This patient is a gentleman on chronic anticoagulation, from whom we have previously removed a sub-galeal lipoma. At that time he was not interested in having his seborrheic keratosis removed from his scalp, although it was offered. He has had a very nice result from his original surgery and is now willing and wishing to undergo removal of what I believe is a seborrheic keratosis. Although, according to the history, it has been there as long as he can remember, it may be an epidermal nevus. A small portion is sent for biopsy to create the definitive diagnosis. The patient understands the risks of bleeding.

Procedure: The patient was brought to the operating room and made comfortable in a supine position on the table. The area to be worked up was infiltrated with 1% lidocaine with 1:100,000 parts epinephrine. The area was then prepped and draped in the usual sterile fashion. A #15 blade was used to remove a small portion of the lesion, which was carefully labeled and sent to pathology for exam. The rest was then shaved off at the level of the dermis, where there was punctate bleeding. Hemostasis was achieved with cautery. A dressing of Gelfoam soaked in thrombin was placed over this, and the patient was allowed to return to the recovery room with stable vital signs. The estimated blood loss was less than 15 cc, which was replaced with crystalloid solution only. Sponge, needle, and instrument counts were reported as correct.

1. Code(s): _____

   What index entries were used to find the code(s)?

   _____

   _____

Wound Repair/Closure

The CPT codebook describes three types of wound repair/closure, as follows:

1. A simple repair is a superficial repair that primarily involves the epidermis, dermis, or subcutaneous tissues without involvement of deeper structures. This repair usually requires simple suturing of only one layer of skin.

2. An intermediate repair, like a simple wound repair, is considered a superficial repair, requiring that one or more of the deeper layers of the subcutaneous tissue and superficial fascia, as well as the skin, be closed in layers. Wounds that are closed with only one layer, but which are so heavily contaminated that they require extensive cleaning or removal of foreign material such as gravel or glass, also may be classified as an intermediate repair.

3. A complex repair of a wound goes beyond a layer closure and requires scar revision, debridement, extensive undermining, stents, or retention sutures. Wounds described as angular, jagged, irregular, or stellate may require complex repair. Layered closure is part of this wound repair.

To accurately code wound closures, the following questions must be answered:

1. What type of repair is being performed: simple, intermediate, or complex?

2. What site or body part is involved, and what is the extent of the wound? The operative report should be reviewed for mention of blood vessel, tendon, or nerve involvement. The wound repair codes include simple ligation of blood vessels and simple exploration of the nerves, vessels, or tendons, so they should not be reported separately. However, a separate code is warranted if the extent of the laceration requires repair of the nerves, vessels, or tendons.

3. What is the length of the repair (in centimeters)?

When multiple wounds are repaired, the coder should add together the lengths of those in the same classification and from all anatomic sites that are grouped together into the same code descriptor. For example, add together the lengths of intermediate repairs to the trunk and extremities. Do not add lengths of repairs from different groupings of anatomic sites (for example, face and extremities). Also, do not add together the lengths of different classifications (for example, intermediate and complex repairs).

> **Example:** Simple wound repair of two lacerations of the arm measuring 2.5 cm and 1.5 cm. The sum of the two lacerations is 4.0 cm, and the code reported is 12002.

When more than one classification of wounds is repaired, the most complicated repair is listed first, followed by the less complicated repairs. Modifier –51 (for Part B providers) also should be reported to identify the performance of more than one procedure. Debridement may be reported separately only when:

*   Gross contamination requires prolonged cleansing.

*   Considerable amounts of devitalized or contaminated tissue are removed, or debridement is carried out separately without immediate primary closure.

49

To report excisional debridement, the coder must have the following information:

- Percentage of body surface debrided (11000–11001)
- Extent of skin debrided: full or partial thickness (11040–11041)
- Depth of the debridement: subcutaneous, muscle, or bone (11042–11044)

A note under the wound repair subheading cross-references the coder to use codes 20100–20103 if the wound required:

- Enlargement
- Extension of dissection
- Debridement
- Removal of one or more foreign bodies
- Ligation or coagulation of minor subcutaneous and/or muscular blood vessel(s)

Superficial wound repairs requiring only Steri-Strips or bandages are reported with the appropriate E/M services code. Surgical codes are inappropriate because no surgical repair was performed. Repairs with tissue adhesive, such as 2-cyanoacrylate (Dermabond), are reported using the appropriate code from the repair category.

It is important to note that Medicare requires a Level II HCPCS code to identify a wound closed with tissue adhesives. Instead of assigning the CPT code for wound repair, the following code should be assigned: G0168 Wound closure utilizing tissue adhesive(s) only.

HCPCS Level II codes are discussed further in chapter 10.

Exercise 4.4

Assign CPT codes and index entries for the following procedures:

1. A child is seen in the physician's office for a superficial laceration of the right knee. The physician repairs the 3.0 cm laceration with simple suturing.

   Code(s) _____ 12001-12021

   Index entries: _____ Repair /Wound /Simple _____

   _____

2. The patient is treated in the emergency department for a deep 3.5 cm wound of the right arm. A routine cleansing and layer closure was required.

   Code(s) _____

   Index entries: _____

   _____

3. A patient is treated for multiple wounds of the right forearm, hand, and knee. The physician sutured the following: simple repair, 2.5 cm forearm; intermediate repair, 1.5 cm hand; 2.0 cm simple repair, knee.

   Code(s) _____

   Index entries: _____

   _____

Exercise 4.5

Emergency Department Record

Chief Complaint:	Laceration left hand
History of Present Illness:	Patient is a 67-year-old female who tripped over a brick. As she tried to break her fall, she somehow cut her left hand. She has a laceration at the base of her fifth finger on the palm side, but no other injuries.
Past Medical History:	Unremarkable
Medications:	None
Allergies:	None
Physical Examination:	
General:	Alert female in no acute distress
Extremities:	Left upper extremity exam reveals a 2.5 cm full-skin-thickness laceration on the palm side of the left hand just at the base of the finger over the volar metacarpal phalangeal joints. She has full active and passive range of motion.
Procedure:	Anesthesia local injection 2 cc 1% lidocaine plain; prepped and routine exploration revealed no foreign body. No neurovascular tendon injury noted. Repaired with six 5-0 nylon sutures. Polysporin ointment and dressing placed on the wound.
Diagnosis:	2.5 cm simple laceration left hand
Disposition and Plan:	Wound care instructions given and advised to have sutures taken out in 10–12 days

1. Code(s): _____

    What index entries were used to find the code(s)?

    _____

    _____

Exercise 4.6

Emergency Department Record

Chief Complaint:	Right arm laceration
History of Present Illness:	This 24-year-old male presents here after attempting to punch out a window in his garage door with his elbow in an attempt to enter his own house
Medications:	None
Allergies:	Keflex
Last Known Tetanus:	Unknown

Review of Systems: No shoulder pain, no wrist pain. Complains of multiple lacerations of the forearm.

Extremities: Right elbow and right forearm reveal multiple lacerations in various lengths from proximal and working distally. Over the area of the olecranon, there is noted to be a 3 cm superficial laceration. There is also noted to be several simple lacerations distally: approximately four measuring 1 cm and three others measuring 2 cm each. There is noted to be a 5 cm laceration involving deeper layers of skin.

Procedure: After adequate anesthesia was obtained with local infiltration of all lacerations with 1% lidocaine with epinephrine, the wounds were explored. No foreign bodies were appreciated. Each wound was vigorously irrigated and draped individually in a sterile fashion individually. Initially, the 3 cm laceration along the area of the olecranon was closed with two interrupted sutures of 4-0 Ethilon. The remaining smaller wounds were closed with simple sutures. The 5 cm laceration required closing with 3-0 Vicryl for the subcutaneous layer and 4-0 Vicryl to close the skin. Wound edges were painted with Benzoin and Steri-Strips applied. The patient tolerated the procedure well.

1. Code(s): _____

    What index entries were used to find the code(s)?

    _____

    _____

Exercise 4.7

Emergency Department Operative Note

Chief Complaint: Head laceration

History of Present Illness: This 85-year-old male was found in his basement with a bleeding head laceration. Exam revealed a laceration on his scalp, which is at the superior occiput. The laceration was approximately 8 cm and required a complex repair. The wound was irrigated as well as possible with normal saline. Subsequently, using 4-0 Vicryl suturing, some of the deeper structures were reapproximated with some hemostasis. Approximately three Vicryl sutures were placed deep in these structures. Four-0 nylon interrupted suturing was used with multiple sutures placed, with eventual control of the hemostasis. Several other staples were placed as well for further cosmetic closure of the skin. The procedure did provide complete resolution of the symptoms. There was a very complex and deep wound with active hemorrhage. Subsequent to this, it was cleansed and Neosporin was placed. Please note that multiple areas of hair were trimmed with scissors prior to this procedure.

1.   Code(s): _____

     What index entries were used to find the code(s)?

     _____

Exercise 4.8

Operative Report

Preoperative diagnosis: Pigmented nevus, arm

Postoperative diagnosis: Melanoma

Operation: Excision 1.5 nevus of arm

The patient was brought into the surgery center and prepped and draped in the usual manner. Local anesthesia was injected under the lesion. The lesion with 0.5 cm margins was excised taking full-thickness skin, transversely oblique. Hemostasis was obtained with cautery. The skin was closed in layers of 3-0 Vicryl in fascia, 5-0 Vicryl subcuticular, and 6-0 nylon in the skin. Dressing was applied.

1.   Code(s): _____

     What index entries were used to find the code(s)?

     _____

Skin Grafting

The first series of codes (14000–14350) includes both the lesion excision and the tissue transfer or rearrangement (also known as local skin flaps), such as Z-plasty, W-plasty, V-Y plasty, rotation, advancement, or double pedicle flap. These codes are categorized first by body part involved and then by size of defect in square centimeters.

An additional code may be reported to describe any skin grafting required to close the secondary defect.

The following definitions are helpful when coding adjacent tissue transfer or arrangement procedures:

- Advancement: The sliding of a pedicle graft into its new position.

- Pedicle graft: Grafted tissue that remains connected to its vascular bed.

- Z-plasty: A tissue transfer that surgically releases tension in the skin caused by a laceration, contracted scar, or a wound along the flexion crease of joint. It is characterized by a Z-shaped incision that is above, through, and below the scar or defect.

- W-plasty: A tissue transfer performed to release tension along a straight scar. A W-shaped incision creates a series of triangular flaps of skin. The triangle flaps on both sides of the scar are removed, and the remaining skin triangles are moved together and sutured into place.

- V-Y plasty: A tissue transfer that begins with a V-shaped skin incision and with advancement and stretching of the skin and tissue. The defect is covered and forms a Y when sutured together.

- Rotational flap: These flaps are curved or semicircular and include the skin and subcutaneous tissues. A base is left, and the remaining portion of the flap is freed and rotated to cover the defect and then sutured into place.

The second series of codes (15000–15401) describes free skin grafts that are completely separated from the donor site in a one-stage procedure. These codes are categorized by type of graft (for example, pinch graft, split-thickness graft, or full-thickness graft), body part involved, and size of defect in square centimeters (except for pinch grafts, which are measured in centimeters). The free skin-grafting procedures include simple debridement of granulations or recent avulsion.

If the donor site requires skin grafting or local flaps, an additional code should be reported. The following definitions are helpful when coding free skin grafts:

- Pinch graft: This is a piece of skin graft about 1/4 inch in diameter that is obtained by elevating the skin with a needle and slicing it off with a knife.

- Split-thickness graft: This graft consists of only the superficial layers of the dermis. See figure 4.2 as an illustration.

Figure 4.2.   Depth of split-thickness and full-thickness grafts

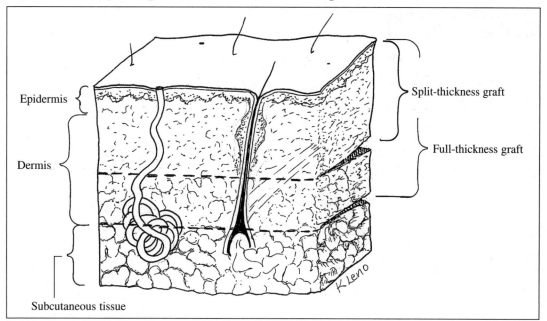

- Full-thickness graft: This graft is composed of skin and subcutaneous tissues.

- Allograft: This graft is obtained from a genetically dissimilar individual of the same species (one individual to another). It is also known as allogenic graft and homograft.

- Xenograft: This graft is obtained from a species different from the recipient (for example, animal to human). It is also called xenogenic graft, heterograft, and heterotransplant.

Removal of Skin Lesion with Free Skin Graft

When an excision of a lesion requires a free skin graft for repair of the defect, the coder is directed to also assign a code to identify the excision of the lesion, using a code in the range of 11400–11471 or 11600–11646.

Flaps (Skin and/or Deep Tissues)

This series of codes (15570–15738) includes procedures describing pedicle flaps, muscle, myocutaneous or fasciocutaneous flaps, and delayed flap transfers. The codes are categorized first by type of flap (for example, pedicle) and then by recipient body part.

Codes 15600–15630, which describe delayed transfer, identify the donor site, not the recipient site. An additional code should be reported when repair of the donor site requires skin grafting or local flaps.

The following definitions are helpful when coding flaps:

- Pedicle flap: This flap consists of detached skin and subcutaneous tissue in which the attached end or base contains an adequate blood supply. It is partially transferred to the recipient site with the base still attached to the donor site. After the recipient site has established a good blood supply, the base or pedicle is cut off and the graft completed.

- Myocutaneous flap: This flap involves the transfer of intact muscle, subcutaneous tissue, and skin as a single unit rotated on a relatively narrow blood supply of the muscle.

Exercise 4.9

Assign CPT codes and index entries for the following procedure:

1. Physician performs a wide resection of a 3.0 cm malignant skin lesion of the left leg. The defect required an adjacent tissue transfer measuring 15 sq cm.

   Code(s) _____

   Index entries: _____

   _____

Exercise 4.10

Operative Report

Preoperative Diagnosis: Basal cell carcinoma of the forehead

Postoperative Diagnosis: Same

Procedure: Excision of basal cell carcinoma with split-thickness skin graft

The patient was given a local IV sedation and taken to the OR suite. The face and left thigh were prepped with Phisohex soap. The cancer was outlined for excision and measured 5 x 4 cm. The forehead was infiltrated with 1% Xylocaine with 1:100,000 epinephrine.

The cancer was excised and carried down to the frontalis muscle. A suture was placed at the 12 o'clock position. The specimen was sent to pathology for frozen section.

Attention was then turned to the skin graft. A pattern of the defect was transferred to the left anterior thigh using a new needle. A local infiltration was performed on the thigh. Using a freehand knife, a split-thickness skin graft was harvested. The thigh was treated with Tegaderm and a wraparound Kerliz and Ace wrap. The skin graft was applied and sutured to the forehead defect with running 5-0 plain catgut.

Xeroform with cotton soaked in glycerin was sutured with 4-0 silk. A sterile dressing was applied. The patient tolerated the procedure well, with no complications or blood loss.

1. Code(s): _____

    What index entries were used to find the code(s)?

    _____

    _____

Exercise 4.11

Operative Report

Preoperative Diagnosis: Open wound, left thigh, status post fasciotomy

Postoperative Diagnosis: Same

Procedure: Split-thickness skin graft, left thigh, donor site from left thigh. Graft was approximately 12 × 5 cm.

Indications for Procedure: The patient is a status post trauma. He had a tree fall on him and sustained a significant injury to his thigh. He had compartment syndrome of his thigh requiring a fasciotomy. He presents today for a skin graft to the fasciotomy site.

Details of Procedure: The patient was brought to the operating room and placed supine on the operating table. Following the adequate induction of general anesthesia, his left thigh and fasciotomy site were prepped and draped in the standard surgical fashion. Attention was first directed to the patient's anterior thigh. The Betadine prep was gently removed with normal saline. We then applied mineral oil to the anterior thigh. We then used a dermatome to harvest an approximately 12 × 5 cm split-thickness skin graft in the depth of 0.015. Following removal of our donor site, an epinephrine-soaked sponge was applied to the donor site. We then went in to the back table and meshed our graft 1:1. Following this, we prepared our graft bed for graft placement. The excellent granulation tissue bed was roughed up using a gauze sponge, and the skin graft was applied and secured in place using surgical staples. The edge of the skin was then trimmed accordingly. Following adequate placement and securing our graft, we then fashioned the dressing. A Bacitracin-coated Adaptic was then applied over the graft and Reston foam was applied over that. Fine mesh gauze was then used to secure it in place, and the Reston and mesh gauze were secured also using surgical staples. There was an excellent compression against the graft. Following this, we turned our attention to the donor site. Epinephrine-soaked gauze was removed, and Calgiswab dressing was applied. There was excellent hemostasis from the donor site. Following this, a Kerlix roll was placed around the left thigh and secured with paper tape. The patient tolerated the procedure without complications. The patient was then taken to the PACU for recovery.

60 sq cm

1. Code(s): _____

    What index entries were used to find the code(s)?

    _____

Skin Graft and Flap/ Split Graft   15100-15 121   (15100)

Surgical Procedures of the Breast

Codes 19000–19499 describe procedures performed on the breast, such as biopsy, mastectomy, and reconstruction. These codes are categorized first by general type of procedure (incision, excision, reconstruction/repair) and then by specific procedure.

The codes describing breast procedures refer to unilateral procedures, and modifiers –LT or –RT should be appended. If a bilateral procedure is performed, modifier –50 should be reported.

Breast Biopsy

In coding breast biopsies, the coder must determine the type of biopsy performed: needle, excisional, or incisional.

Percutaneous (needle) biopsy of the breast is reported with code 19100.

Excisional biopsy involves total removal of the lesion, whether malignant or benign, from the breast. To make this determination, the coder should review both the operative report and the pathology report. The operative report may indicate that the lesion was removed completely. In the case of malignant lesions, the pathology report may indicate that the margins of the specimen are negative for malignancy or free of tumor.

If the excisional biopsy was performed with identification by preoperative placement of radiological marker, codes 19125–19126 should be reported. When appropriate, an additional code(s) to describe placement of the needle localization wire (19290–19291) or metallic localization clip (19295) should be reported.

An incisional biopsy (19101) is typically one in which only a portion of the lesion is removed for pathologic examination.

Mastectomy

Codes 19140–19240 describe the various types of mastectomy:

- Code 19160, Partial mastectomy, refers to the partial removal of part of the breast tissue, leaving the breast almost intact. This also may be referred to as a lobectomy or lumpectomy.

- Code 19180, Simple, complete mastectomy, is assigned for the excision of all the breast tissue, with the lymph nodes and muscle left intact.

- Code 19182, Subcutaneous mastectomy, is used for excision of breast tissue with the skin and nipple intact.

- Code 19200, Radical mastectomy, refers to the excision of breast tissue including the pectoral muscles and the axillary lymph nodes.

- Code 19220, also described as a radical mastectomy, is assigned for the excision of breast tissue including the pectoral muscles and axillary and internal mammary lymph nodes.

- Code 19240, Modified radical mastectomy, is used for the excision of breast tissue including the axillary lymph nodes. The pectoralis minor muscles may or may not be removed, but the pectoralis major muscles are left intact.

Insertion of breast prosthesis may be reported as an additional code when performed at the same time as the mastectomy (19340) or when performed at a later date (19342).

Exercise 4.12

Physician Office Operative Note

This patient has come to see me for follow-up for a cyst present in the left breast area. I did a needle aspiration biopsy, and fluid was sent out for cytology. If the biopsy is negative, I can see him back in the office in four months, or earlier if there are any problems.

The right breast feels benign. There is no axillary adenopathy. No cervical adenopathy.

Hospital Pathology: Left breast aspiration
                        —few benign lipocytes present only

1. Code(s): _____

    What index entries were used to find the code(s)?

    _____

    _____

Exercise 4.13

Operative Report

Preoperative Diagnosis: Abnormal mammogram, left breast

Postoperative Diagnosis: Same

Indications for Procedure: The patient is a 61-year-old G3, P3 female with a family history of positive carcinoma of the breast. She underwent a screening mammogram in the spring of this year that demonstrated a localized density in the subareolar tissue of the left breast. Physical exam demonstrated no palpable abnormality in the area.

Description of Procedure: The patient was brought to the OR after undergoing placement of a hook wire localizing needle in the mammography suite by the radiologist. She was placed on the OR table in a supine position. After ensuring an adequate level of conscious sedation, her left breast and chest wall were prepped and draped in a sterile fashion. A needle/wire complex was protruding from the left breast approximately 2 centimeters above the nipple. The skin surrounding the needle in the breast tissue in the subareolar area was infiltrated with 1% Xylocaine to achieve local anesthesia. A 5-centimeter incision was made around the localizing wire. Small superior and inferior skin flaps were elevated, exposing the underlying subcutaneous fat. Dissection with electrocautery was begun into the breast about the wire. The needle wire complex was grasped using Allis clamps and drawn into the operative wound. The breast tissue and subcutaneous fat surrounding the needle were excised in this fashion until all the tissue surrounding the needle/wire complex was excised. The specimen was then forwarded to the radiology suite for specimen mammography.

As the specimen mammogram was being obtained, the wound was examined for hemostasis, which was felt to be complete. The deeper breast tissues were closed using interrupted 3-0 Vicryl figure-of-eight sutures. Subcutaneous tissues were approximated in a similar fashion. The wound was irrigated and again examined for hemostasis, which was felt to be complete. The skin was closed using a running 5-0 Maxon subcuticular suture. The wound was washed and dried and sterile dressings applied. The operative field was not disturbed until a call was received from the radiology suite indicating that the specimen contained the area of interest identified on the patient's original mammogram. At this point, the patient was transferred to the recovery area in stable condition.

1. Assign codes for the surgeon's services:

    _____

    What index entries were used to find the code(s)?

    _____

    _____

ch 3&4

Exercise 4.14

Operative Report

Preoperative Diagnosis: Probable carcinoma of the right breast

Postoperative Diagnosis: Carcinoma of the right breast

Operation: Excisional biopsy

Procedure: The patient was brought to the OR. Under satisfactory general endotracheal anesthesia, the right breast was prepped and draped in the usual manner. Through an elliptical incision in the upper outer quadrant, a small nodule was excised. Bleeders were electrocoagulated. The deep layer was closed with interrupted 3-0 Vicryl. The skin was closed with clips. A dry sterile dressing was applied, and the patient returned to the recovery room in good condition.

Pathology Report

Clinical Diagnosis: Right breast mass

Specimen: Mass, right breast, frozen section

Pathological Diagnosis: Breast mass, right: infiltrating ductal carcinoma, Grade 2/3, 0.7 cm.

Resected margins negative for carcinoma

1.   Code(s): _____

    What index entries were used to find the code(s)?

_____

_____

Musculoskeletal Subsection

The musculoskeletal subsection is categorized first by body part and then by general type of procedure, with the individual codes describing the specific procedure performed. The first series of codes (20000–20999) describes general musculoskeletal procedures such as bone biopsy, application of fixation device, bone graft, replantation of body part, wound exploration, and arthrocentesis. A lengthy note at the beginning of this subsection defines terms related to the treatment of fractures.

The codes listed in this subsection include the application and removal of the first cast and/or traction device. Subsequent replacement of the cast and/or traction device may be reported with codes 29000–29799 and codes located at the beginning of the general subsection.

Fractures and Dislocations

To report the diagnosis and treatment of fractures and dislocations accurately, coders must answer the following questions:

1.   What body site is involved? The operative report and/or any diagnostic tests performed, such as X rays or computed tomography (CT) scans, should be reviewed.

2.   Was the fracture/dislocation treatment open or closed or with percutaneous skeletal fixation? Closed treatment refers to treatment of the fracture/dislocation without a surgical incision into the site. Open treatment refers to the treatment of a fracture or dislocation that includes exposing the site via a surgical incision or when a fractured

bone is opened remote from the fracture site in order to insert an intramedullary nail across the fracture site (fracture site is not opened and visualized). Percutaneous skeletal fixation involves treatment of a fracture by placing fixation devices such as pins across the fracture site, usually under X-ray imaging.

3. Was the fracture/dislocation manipulated? Manipulation refers to the attempted reduction or restoration of a dislocated joint or fracture. CPT codes are available for reporting nondisplaced fractures treated without manipulation.

   Example: Code 27238 is used for reporting closed treatment of an intertrochanteric fracture, without manipulation.

4. Did the procedure include internal or external fixation?

Application of Casts and Strapping

The series of codes (29000–29750) describing the application of casts and strapping can be reported in the following scenarios:

- To identify replacement of a cast or strapping during or after the period of normal follow-up care (global postoperative period)

- To identify an initial service performed without any restorative treatment or stabilization of the fracture, injury, or dislocation and/or to afford pain relief to the patient

- To identify an initial cast or strapping when the same physician does not perform or is not expected to perform any other treatment or procedure

- To identify an initial cast or strapping when another physician provided or will provide restorative treatment

CPT guidelines for hospital outpatient reporting of casting/strapping/splinting can be found in *CPT Assistant,* Vol. 12, Issue 4, April 2002.

Exercise 4.15

Assign CPT codes and index entries for the following procedures. Append modifiers if applicable.

1. Diagnosis: Closed fracture of ulnar shaft, left
   Procedure: Open reduction of ulnar shaft fracture

   Code(s) _____

   Index entries: _____

   _____

2. Closed treatment of two uncomplicated rib fractures

   Code(s) _____

   Index entries: _____

   _____

3. Closed reduction of proximal humerus fracture, right

   Code(s) _____

   Index entries: _____

   _____

4. The orthopedic surgeon reduces a fracture of the right proximal tibia. After closed treatment and skeletal traction, the physician applies a short leg cast.

   Code(s) _____

   Index entries: _____

   _____

5. The patient was diagnosed with a dislocated right patella. Under anesthesia, the surgeon performed a closed reduction.

   Code(s) _____

   Index entries: _____

   _____

6. Open reduction with internal fixation, fracture of distal end (medial condyle) of left femur

   Code(s) _____

   Index entries: _____

   _____

7. Patient is diagnosed with right humeral shaft fracture. The orthopedic surgeon performs an open treatment of the fracture using an intramedullary implant and locking screws

   Code(s) _____

   Index entries: _____

   _____

Exercise 4.16

Emergency Department Record

Chief Complaint:	Right ankle injury
History of Present Illness:	The patient is a 39-year-old female who injured her right ankle yesterday. While stepping around some puppies to avoid hitting them, she suffered an inversion injury to her ankle. She complains of lateral ankle and foot pain, and has pain on weight bearing.
Past Medical History:	Status post hysterectomy
Medications:	None
Allergies:	Codeine, which causes nausea
Physical Examination:	Alert female in no acute distress. Right lower extremity: proximal mid tibia-fibula are nontender. Ankle shows moderate diffuse swelling over the lateral ankle extending onto the dorsolateral foot with ecchymoses. Good distal neurovascular status. Decreased range of motion secondary to pain and swelling.
Emergency Department Course:	X ray of right foot and ankle shows an avulsion fragment off of the distal fibula, otherwise soft tissue swelling
Diagnosis:	Acute right ankle sprain with avulsion fracture
Disposition and Plan:	Short leg splint applied. Crutches. No weight bearing. Ice and elevate. Vicodin #30 one- to two-q 4-6 h. She tolerates it well. Orthopedic referral.

1. Code(s): _____

   What index entries were used to find the code(s)?

   _____

   _____

Exercise 4.17

Operative Report

Preoperative Diagnosis:	Fracture of distal fibula, left
Postoperative Diagnosis:	Same
Procedure:	Closed reduction of fibular fracture

This 14-year-old gymnast feels pain in her left leg after vaulting at practice. She is unable to bear any weight on her foot.

Physical examination showed foot and ankle to be normal. The neurovascular status of the foot was normal. The ankle was nontender and not swollen. Findings were confined to the distal fibula, two inches proximal to the lateral malleolus. There was point tenderness in this area. An X ray of the tibia and fibula shows a displaced fracture of the distal fibula.

The fracture was reduced and the patient placed in a short leg splint with extensive padding over the fracture site. She was given Tylenol #3 for pain and instructed to follow up with her physician in 10 days.

1. Code(s): _____

   What index entries were used to find the code(s)?

   _____

Arthroscopy

Procedures describing both diagnostic and therapeutic arthroscopy are reported with codes 29800–29909. These codes are categorized first by body part involved and then by type—

surgical or diagnostic. The surgical arthroscopic codes are further divided to identify the specific procedure performed, such as synovectomy or debridement. A surgical arthroscopy always includes a diagnostic component that should not be reported separately.

Exercise 4.18

Assign CPT codes and index entries for the following procedures. Append modifiers if applicable.

1. Arthroscopic synovectomy (limited) of the left knee

   Code(s) _____

   Index entries: _____

   _____

2. Arthroscopy of right shoulder with rotator cuff repair

   Code(s) _____

   Index entries: _____

   _____

3. Arthroscopy of the left wrist with repair of triangular fibrocartilage and joint debridement

   Code(s) _____

   Index entries: _____

   _____

4. Arthroscopy of the left elbow with limited debridement

   Code(s) _____

   Index entries: _____

   _____

Exercise 4.19

Operative Report

Preoperative Diagnosis: Tear of the right medial meniscus

Postoperative Diagnosis: Same

Operation: Meniscus repair

Procedure: The patient was brought to the OR and anesthetized. An inflatable tourniquet was placed about the proximal thigh, and the operative area was prepped and draped in a sterile fashion with the leg placed in the instrument maker leg holder. Following this, incisions were made for insertion of the arthroscope inflow cannula and probe. Video arthroscopy was then carried out. He was found to have a tear of the posterior horn of the medial meniscus, and this was repaired. The anterior cruciate ligament was examined and found to be intact. The lateral meniscus also appeared to be intact. The patellofemoral joint was within normal limits. While the patient was asleep, the knee was examined and stressed. There was no opening of the medial collateral ligament region and no instability in that area. After completion of the arthroscopy, the instruments were withdrawn from the wound and the incisions closed. The incisions were injected marginally with local anesthetic for postoperative analgesia. After closure of the incisions, Betadine ointment and dressings were placed over the knee and the patient was returned to the recovery room in stable condition.

1. Code(s): _____

   What index entries were used to find the code(s)?

   _____

   _____

Respiratory Subsection

The respiratory subsection includes surgical procedures involving the nose and sinuses, larynx, trachea and bronchi, and lungs and pleura. Figures 4.3 and 4.4 depict the respiratory system.

Nasal Sinus Endoscopy

Codes 31231–31294 describe nasal sinus endoscopic procedures. These procedures allow the physician to visualize the interior of the nasal cavity, the middle and superior meatus, the turbinates, and the sphenoethmoid recess. The purpose of the procedures may be either diag-

Figure 4.3. **The upper respiratory system**

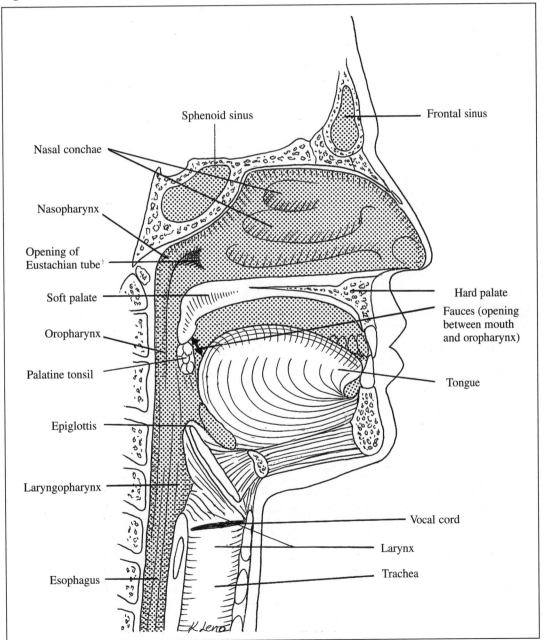

Figure 4.4. **The lower respiratory system**

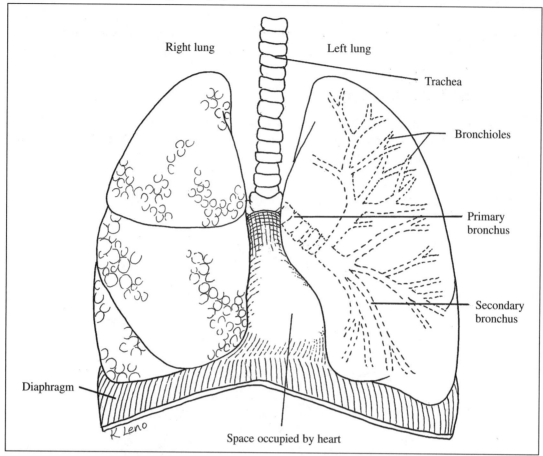

nostic or surgical in nature. A surgical endoscopy may be performed to control a nosebleed or to perform a maxillary antrostomy or sphenoidotomy. The coder should always review the documentation carefully to clarify the extent of the procedure. A surgical endoscopy includes the diagnostic component. The diagnostic endoscopy should not be reported separately when performed during the same operative episode. Also, if performed, a sinusotomy is considered part of the endoscopic procedure and not reported separately.

Unless otherwise stated, codes in the 31231–31294 range are assumed to be unilateral. When the documentation indicates that a bilateral procedure was performed and the specific code does not state bilateral, modifier –50 may be assigned. Key points to remember include:

- Do not assign a separate code to identify a diagnostic nasal/sinus endoscopy when it is performed in conjunction with a surgical nasal/sinus endoscopy.

- A surgical endoscopy includes a sinusotomy. Assign only the code for the surgical endoscopy when both are performed during the same operative episode.

- Use modifier –50 to identify a bilateral procedure only if the code does not specify bilateral.

Exercise 4.20

Assign CPT codes and index entries for the following procedures. Append modifiers if applicable.

1. Bilateral nasal endoscopy with total ethmoidectomy

   Code(s) _____

   Index entries: _____

   _____

2. Left nasal endoscopy for control of epistaxis

   Code(s) _____

   Index entries: _____

   _____

3. Diagnostic maxillary sinusoscopy, bilateral

   Code(s) _____

   Index entries: _____

   _____

Exercise 4.21

Operative Report

Preoperative Diagnosis: Deviated nasal septum, chronic maxillary sinusitis, turbinate hypertrophy, nasal obstruction

Postoperative Diagnosis: Same

Procedure Performed:

1. Septoplasty

2. Nasal endoscopy, with bilateral maxillary antroscopy, removal of maxillary polyp

3. Submucous resection of the inferior turbinates, bilaterally

Indication for Surgery: This twenty-six-year-old female was seen by ENT Service for complaints of chronic sinusitis and difficulty breathing through the nose. She was noted to have a severely deviated septum toward the right with turbinate hypertrophy, nasal obstruction (CT scans confirmed this), as well as obstruction of the ostiomeatal complexes with mucosal thickening. A decision for the above-stated procedure was then made after she had failed conservative care.

Procedure: The patient was brought to the operative suite, given general anesthetic, and properly prepped and draped. 5% cocaine pledgets were placed in each nasal chamber. 1% lidocaine with 1:100,000 epinephrine were injected into the caudal columnar region into the septum, as well as the middle uncinate middle turbinate region. Then, with the #1 scalp blade, an incision was made along the left caudal columnar region in the septum, down to the mucoperichondrium. The mucoperichondrium was carefully elevated off the nasal septum cartilage, exposing a portion of the deviation. The contralateral portion was also freed up. With a Seiler knife, a portion of the deviation was removed. A large septal spur, touching the lateral wall, was carefully freed up and removed.

After the patient exhibited a much improved nasal septum, a piece of cartilage was morselized and inserted between the septal mucosa layers and the submucosa was closed with 4-0 plain suture in interrupted form. Attention was then brought to the middle turbinates, which were found to be lateralized. A decision to medialize them was made by placing 4-0 Vicryl to the left middle turbinate, sent through the right middle turbinate, back to the septum, and tied off on the left side.

Next, with the scope, the left nasal chamber was examined. The natural os was located. With the frontal probe, it was further enlarged with microbiter straight shot and back-biters. There was a moderate amount of mucosal thickening around this opening, just on the inside. After it was widely patent and cleaned out, attention was brought to the right side. The right os was located in a similar fashion and widely enlarged with the microbiter straight shot and back-biters. Again, a moderate amount of mucosal thickening was noted around this opening. When this was completed, attention was brought to the inferior turbinates.

The inferior turbinates were infractured and clamped with a Carmel clamp for five minutes, then submucosal resection was performed in the usual fashion. The rods of the turbinates were then cauterized with suction cautery. This was repeated in a similar fashion bilaterally. Silastic splints were sewn into place along the septum with 3-0 Ethilon, and tampons coated in Bactroban were inserted into both nasal chambers. The oral cavity was suctioned of all serosanguineous debris, and the patient exhibited good hemostasis. She was taken out of her anesthetic and transferred to the recovery room in stable condition.

1. Code(s) to be submitted for the *hospital* services:

   _____

   What index entries were used to find the code(s)?

   _____

   _____

Laryngoscopy

A laryngoscopy is an endoscopic procedure that allows the physician to visualize the larynx, or voice box. This examination may be diagnostic only or may be performed for surgical purposes such as for a biopsy or removal of a lesion. Codes 31505–31579 describe these diagnostic and surgical endoscopic procedures.

Codes 31505–31513 refer to an indirect laryngoscopy. An indirect laryngoscopy is the simplest way to examine the larynx. One technique involves the use of a small mirror placed in the back of the throat. With the aid of a light source, the image of the larynx can be visualized in the mirror. The physician may view the image of the oropharynx, posterior third of the tongue, lateral laryngeal walls, posterior pharyngeal wall, epiglottis, valleculae, and piriform sinuses. He or she also may be able to view the aryepiglottic folds, posterior epiglottis, and vocal cords. Although an indirect laryngoscopy is the simplest and least expensive way to examine the larynx, it does require a great deal of skill on the part of the physician. Moreover, this technique may be impossible to perform on a patient who has a strong gag reflex and t cannot be used on small children.

Codes 31515–31571 are used to identify a direct laryngoscopy. This range of codes identifies the performance of procedures such as biopsy, removal of a lesion, arytenoidectomy, and removal of a foreign body. Laryngoscopes that are commonly used include Kleinsasser, Jako, Dedo, Jackson, Lindholm, Nagashima, Holinger, and Benjamin. During this complex procedure, the physician looks directly at the larynx. The patient is usually placed under general anesthesia to avoid the difficulties associated with the gag reflex. A microscope also may be used during the procedure to magnify the image of the larynx. Because the code assignment will be affected, the coder should review the operative report carefully for any mention of a microscope or for terms such as "microlaryngoscopy." It is inappropriate to use code 69990, Use of operating microscope, in addition to any laryngoscopy code identified as being done with an operating microscope.

Codes 31575–31578 are used for a laryngoscopy performed with flexible fiberoptic equipment. After administration of a topical anesthesia and vasoconstrictor, the instrument is passed through the nasal cavity. This type of laryngoscope provides a more comfortable approach to visualizing the larynx, the pharynx, and the nasal cavity.

Code 31579 identifies a laryngoscopy with stroboscopy. A strobe light provides a very bright light in short flashes. Because of the flashing produced by the stroboscopy, the physician is better able to examine moving vocal cords.

Points to remember:

- Determine the purpose of the laryngoscopy.

- Determine whether a direct, indirect, or flexible fiberoptic laryngoscope was used.

- Determine whether a stroboscopy was used.

- If an operating microscope was used, use the combination code. Do *not* assign code 69990.

Exercise 4.22

Assign CPT codes and index entries for the following procedures:

1. Direct laryngoscopy with stripping of vocal cords

   Code(s) _____

   Index entries: _____

   _____

2. Flexible fiberoptic laryngoscopy performed for removal of a dime lodged in the patient's larynx

   Code(s) _____

   Index entries: _____

   _____

3. Indirect laryngoscopy with biopsy

   Code(s) _____

   Index entries: _____

   _____

4. Using an operating microscope, the surgeon performs a laryngoscopy with excision of a polyp

   Code(s) _____

   Index entries: _____

   _____

Exercise 4.23

Operative Report

Preoperative Diagnosis: Laryngeal lesion

Postoperative Diagnosis: Same

Operation: Direct laryngoscopy and biopsy of vocal cord lesion using an operating microscope

Procedure: The patient was placed on the OR table in the supine position, induced under general anesthesia, and intubated. The Dedo laryngoscope was introduced into the oral cavity, slipped under the tip of the epiglottis, and suspended from the Lewy suspension apparatus. The lesion involved the entire left vocal cord and extended through the ventricle to the false vocal cord and into the anterior commissure area. It also slightly involved the anterior portion of the right vocal cord. In addition, some subglottic extension was present. A biopsy was taken and sent out for frozen section. The laryngoscope was then removed and the procedure terminated. The patient tolerated the procedure well and left the room in good condition.

1. Code(s): _____

   What index entries were used to find the code(s)?

   _____

   _____

Bronchoscopy

A bronchoscope is an instrument that can be inserted into either the nose or the mouth and passed through the trachea, past the larynx, and into the bronchial tubes. Indications for this procedure include hemoptysis, a persistent cough that is unresponsive to medication, shortness of breath, an acute upper airway obstruction, or an abnormal chest X ray or infection.

A physician may elect to use a flexible or rigid bronchoscope. The rigid scope, also referred to as an open-tube bronchoscope, is inserted through the mouth and most often is used to remove foreign objects or to secure a larger-than-normal biopsy sample. The more commonly performed flexible bronchoscopy consists of a flexible tube with many small glass fibers that allow the transmission of light. Codes in the 31622–31656 range are used to identify a variety of procedures using either type of bronchoscope.

The note at the beginning of this section advises coders that a surgical bronchoscopy includes a diagnostic bronchoscopy. It is important to note that codes 31622–31646 include fluoroscopic guidance. Fluoroscopic equipment serves as an image intensifier and is frequently used during bronchoscopies. It is incorrect to use an additional code to identify fluoroscopy.

Frequently, the purpose of the bronchoscopy is to obtain tissue to allow the physician to make an accurate diagnosis. Specimens may be collected in several ways. Cell washings may be obtained by introducing saline solution into the airways, which then is removed and sent to the lab for cytological examination. Code 31622 identifies a bronchoscopy *with or without* cell washings.

Brushings of tissue is another method of specimen collection. One advantage to this method is that brushings allow the diagnosis to be made on the basis of tissue that could not be obtained normally with biopsy forceps. Either a fixed brush or a protected specimen brush (PSB) may be introduced through the bronchoscope. A PSB is a brush contained in a double catheter. A wax plug at the top prevents contamination of the specimen by upper airway flora. Code 31623 is assigned when a bronchoscopy is performed to collect specimen(s) with either a fixed brush or a PSB.

Code 31624 identifies a bronchoscopy with bronchial alveolar lavage (BAL). This procedure is performed to collect cells from peripheral lung tissue. During a BAL, sterile saline is instilled into the airway in aliquots of 20 ml up to 50 ml. The saline is suctioned out and sent for cytological examination. Code 32997 is assigned for total lung lavage (unilateral).

When a lesion can be visualized with the bronchoscope, the physician may elect to use forceps to obtain a sample of tissue. This procedure allows a more precise piece of tissue to be obtained for pathological diagnosis. Code 31625 is used to identify a bronchoscopy with bronchial or endobronchial biopsy, single or multiple sites.

When the diagnosis of a lung disease requires a sample of lung tissue, a transbronchial lung biopsy may be performed. During the bronchoscopy, forceps are used to puncture the bronchus and take samples of the lung tissue. This procedure is less invasive than an open-lung biopsy and thus carries less risk of morbidity. Code 31628 is assigned to identify a bronchoscopy with a transbronchial lung biopsy of a single lobe. To report transbronchial lung biopsies performed in additional lobes, assign add-on code 31632.

Points to remember:

- Determine the purpose of the bronchoscopy.

- Do not assign a separate code to identify a diagnostic bronchoscopy when performed in conjunction with a surgical bronchoscopy.

- Because fluoroscopic guidance is considered part of the procedures identified by codes 31622–31646, a separate code to identify fluoroscopy is not needed.

Exercise 4.24

Assign CPT codes and index entries for the following procedures:

1. Bronchoscopy with transbronchial biopsy of lung

   Code(s) _____

   Index entries: _____

   _____

2. Bronchoscopy with laser destruction of a lesion of the bronchus

   Code(s) _____

   Index entries: _____

   _____

3. Flexible bronchoscopy with cell washings, brushings, and biopsy

   Code(s) _____

   Index entries: _____

   _____

Exercise 4.25

Operative Report

Preoperative Diagnosis:	Persistent cough, dyspnea
Postoperative Diagnosis:	Probable bronchitis
Procedure:	Bronchoscopy
Medications:	Versed 13 mg given just prior to and during the procedure. Topical aerosolized lidocaine and atropine 0.4 mg IM and aerosolized albuterol 2.5 mg

Details of Procedure: The left nares was cannulated. The posterior nasopharynx was normal. The vocal cords, although with exogenous tissue consistent with obesity, were normal and normally apposed. The main carina was normal as was the trachea itself. The left lower lobe anatomy was a variant of normal with two main sub-segments, each having three sub-subsegments in the left upper lobe. Very slight erythema is seen in the medial aspect of the left upper lobe subsegment. Brushings were obtained from this area.

The right inside anatomy was entirely normal. No endobronchial lesions were seen throughout.

Pathology

Gross Description: Received are two prepared slides

Microscopic Description: The bronchial brushing slides demonstrate benign bronchial epithelial cells and macrophages. The background contains mucus with minimal inflammation. There is no atypia or malignancy.

Diagnosis: Lung, left upper lobe, bronchial brushings. Negative for malignant cells.

1. Code(s): _____

   What index entries were used to find the code(s)?

   _____

   _____

Cardiovascular

The cardiovascular subsection includes surgical procedures involving the heart and peri-cardium, arteries, and veins. Figure 4.5 displays the heart, veins, and arteries. The codes are

Figure 4.5.   The heart and the veins and arteries that branch from it

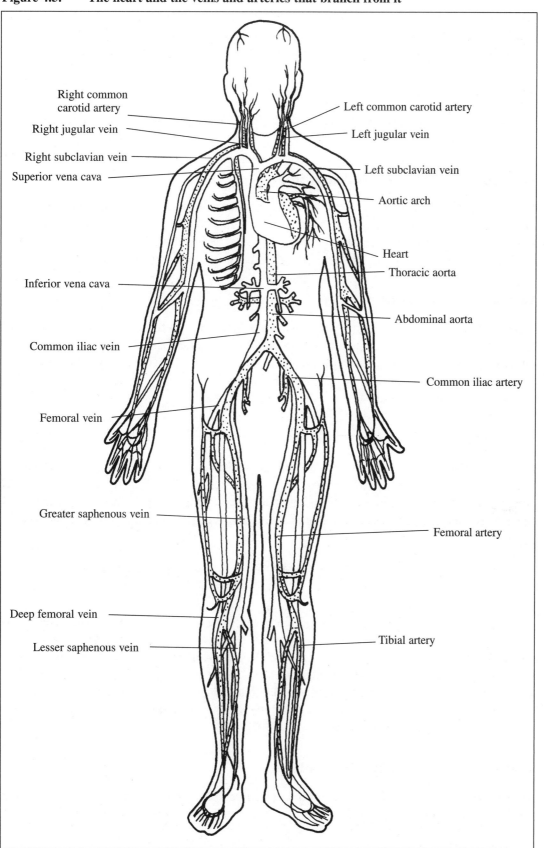

Right common
carotid artery

Right jugular vein

Right subclavian vein

Superior vena cava

Inferior vena cava

Common iliac vein

Femoral vein

Greater saphenous vein

Deep femoral vein

Lesser saphenous vein

Left common carotid artery

Left jugular vein

Left subclavian vein

Aortic arch

Heart

Thoracic aorta

Abdominal aorta

Common iliac artery

Femoral artery

Tibial artery

categorized first by body part involved and then by procedure performed, such as insertion of pacemaker, coronary artery bypass, embolectomy, and venipuncture. Assignment of codes for many of the cardiac procedures requires advanced knowledge and skill. The reference section of this book provides a list of recommended resources for coding cardiac procedures.

Vascular Injection Procedures

Careful review of the note at the beginning of this subsection will help the coder select the appropriate codes.

Intra-Arterial/Intra-Aortic Injections

Selective arterial catheterizations require that the catheter be removed, manipulated, or guided into a part of the arterial system other than the aorta or the vessel punctured. Nonselective arterial catheterizations involve placement of a catheter or needle directly into an artery, or a needle is negotiated only into the thoracic or abdominal aorta from any approach.

Intravenous Injections

Selective venous catheterizations include catheter placement in those veins that rise directly from the vena cava or the vein punctured directly (primary branches) and any subsequent (secondary) branches of the primary venous branches. Nonselective venous catheterizations involve direct puncture of peripheral veins and the vena cavae or placement of the catheter in the inferior or superior vena cavae by any route.

Coronary Artery Bypass Grafting

Codes 33510–33545 describe procedures related to coronary artery bypass grafting (CABG). The first series of codes (33510–33516) is reported when the CABG uses only venous grafts, such as those obtained from the saphenous vein. To code this procedure accurately, the coder must review the operative report to determine the number of coronary venous grafts that were performed.

> **Example:** CABG of two coronary arteries using saphenous vein grafts. The code reported is 33511.

The second series of codes (33517–33530) describes a CABG that uses both arterial and venous grafts. As already mentioned, the saphenous vein usually provides the venous grafts and the arterial graft is usually created from the internal mammary artery. To fully code arterial-venous bypass grafting, two codes must be assigned: one from the 33517–33523 series to identify the number of venous grafts performed, and one from the 33533–33545 series to identify the number of arterial grafts. Careful review of the operative report is required to determine the type and number of grafts performed.

Pacemakers and Defibrillators

Pacemakers, pacing cardioverters, and defibrillator systems are classified with codes 33200–33249. Guidelines in this section should be reviewed for descriptions of what comprises the various kinds of pacemaker and defibrillator systems. Repositioning or replacement of leads or devices within fourteen days is included in the reporting of these codes. Modifiers –76 and –77 are not appended to pacemaker or defibrillator codes after fourteen days because these are considered new, and not repeat, services.

Catheter Insertion

Many therapies now are administered by various types of catheters and ports. CPT coding for catheterization procedures depends on the type and use of the catheter in question. In general, CPT codes are assigned only to catheters inserted by physicians and not to catheters inserted by nursing personnel.

Central Venous Access Procedures

Central venous access devices (CVADs) are small, flexible tubes placed in large veins for patients who require frequent access to their bloodstream. CVADs are commonly used for the following purposes:

- Administration of medications (i.e., antibiotics, chemotherapy)

- Administration of fluids and nutritional compounds (hyperalimentation)

- Transfusion of blood products

- Multiple blood draws for diagnostic testing

Before assigning codes in this section, it is important to read the note that precedes code 36555. First, CPT classifies venous access procedures into five distinct categories:

- Insertion

- Repair

- Partial replacement

- Complete replacement

- Removal

The definitions for each of these categories are provided in CPT. Additional information must be abstracted from the health record to determine the correct code. As an example, refer to the decision tree in figure 4.6 for insertion of a central venous access device. From this decision tree, documentation is needed to determine the following:

- Catheter inserted centrally or peripherally

- Tunneled or nontunneled

- Pump or port

- Age of patient

Figure 4.6.   Central venous access procedures coding decision tree

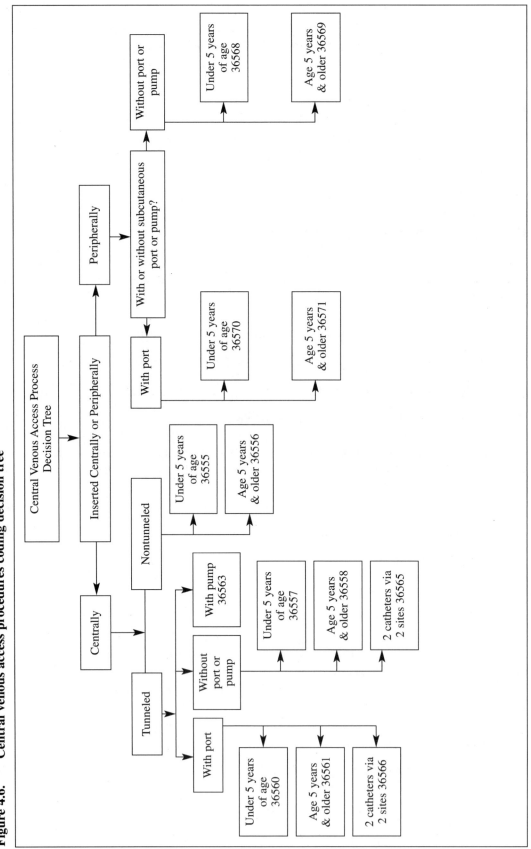

Centrally Inserted Catheter

A centrally inserted catheter is placed in the jugular, subclavian, femoral vein, or inferior vena cava. The peripherally inserted catheters are typically placed in the arm and advanced forward into the larger subclavian vein. The documentation may state that the catheter was inserted into the basilic or cephalic vein. For the centrally inserted catheter, the coder must check the documentation to determine whether the catheter was tunneled. Tunneled catheters have an entrance site at a distance from where they enter the vascular system. These are "tunneled" through the skin and subcutaneous tissue to a great vein. Typically, these catheters are for long-term use. The code descriptions also differentiate between the use of subcutaneous ports or pumps. Implanted ports are placed below the skin, and blood is drawn or medication is delivered by placing a tiny needle through the overlying skin into the port or reservoir. Pumps use a computerized mechanism for infusion.

Peripherally Inserted Catheter

Unlike central catheters, peripherally inserted central catheter (PICC) lines are not inserted into the central vein.

CPT provides codes for the removal of CVADs (36589–36590) but instructs the coder not to assign the codes for nontunneled central venous catheters. Removal of some catheters does not warrant a separate code if no surgical procedure is required and the catheter is simply pulled out.

Exercise 4.26

Operative Report

Preoperative Diagnosis: Heart block

Postoperative Diagnosis: Same

Procedure: Insertion of permanent pacemaker

The patient was premedicated before arriving at the OR. The patient was prepped and draped in the usual manner. Through the percutaneous route, the needle was inserted into the subclavian vein. The bipolar electrode was introduced, taken to the pulmonary artery, and brought out slowly to the apex of the right ventricle. Measurements were taken, and the position was excellent. The electrode was anchored to the fascia over the sleeve and connected to the pacemaker battery. The wound was closed. Patient tolerated the procedure well and returned to the outpatient recovery area.

1. Code(s): _____

   What index entries were used to find the code(s)?

   _____

   _____

Exercise 4.27

Operative Report

Preoperative Diagnosis: Breast carcinoma

Postoperative Diagnosis: Same

Operation: Removal of venous access port

Indications: The patient is a 44-year-old woman who had a left, modified radical mastectomy in 2002. In August, she had a Port-a-Cath placed in the right side. However, it has caused an extreme amount of discomfort so she has requested that it be removed.

Procedure: The patient was taken to the OR and placed in a supine position on the table. She was then prepped and draped in the usual sterile fashion. The area was anesthetized with 1% Carbocaine. An incision was made over the venous access device and carried down to the place of the device. After freeing it up and cutting the retention sutures, the venous access device was removed. Hemostasis was obtained with cautery and pressure. The wound was then closed in layers and a dressing applied. The patient tolerated the procedure well and was returned to the surgicenter in stable condition.

1. Code(s): _____

   What index entries were used to find the code(s)?

   _____

   _____

Exercise 4.28

Operative Report

Preoperative Diagnosis: Renal failure

Postoperative Diagnosis: Same

Operation: Insertion of subclavian venous catheter

With this elderly patient in the head-down position, the entire left upper chest was prepared with Betadine scrub and painting, and draped in the usual sterile fashion. Then, 1% Xylocaine was used for local anesthetic. A percutaneously subclavian venous catheter was inserted without difficulty and secured at the skin level with 3-0 Nylon, and a sterile dressing was applied. The catheter also was irrigated with Heparin solution. Patient tolerated the procedure well. Will follow with a chest X ray.

1. Code(s): _____

   What index entries were used to find the code(s)?

   _____

   _____

Digestive Subsection

The digestive subsection includes surgical procedures involving the lips, mouth and tongue, palate and uvula, salivary glands and ducts, pharynx, adenoids and tonsils, esophagus, stomach, intestines, appendix, rectum, biliary tract, abdomen, peritoneum, and omentum. The codes are categorized first by body part involved and then by procedure, such as herniorrhaphy, esophagotomy, ileostomy, cholecystectomy, and hemorrhoidectomy. Figure 4.7 shows the digestive system.

Figure 4.7.   The digestive system

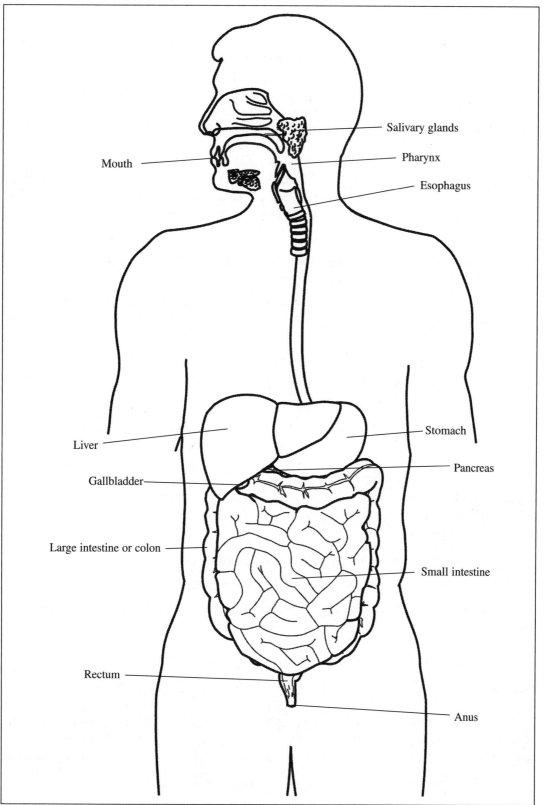

Endoscopies

In general, gastrointestinal endoscopies are categorized by body part involved, type or purpose of endoscopy (diagnostic or surgical), and specific procedure performed, such as biopsy, ablation of tumor or polyp, and removal of foreign body. The endoscopy should always be coded as far as the scope was passed.

An esophagoscopy allows the physician to visualize the esophagus. Codes in the 43200–43232 range are used to report esophagoscopies.

An upper gastrointestinal endoscopy, also known as an esophagogastroduodenoscopy, or EGD, or upper endoscopy, involves the visual examination of the esophagus, stomach and upper duodenum, and/or jejunum. Indications for these procedures include gastrointestinal (GI) bleeding, ulceration, or inflammation; abdominal pain; narrowing of the esophagus; and suspected tumors or polyps. EGDs are reported with codes in the 43234–43259 range. The code ranges can be located in the alphabetic index under Endoscopy, Gastrointestinal, Upper.

Lower GI endoscopies can be classified by the area of the intestine examined, as follows:

- A proctosigmoidoscopy is limited to an examination of the rectum and sigmoid colon. See codes in the 45300–45327 range.

- A sigmoidoscopy involves examination of the entire rectum and sigmoid colon but also may include examination of a portion of the descending colon. See codes in the 45330–45345 range.

- A colonoscopy pertains to the examination of the entire colon, from the rectum to the cecum, and may include examination of the terminal ileum. See codes in the 45355–45387 range.

Indications for these lower GI procedures include: evaluation of an abnormal barium enema, lower gastrointestinal bleeding, iron deficiency anemia of unknown etiology, diarrhea, or follow-up examination after removal of a neoplastic growth.

When coding a colonoscopy, the coder must review the operative report to determine the approach: through an existing colostomy (44388–44397), a colotomy (45355), or the rectum (45378–45387).

Points to remember:

- A surgical endoscopy includes a diagnostic endoscopy.

- The purpose of the endoscopy should be determined.

- When coding a colonoscopy, select the code that reflects the approach used to insert the instrument.

Removal of Tumors or Polyps

Because the endoscopic removal of a tumor or polyp can be accomplished with several techniques, the coder should review the documentation carefully before selecting a code. One technique uses hot biopsy forceps or bipolar cautery. Hot biopsy forceps resemble tweezers connected to an electrosurgical unit. Grasping the polyp, the physician pulls the growth away from the wall of the structure. A portion of the neoplasm may be removed for pathological analysis. The remaining portion is destroyed with the electrocoagulation current. Bipolar cautery also uses electrical current to remove the polyp.

The snare technique uses a wire loop that is slipped over the polyp or tumor. The stalk is then cauterized and the growth removed.

Finally, the physician may elect to use a neodymium yttrium aluminum garnet (Nd:YAG) laser to remove the lesion. When a laser is used during the endoscopy, the coder should assign the code for the endoscopy that states "with ablation of tumor(s), polyp(s), or other lesion(s) not amenable to removal by hot biopsy forceps, bipolar cautery or snare technique."

Note: It is possible for a physician to use different techniques to remove polyps during the same operative episode. In this case, the appropriate CPT code would be assigned to identify each technique.

Incomplete Colonoscopies

There are several guidelines for coding discontinued procedures for physicians and hospitals. (See chapter 3 of this book and appendix A of the CPT codebook for descriptions of modifiers –52, –53, –73 and –74.) In the case of a colonoscopy, the procedure may be attempted, but circumstances may prevent the entire colon from being visualized (for instance, poor prep). In this case, CPT guidelines instruct the coder to assign the colonoscopy code with modifier –52 for Reduced Services (for physician services).

It should be noted that some Medicare carriers have different guidelines for reporting incomplete colonoscopies.

According to Program Memorandum AB-03-114 issued August 1, 2003, Medicare covers colorectal cancer screening test/procedures for the early detection of colorectal cancer when coverage conditions are met. Among the screening procedures covered are screening colonoscopies:

- G0105, Colorectal cancer screening; colonoscopy on individual at high risk

- G0121, Colorectal screening; colonoscopy on individual not meeting criteria for high risk

Coverage of these services is subject to certain frequency limitations.

The memorandum further explains that when a covered colonoscopy is attempted but cannot be completed the *professional provider* should add the modifier of –53 to the colonoscopy code to indicate that the procedure was interrupted. When submitting a *facility* claim for the interrupted colonoscopy, providers are to suffix the colonoscopy codes with a modifier of –73 or –74 as appropriate.

Biopsies and Lesion Removal

When performing a GI endoscopy, the physician may encounter one or many lesions. Biopsies of some or all lesions may be taken. Lesion removal may be performed after a biopsy or without a biopsy. Therefore, the following guidelines should be applied:

- When a biopsy of a lesion is taken and the remaining portion of the *same* lesion is excised during the same operative episode, assign a code for the excision only (*CPT Assistant,* February 1999).

- When one lesion is biopsied and a *different* lesion is excised, assign a code for the biopsy and a code for the excision. This rule is applicable unless the excision code narrative includes the phrase "with or without biopsy." In this case, only the excision code is assigned. It would be appropriate to append the biopsy code with modifier –59, Distinct Procedural Service.

- Biopsy codes use the terminology "with biopsy, single or multiple." These codes are to be used only once, regardless of the number of biopsies taken.

Exercise 4.29

Assign CPT codes and index entries for the following procedures:

1. Esophagoscopy with biopsy of a small lesion in the esophagus and a snare removal of a polyp from another area of the esophagus

   Code(s) _____

   Index entries: _____

   _____

2. Proctosigmoidoscopy with biopsy of four separate lesions

   Code(s) _____

   Index entries: _____

   _____

3. EGD with laser removal of duodenal polyp

   Code(s) _____

   Index entries: _____

   _____

4. Endoscopic biopsy of a lesion of the transverse colon

   Code(s) _____

   Index entries: _____

   _____

5. ERCP with removal of bile duct stones

   Code(s) _____

   Index entries: _____

   _____

Exercise 4.30

Operative Note

Procedure: EGD with foreign body removal

Clinical Note: This patient is a 47-year-old male who experienced acute odynophagia after eating a meal consisting of fish. The patient felt a foreign body-like sensation in his proximal esophagus. He was evaluated with lateral, C-spine films, and soft tissue films without any evidence of perforation.

Findings: After obtaining informed consent, the patient was endoscoped. He was premedicated without any complication. Under direct visualization, an Olympus Q20 was introduced orally and the esophagus was intubated without any difficulty. The hypopharynx was carefully reviewed, and no abnormalities were noted. There were no foreign bodies and no lacerations to the hypopharynx. The proximal esophagus was normal. No active bleeding was noted. The endoscope was advanced farther into the esophagus, where careful review of the mucosa revealed no foreign bodies and no obstructions. However, the gastroesophageal junction did show a very small fish bone, which was removed without any complications. The endoscope was advanced into the stomach, where partially digested food was noted. The duodenum was normal. The endoscope was then removed. The patient tolerated the procedure well, and his postprocedural vital signs are stable.

1.   Code(s): _____

     What index entries were used to find the code(s)?

     _____

     _____

Exercise 4.31

Operative Report

Procedure: Colonoscopy

Instrument used: Olympus CF100L

Indications: The patient has a family history of carcinoma of the colon and colonic polyps.

Procedure: The digital and anal exams were normal. The colonoscope was inserted to the cecum. The prep was good. Eight to ten very sessile and diminutive polyps were identified, all but one located in the rectum. The other polyp was located in the proximal transverse colon. All were coagulated and removed with the hot biopsy forceps. No other mucosal lesions were identified.

Pathology Report

Gross:
1.   The specimen labeled biopsy of polyp, transverse colon, consists of a pale tan, slightly firm tissue measuring 0.2 cm in greatest diameter; completely submitted.

2.   The specimen labeled biopsy of polyp, rectum, consists of six pieces of slightly firm pinkish-tan tissue ranging from 0.2 to 0.3 cm in greatest diameter; completely submitted.

Micro:
No high-grade dysplasia or malignant change is seen in the colorectal polyps.

Pathological Diagnosis:
1.   Biopsy of polyp, transverse colon: Hyperplastic polyp
2.   Biopsy of polyp, rectum: Hyperplastic polyp

1.   Code(s): _____

     What index entries were used to find the code(s)?

     _____

     _____

Exercise 4.32

Operative Report

Preoperative Diagnosis: Evaluate for residual inflammatory changes

Postoperative Diagnosis: See assessment

Operation: Flexible fiberoptic sigmoidoscopy

Findings: The sigmoidoscope was inserted into the rectum and eventually advanced up to a level 60 cm from the anus. The mucosa throughout the colon and rectum were examined and appeared completely normal with no inflammation, ulceration, or exudate. There was no bleeding. I did not see any narrowed areas, polyps, or masses. I did see a few sigmoid diverticula.

Assessment: With the exception of a few sigmoid diverticula, the examination up to a level of 60 cm from the anus was noted to be normal. The previous inflammatory changes have completely subsided.

1. Code(s): _____

    What index entries were used to find the code(s)?

    _____

Hernia Repairs

An abdominal hernia occurs when internal organs, such as the intestines, break through a hole or tear in the musculature of the abdominal wall. This protrusion produces a bulge that can be seen or felt. Symptoms include burning and pain with activity.

Codes 49491–49659 describe procedures related to hernia repair. To assign these codes accurately, the coder must be able to specify the type and/or site of the hernia, the history of the hernia, the age of the patient, and the clinical presentation of the hernia.

The following terms are used to describe the type and/or location of different hernias:

*   Inguinal hernia: A common herniation of the inguinal canal in the groin area

*   Lumbar hernia: A rare herniation occurring in the lumbar region of the torso

*   Incisional hernia: A herniation occurring at the site of a previous surgical incision

*   Femoral hernia: A common herniation occurring in the femoral canal in the groin area

*   Epigastric hernia: A herniation located above the navel

*   Umbilical hernia: A herniation occurring at the navel

*   Spigelian hernia: A herniation usually located above the inferior epigastric vessel along the outer border of the rectus muscle

Some codes provide historical information specifying whether the hernia is an *initial* repair (first surgical repair of the hernia) or a *recurrent* repair (hernia has been surgically repaired previously). Other codes differentiate patients by age: any age, under six months, six months to under five years, or five years or over.

Finally, a number of terms are used to describe the clinical presentation of hernias. These include:

*   Reducible: The protruding organs can be returned to normal position by surgical (not medical) manipulation.

- Sliding: The colon or cecum is part of the hernia sac. (In some cases, the urinary bladder also may be involved.)

- Incarcerated: The hernia cannot be reduced without surgical intervention.

- Strangulated: The hernia is an incarcerated hernia in which the blood supply to the contained organ is reduced. A strangulated hernia presents a medical emergency.

The following example illustrates how the different variables describing hernias can be represented in a specific code assignment:

49550   Repair initial femoral hernia, any age; reducible

49553   incarcerated or strangulated

More than 600,000 hernia repairs (herniorrhaphies) are performed each year. A physician may perform one of three common types of repairs. The first type is the traditional or conventional repair. Under general anesthesia, the physician pushes the bulging tissue back into the abdominal cavity. The defect is closed by pulling together and stitching the surrounding muscles and ligaments. A recovery period of four to six weeks is usually needed.

The second type of herniorrhaphy uses mesh rather than stitches to repair the abdominal defect. Because stitches are not used, the patient experiences less postoperative pain. Commonly used meshes are Marlex and Prolene. When coding a mesh repair of an incisional or ventral hernia, code 49568, Implantation of mesh or other prosthesis for incisional or ventral hernia repair, must be assigned in addition to the repair code. The use of mesh with other hernia repairs is not coded.

The third type of hernia repair is performed by a laparoscope. A laparoscopic repair is commonly performed to repair bilateral and recurrent hernias. Less discomfort and faster recovery are the main advantages of this approach. As with other endoscopies, a surgical laparoscopy includes a diagnostic laparoscopy.

It is important to note that diaphragmatic and hiatal hernias are not assigned to the digestive system. To identify these hernias, the coder should use codes from the 39502–39541 range in the diaphragm subsection of the CPT codebook.

Exercise 4.33

Assign CPT codes and index entries for the following procedures. Append modifiers if applicable.

1. A four-year-old patient undergoes an initial herniorrhaphy for repair of an inguinal hernia and a unilateral hydrocelectomy of the spermatic cord.

    Code(s)   _____

    Index entries: _____

    _____

2. Right incarcerated initial incisional hernia repair with mesh. Patient is 49 years old.

    Code(s)   _____

    Index entries: _____

    _____

3. Diagnosis: Recurrent inguinal hernia
    Procedure: Laparoscopic hernia repair

    Code(s)   _____

    Index entries: _____

    _____

4. Recurrent incarcerated inguinal hernia repair with implantation of mesh. Patient is 56 years old.

    Code(s)   _____

    Index entries: _____

    _____

5. A 35-year-old patient undergoes an umbilical herniorrhaphy.

    Code(s)   _____

    Index entries: _____

    _____

Exercise 4.34

Operative Report

Preoperative Diagnosis: Left inguinal hernia

Postoperative Diagnosis: Same

Procedure: Left initial inguinal hernia repair with mesh

Anesthesia: General

Indications: The patient is a 23-year-old male who presented with several weeks' history of pain in his left groin associated with a bulge. Examination revealed that his left groin did indeed have a bulge and his right groin was normal. We discussed the procedure as well as the choice of anesthesia.

Operative Summary: After preoperative evaluation and clearance, the patient was brought into the operating suite and placed in a comfortable supine position on the OR table. Monitoring equipment was attached, and general anesthesia was induced. His left groin was sterilely prepped and draped, and an inguinal incision made. This was carried down through the subcutaneous tissues until the external oblique fascia was reached. This was split in a direction parallel with its fibers, and the medial aspect of the opening included the external ring. The ileo inguinal nerve was identified, and care was taken to retract this inferiorly out of the way. The cord structures were encircled and the cremasteric muscle fibers divided. At this point, we examined the floor of the inguinal canal, and the patient did appear to have a weakness here. We then explored the cord. There was no evidence of an indirect hernia. A piece of 3 × 5 mesh was obtained and trimmed to fit. It was placed down in the inguinal canal and tacked to the pubic tubercle. It was then run inferiorly along the pelvic shelving edge until lateral to the internal ring and tacked down superiorly using interrupted sutures of 0-Prolene. A single stitch was placed lateral to the cord to recreate the internal ring. Details of the mesh were tucked underneath the external oblique fascia. The cord and the nerve were allowed to drop back into the wound, and the wound was infiltrated with 30 cc of half percent Marcaine. The external oblique fascia was then closed with a running suture of 0-Vicryl. Subcutaneous tissues were approximated with interrupted sutures of 3-0 Vicryl. The skin was closed with a running subcuticular suture of 4-0 Vicryl. Benzoin and Steri-Strips and a dry sterile dressing were applied. All sponge, needle, and instrument counts were correct at the end of the procedure. The patient tolerated the procedure well and was taken to the recovery room in stable condition.

1. Code(s): _____

   What index entries were used to find the code(s)?

   _____

   _____

Urinary Subsection

The urinary subsection includes surgical procedures involving the kidney, ureter, bladder, and urethra. These codes are categorized first by body part involved and then by procedure performed, such as cystourethroscopy, percutaneous renal biopsy, transurethral resection of the prostate, and urethroplasty. Figure 4.8 displays the urinary system.

Urodynamics

Codes 51725–51797 describe urodynamic procedures that may be reported separately or in combination when more than one procedure is performed. Modifier –51 should be reported when multiple procedures are performed. These procedures are performed either by the physician or under his or her direction. The following services/supplies are considered part of the procedure and should not be reported separately: instruments, equipment, fluids, gases, probes, catheters, technicians' fees, medications, gloves, trays, tubing, and other sterile supplies.

If the physician is providing only the professional component (that is, the supervision and interpretation), modifier –26 also should be reported for physician services.

Figure 4.8.   The urinary system

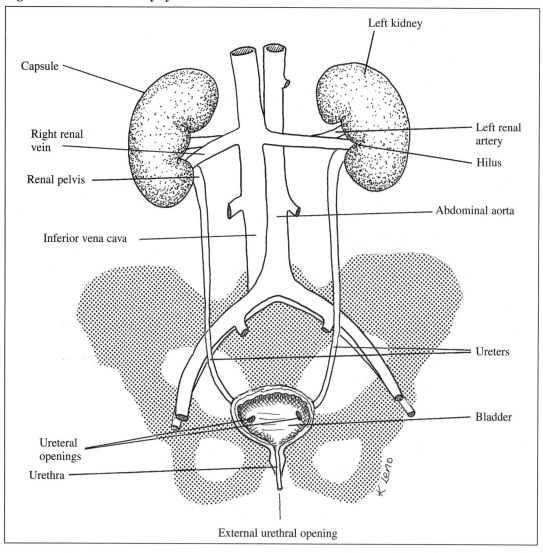

The following definitions (Rogers 2001) describing the various urodynamic procedures will help the coder assign the appropriate CPT code:

- A *simple* cystometrogram is the measurement of the bladder's capacity, sensation of filling, and intravesical pressure. A *complex* cystometrogram involves measurement of the bladder's capacity, sensation of filling, and intravesical pressure using a rectal probe to distinguish between intra-abdominal pressure and bladder pressure.

- *Simple* uroflowmetry is the measurement of the voiding time and peak flow. *Complex* uroflowmetry involves the measurement and recording of mean and peak flow and the time taken to reach peak flow during continuous urination.

- A urethral pressure profile (UPP) involves the recording of pressures along the urethra as a special catheter is slowly withdrawn.

- Electromyography studies are performed to record muscle activity during voiding while simultaneously recording urine flow rate.

bladder cystoscopy
cystourethrascopy

Endoscopies

In general, genitourinary endoscopies are categorized by body part involved(urethra, prostate, ureter(and specific procedure performed, such as cystourethroscopy with biopsy of the bladder or urethra, transurethral incision of prostate, cystourethroscopy with ureteral meatotomy, and cystourethroscopy with insertion of indwelling ureteral stent. The endoscopic procedures described in codes 52000–52700 are listed so that the main procedure can be identified without having to list all the minor related functions performed at the same time.

> **Example:** Code 52647 describes noncontact laser coagulation of the prostate, including control of postoperative bleeding. The description indicates a complete procedure that includes vasectomy, meatotomy, cystourethroscopy, urethral calibration and/or dilatation, and internal urethrotomy. Minor procedures such as meatotomy, calibration, and so on are part of code 52647 and should not be reported separately.

Exercise 4.35

Assign CPT codes and index entries for the following procedures:

1. Cystoscopy for insertion of double-J ureteral stent

   Code(s) _____

   Index entries: _____

   _____

2. Cystoscopy with fulguration of 1.0 cm lesion of bladder

   Code(s) _____

   Index entries: _____

   _____

3. Cystoscopy, left ureteroscopy with laser lithotripsy

   Code(s) _____

   Index entries: _____

   _____

4. Cystoscopy with insertion of urethral stent

   Code(s) _____

   Index entries: _____

   _____

Exercise 4.36

Operative Report

Preoperative Diagnosis: Right ureteral stone

Postoperative Diagnosis: Same

Procedure: Right ureteroscopy, stone extraction, stent

Details of Procedure: The patient was taken to the operating suite and placed in the dorsal lithotomy position, and then sterilely prepped and draped in the usual fashion. Cystoscope was then inserted into the urethra; it was normal. The prostate was nonobstructed, and the bladder was free of neoplasm, infection, or calculus. There was some edema of the right intramural ureter. A guide wire was introduced into the right ureteral orifice, advanced to the right renal-collecting system without difficulty. A balloon was used to dilate the ureter, and a scope was introduced. The gravel was noted from the stone being fragmented from the balloon. This was washing out. The remainder of the ureter was examined and found to be free of neoplasm, perforation, or calculus. The stent was inserted. A string was kept attached. The patient was transferred to the recovery room in satisfactory condition.

1. Assign code(s) for the physician's services:

    _____

    What index entries were used to find the code(s)?

    _____

    _____

Exercise 4.37

Operative Report

Preoperative Diagnosis: Recurrent bladder cancer

Postoperative Diagnosis: Recurrent bladder cancer

Procedure Performed: Cystoscopy with bladder biopsies and fulguration

Anesthesia: General

Procedure: The patient has prior transitional cell carcinoma of the bladder and also carcinoma in situ. He has received MVAC therapy and BCG. Surveillance cystoscopy demonstrated erythema of the bladder wall. He is being admitted for cystoscopy, bladder biopsy, and fulguration now. Procedure, reasons, risks, and complications were reviewed and consent was granted.

He was brought to the Operating Room under general anesthesia, placed in the dorsolithotomy position, and prepped and draped in a sterile manner. A #21 French cystoscope was inserted, urethra was normal, verumontanum intact. Prostate revealed evidence of prior transurethral resection and moderate outlet obstruction. There were erythematous areas throughout the bladder, and a 0.5 cm lesion was fulgurated. Both ureteric orifices were normal size, shape, and caliber with clear efflux. The erythematous areas were then biopsied with flexible biopsy forceps. After obtaining biopsies, the area was then fulgurated with Bugbee electrode. Reinspection was carried out; no gross bleeding was noted. The bladder was drained, cystoscope was withdrawn, and the patient was transferred to the Recovery Room in satisfactory condition with all vital signs stable.

Pathology Report

Final Diagnosis

Urinary Bladder, Biopsies:
      —Urothelial carcinoma in situ, focal
      —Chronic nonspecific cystitis

1. Code(s): _____

    What index entries were used to find the code(s)?

    _____

    _____

Male Genital System Subsection

The codes in the male genital system subsection are used to report procedures on the penis, testis, epididymis, tunica vaginalis, scrotum, vas deferens, spermatic cord, seminal vesicles, and prostate. Figure 4.9 displays these structures.

Removal of lesions (for example, condyloma, papilloma, molluscum contagiosum, herpetic vesicle) of the penis is not located in the integumentary system subsection but, rather, in the male genital system (54050–54065) subsection. The code selection is determined by the method of removal. For destruction or excision of other lesions, reference the integumentary system subsection of the surgery section.

Figure 4.9.   The male genital system

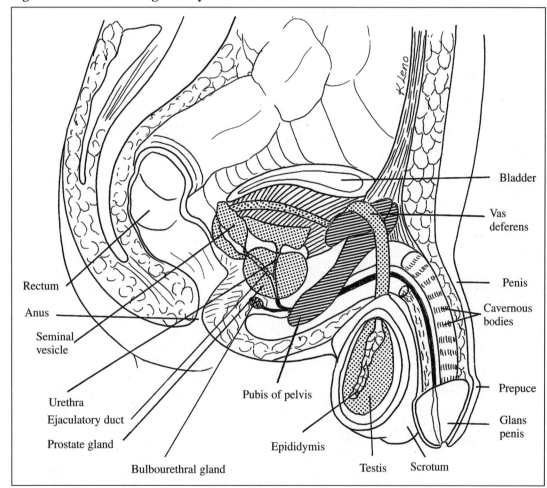

Exercise 4.38

Assign CPT codes and index entries for the following procedures:

1. Laser destruction of 4 condylomas of the penis

    Code(s) _____

    Index entries: _____

    _____

2. Incision and drainage of subcutaneous abscess of the penis

    Code(s) _____

    Index entries: _____

    _____

3. Punch biopsy of prostate

    Code(s) _____

    Index entries: _____

    _____

4. Bilateral epididymectomy

    Code(s) _____

    Index entries: _____

    _____

5. Clamp circumcision, newborn

    Code(s) _____

    Index entries: _____

    _____

Exercise 4.39

Operative Report

Preoperative Diagnosis:	Adenocarcinoma of the prostate
Postoperative Diagnosis:	Same
Operative Procedure:	Transrectal ultrasound Transperineal implant of I-125 seeds into the prostate
Anesthesia:	General

Procedure: The patient was brought to the cysto suite and placed in the lithotomy position at a 90∫ angle. General anesthesia was induced, and a Foley catheter was placed. The ultrasound probe was positioned in the rectum, and the appropriate reference points were identified and compared to his previous volumetric studies.

Under fluoroscopic and ultrasound guidance, 19 needles were inserted into the prostate based on a pre-measured template. Approximately 70 seeds were placed.

A cystoscopic examination was performed at the end of the case, and no seeds were identified within the urinary bladder.

A Foley catheter was replaced into the bladder and will be removed later today. The appropriate postimplantation radiation and postoperative instructions were given. He tolerated the procedure well and was taken to the recovery room in satisfactory condition.

1. Assign code(s) for the physician's services:

   _____

   What index entries were used to find the code(s)?

   _____

   _____

Exercise 4.40

Operative Report

Preoperative Diagnosis: Chronic left orchialgia
                            Chronic epididymitis

Operation: Left inguinal orchiectomy

Anesthesia: Local standby; one-quarter percent Marcaine, 1%, Xylocaine, 1/1 dilution. Total
                            25 cc used as inguinal block

Estimated Blood Loss: Minimal

Indications: This is an 82-year-old male with chronic left gonadal pain due to chronic granulomatous epididymitis. This has failed to respond to conservative measures and has caused him marked discomfort in the left groin. As a result, we recommended that he consider outpatient orchiectomy. The risks and potential complications were discussed and informed consent obtained.

The patient was given Ancef IV as well as IV sedation and placed on the operating table in the supine position. The lower groin and abdomen were shaved, prepped, and draped in the standard fashion. The external inguinal ring was identified, and an area just distal to the external inguinal ring was anesthetized with the local anesthetic, and a small transverse incision was made down to the spermatic cord. The testis was then brought out through the inguinal incision after the spermatic cord blockade with local anesthetic. The testis was separated from the scrotum by incision in the gubernaculum with needle tip Bovie. The spermatic cord was identified, dissected back to the external inguinal ring, and bisected with a curved Kelly clamp and then clamped and transected with Metzenbaum scissors. The spermatic cord was closed with suture ligature of 0 Vicryl and a free tie of 0 Vicryl proximal to this on each side of the spermatic cord. The incision was inspected for hemostasis. No further bleeding was noted, and the testis was delivered for pathologic evaluation. The Scarpa's fascia was closed with interrupted 2-0 Vicryl, and the skin was closed with a running 4-0 Vicryl subcuticular closure. Steri-Strips and four by fours were applied as a dressing. He was returned to the recovery room in stable condition. Estimated blood loss was minimal.

1. Code(s): _____

    What index entries were used to find the code(s)?

    _____

    _____

Laparoscopy/Hysteroscopy Subsection

Laparoscopic procedures are found within the specific body system sections. For example, laparoscopic procedures of the abdomen, peritoneum, and omentum are located in the code range of 49320–49329. A vaginal hysterectomy performed laparoscopically is assigned a code from 58550–58554.

Female Genital System Subsection

Codes listed in the female genital system subsection of CPT include those for various surgical repairs, dilatation and curettage, and hysterectomies and hysteroscopies. This section also contains codes for maternity care and delivery. Figure 4.10 displays the female genital system.

Hysteroscopy (58550–58579)

A hysteroscope is a thin, telescope-like instrument that allows the physician to look inside the uterus. After insufflation of the uterine cavity with CO_2, the hysteroscope is inserted through

Figure 4.10.   The female genital system

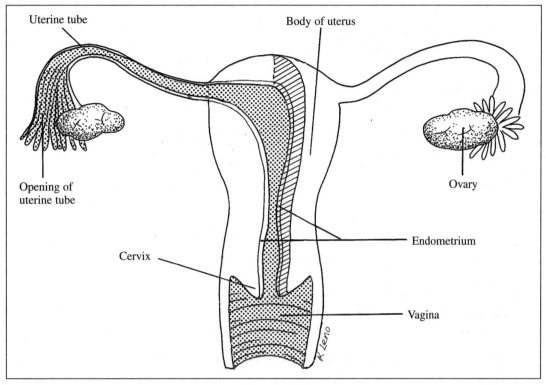

the cervical canal and into the uterus. This direct visualization improves the accuracy of diagnosis and treatment. Accessory instruments that may be used with a hysteroscope procedure include scissors, forceps, lasers, and various electrodes. A dilatation and curettage (D&C) is commonly performed with a hysteroscopic biopsy or polypectomy. Therefore, no additional code is assigned to identify the D&C.

Maternity Care and Delivery Subsection

Along with codes for surgery and other procedures involving the female reproductive organs, the female genital system subsection includes CPT codes for maternity care and delivery services. Antepartum care includes initial and subsequent history, physical examination, recording of clinical information, and monthly visits up to 28 weeks' gestation, biweekly visits to 36 weeks' gestation, and weekly visits to the time of delivery. According to the CPT codebook, any additional visits are to be coded separately using E/M codes. Health plans may have specific rules about the reporting of services beyond those included in the global service package that often accompanies maternity coverage. This may affect the reporting of services, particularly if more than one physician is required to care for the patient, as may occur with unexpected C-section delivery.

Postpartum care codes include both hospital and office visit codes following either vaginal or Cesarean delivery.

Some CPT codes address global care, and some are used to report only a portion of care.

Example: CPT code 59425 is for antepartum care only, four to six visits. It may be used by a family practice physician who refers a patient in the second trimester of pregnancy to an obstetrician due to a high risk of complications.

Code 59510 would be reported by a physician providing global care for a Cesarean delivery from start to finish.

Patients who attempt vaginal delivery after previous C-section delivery or who successfully deliver vaginally after previous C-section delivery have specific CPT codes assigned from the 59610–59622 range. These codes should always be used when they apply.

Exercise 4.41

Assign CPT codes and index entries for the following procedures:

1. Laparoscopic fulguration of fallopian tubes

   Code(s) _____

   Index entries: _____

   _____

2. D&C performed for a patient with dysfunctional bleeding

   Code(s) _____

   Index entries: _____

   _____

3. D&C performed for patient with diagnosis of incomplete abortion (8 weeks pregnant)

   Code(s) _____

   Index entries: _____

   _____

4. Laparoscopy with aspiration of ovarian cyst

   Code(s) _____

   Index entries: _____

   _____

5. Laparoscopic removal of two fibroids (total weight 150 grams)

   Code(s) _____

   Index entries: _____

   _____

6. Vaginal hysterectomy with salpingo-oophorectomy (uterus weight 250 grams).

   Code(s) _____

   Index entries: _____

   _____

Exercise 4.42

Operative Report

Preoperative Diagnosis: Moderate dysplasia of the cervix

Postoperative Diagnosis: Same

Procedure: LEEP

Anesthesia: General inhalation anesthesia per mask

Procedure: The patient was brought to the OR with IV fluids infusing and placed on the table in the supine position. General inhalation anesthesia per mask was administered after acquisition of an adequate anesthetic level, and the patient was placed in the lithotomy position. The perineum was draped. A laser speculum was placed in the vaginal vault. The cervix was rinsed with a solution of acetic acid, and colposcopic examination of the cervix showed areas of wide epithelium across the anterior lip of the cervix, consistent with the previous biopsy showing moderate dysplasia. Using the 2 cm electrosurgical loop excision, the endocervical canal was cauterized with bipolar cautery. Then the procedure was completed. The speculum was removed. The patient was taken out of the lithotomy position. Her anesthesia was reversed. She was awakened and taken to the recovery room in stable condition. Sponge, instrument, and needle counts were correct times three. Estimated blood loss was less than 25 cc.

1. Code(s): _____

    What index entries were used to find the code(s)?

    _____

    _____

Exercise 4.43

Operative Report

Preoperative Diagnosis: Dysfunctional uterine bleeding, failed hormonal therapy

Postoperative Diagnosis: Same

Procedure Performed: Diagnostic hysteroscopy
                            Fractional dilatation and curettage

Indications for Procedure: The patient is a 35-year-old Gravida V Para IV AB I female from the Towne Health Center. She has been bleeding the majority of each month over the past four months. She has been tried on Ortho-Novum 7/7 to control the bleeding, but this has been of no help. The patient is here for the above procedure.

Description of Procedure: With the patient under satisfactory general anesthesia in the dorsal lithotomy position, a pelvic exam revealed a cervix that came down to the introitus, constituting a second-degree uterine prolapse. The patient had many hymenal tags on both the right and left side. A large speculum was placed inside the vagina. The anterior lip of the cervix was grasped with a single-toothed tenaculum. The cervix was sounded to 8.5 cm. The endocervical canal was now serially dilated. Using the hysteroscope and Ringer's Lactate as a distending solution, the hysteroscope was passed through the internal os into the uterine cavity. Inspection of the uterine contents revealed both right and left ostia identified. Some lining was on the floor of the uterus and some on the roof. The fundus was devoid of any lining. There were no submucosal fibroids and no submucosal septa. The hysteroscope was removed, and the next procedure was fractional dilatation and curettage. Using a Kevorkian-Younge curet, the endocervical canal was curetted and the cervical canal was further dilated using a medium-size curet. The endometrial cavity was curetted with moderate curettings obtained. These were sent for pathological diagnosis. The patient tolerated the procedure fairly well and was escorted to the recovery room in satisfactory condition.

1. Code(s): _____

    What index entries were used to find the code(s)?

    _____

    _____

Endocrine System Subsection

No specific coding guidelines apply to this subsection.

Nervous System Subsection

The nervous system subsection includes craniectomy and craniotomy procedures, in addition to procedures involving injection and catheter insertion into nerves and the spinal cord. Pain management codes such as nerve blocks and epidural procedures also are part of this subsection. Figure 4.11 illustrates the spinal column.

Laminotomy and Laminectomy

The codes for laminotomy and laminectomy procedures are determined based on the surgical approach, anatomic location within the spine, and specific procedures performed.

Laminotomy (hemilaminectomy) codes are based on an interspace in a specific area of the spine. If the procedure is performed on additional interspaces, the coder should locate the appropriate code(s) in that section of *CPT* for each additional interspace.

Injections

Spinal injections (or infusions) involve injecting medications through a needle placed into a structure or space in the spine in order for the physician to be able to diagnose the source of pain or to reduce it. Typical medications used include local anesthetics and corticosteroids. Local anesthetics numb the nerves and corticosteroids help reduce inflammation.

Injections into joints are sometimes referred to as blocks.

To accurately assign codes for these procedures, coders must abstract documentation from the operative report to determine the injection site (cervical, lumbar) and the substance injected (neurolytic).

➡ For example, a single, steroid injection into the lumbar spine would be assigned CPT code 62311.

Figure 4.11.   **The spinal column**

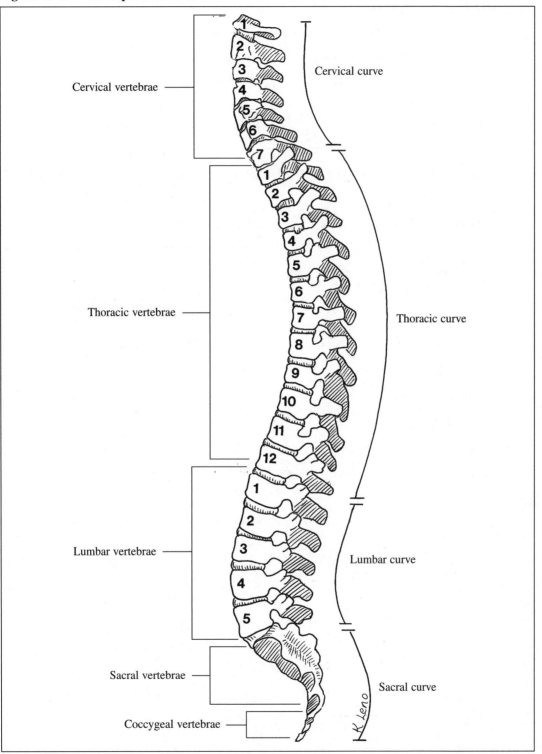

Cervical vertebrae

Cervical curve

Thoracic vertebrae

Thoracic curve

Lumbar vertebrae

Lumbar curve

Sacral vertebrae

Sacral curve

Coccygeal vertebrae

K. Leno

Exercise 4.44

Assign CPT codes and index entries for the following procedures. Append modifiers if applicable.

1. Patient with chronic pain receives a nerve block; anesthetic agent into the branch of sciatic nerve

    Code(s) _____

    Index entries: _____

    _____

2. Using an operating microscope, the physician performs a neuroplasty of the right ring finger

    Code(s) _____

    Index entries: _____

    _____

3. Cervical epidural spinal injection of phenol

    Code(s) _____

    Index entries: _____

    _____

4. Neurorrhaphy of digital nerves of right thumb and ring finger

    Code(s) _____

    Index entries: _____

    _____

Exercise 4.45

Operative Report

Preoperative Diagnosis: C5-C6 Disc herniation

Postoperative Diagnosis: Same

Operative Procedure: Anterior cervical discectomy

Indications and Details of This Procedure: This 45-year-old gentleman presents with a six-month history of neck pain, right shoulder pain, right intra-scapular pain, and pain radiating on the outer aspect of the right arm. He was found to have wasting of the supra and infra-spinatus muscles and EMG confirmed an C-6 radiculopathy. Magnetic resonance imaging scan showed a lateral disc herniation at the level of C5-6. The patient tried initial conservative measures, which did not help him; hence recommendation of surgery was made. The risks and benefits included infection, hemorrhage, injury to the nerve roots, paralysis, injury to the spinal cord with paralysis, failure to improve, or even death. The patient fully understands and agrees to go ahead with the procedure.

The patient was anesthetized and positioned supine with a shoulder support, and the neck was prepared and draped in the usual manner. Mid cervical crease incision was marked, both four cm. Incisions were placed transversely and the skin was sharply cut, and then the platysma was cut in the line of incision. The cervical fascia was dissected. Then we entered the plane between the trachea and the carotid sheath by blunt dissection reaching the prevertebral space. The prevertebral fascia was incised longitudinally. The disc bulge at 5-6 was easily identified, and a spinal needle placed confirmed the position to be at 5-6. The anterior osteophytes were prominent. They were removed and then we entered the disc space. The disc space itself had collapsed, and there was only dessicated disc material. We curetted out the disc and the cartilage plate, and the vertebral spreader was put in. More disc was removed from the lateral parts of the disc extending toward the uncas on both sides. As we moved posteriorly toward the ligament, there was subligamentous disc herniation to the right side. It was removed, and the ligament was reached. The ligament was lifted with a blunt hook and opened with micro-punches. Using a Midas Rex drill, the posterior parts of the bone in this region were drilled doing a right foraminotomy on the right, and the nerve root was decompressed. A no-free fragment was identified inside the canal, and the entire ligamentum disc was removed over the nerve root. The bone was punched in those corners to give adequate space. The ligament was cut across the width of the space, and on the left side also foraminotomy was done removing the osteophytes in the corner and decompressing the nerve root. After we were satisfied with the decompression, the space was irrigated with antibiotic solution and hemostasis was achieved with some Gelfoam powder, and the wound was thoroughly irrigated. Hemostasis was achieved in the muscle plane, and closure was done with 3-0 Vicryl for the platysma and subcutaneous layer, and the skin was closed with 4-0 subcuticular Vicryl. Dressings were applied in the usual manner with Steri-Strips, Telfa gauze, and Tegaderm. The patient was reversed from anesthesia and had an uneventful recovery. He was moving all the limbs well and was transferred in a stable condition to the Recovery Room.

1. Code(s): _____

    What index entries were used to find the code(s)?

    _____

Eye and Ocular Adnexa Subsection

The eye and ocular adnexa subsection includes procedures involving the eyeball, anterior and posterior segment, ocular adnexa, and conjunctiva. Figure 4.12 shows the structure of the eye.

    The codes are categorized first by body part involved and then by type of procedure, such as retinal and choroid repair, conjunctivoplasty, cataract removal, and removal of foreign body.

    Many of the refractive procedures performed for vision correction (such as Lasik procedures) are categorized in the unlisted category for the anterior segment, CPT code 66999, rather than having specific CPT codes.

Figure 4.12.   The structure of the eye

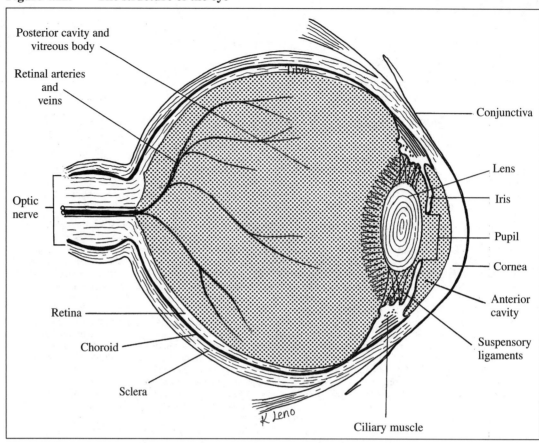

Posterior cavity and vitreous body

Retinal arteries and veins

Optic nerve

Iris

Conjunctiva

Lens

Iris

Pupil

Cornea

Anterior cavity

Suspensory ligaments

Retina

Choroid

Sclera

Ciliary muscle

Cataract Extraction

The note at the beginning of the cataract extraction subsection (66830–66986) identifies the following procedures as part of the extraction: lateral canthotomy, iridectomy, iridotomy, anterior capsulotomy, posterior capsulotomy, use of viscoelastic agents, enzymatic zonulysis, use of other pharmacologic agents, and subconjunctival or sub-Tenon injections. When performed as part of the cataract extraction, these procedures should not be coded separately because they are incorporated into the bigger procedure of the cataract removal.

The two types of cataract extraction are extracapsular and intracapsular. *Extracapsular* extraction, which includes removal of the lens material without removing the posterior capsule, is reported with codes 66840–66852, 66940, 66982, and 66984. *Intracapsular* extraction, which involves removal of the entire lens including the capsule, is reported with codes 66920, 66930, and 66983.

Codes 66982, 66983, and 66984 describe cataract extraction with insertion of intraocular lens (IOL) prosthesis during the same operative episode. Insertion of IOL prosthesis performed during a subsequent encounter is reported with code 66985.

Combo code if lens inserted at time of cataract removal

Exercise 4.46

Assign CPT codes and index entries for the following procedures. Append modifiers if applicable.

1. With the use of a slit lamp, the physician removes a piece of metal from the patient's cornea

   Code(s) _____

   Index entries: _____

   _____

2. Biopsy of left upper eyelid

   Code(s) _____

   Index entries: _____

   _____

3. Excision of 0.5 cm lesion of conjunctiva

   Code(s) _____

   Index entries: _____

   _____

4. Excision of a chalazion, right upper eyelid

   Code(s) _____

   Index entries: _____

   _____

Exercise 4.47

Operative Report

Preoperative Diagnosis:	Cataract of the left eye
Postoperative Diagnosis:	Cataract of the left eye
Operative Procedure:	Phacoemulsification of cataract of the left eye with lens implantation
Complications:	None

Indications: The patient is a 77-year-old female with a history of decreasing vision to a level of 20/100 in her left eye. Slit lamp examination showed a nuclear sclerotic cataract. Fundus examination view appeared to be normal. The patient requested removal of the cataract for improvement in her vision.

Procedure: The patient was brought to the OR and placed on the operating table in the supine position. A small amount of Brevital was given intravenously for relaxation, and then a local anesthetic using 0.75% Marcaine in a peribulbar manner and a modified Van Lint manner was administered. After obtaining proper anesthetic effect, the eye was prepped and draped in the usual manner. A blepharostat was placed between the lids of the eye, and a bridle suture using 4-0 silk was placed through the superior rectus tendon. A peritomy was performed from the 2 to 10 o'clock position superiorly with cautery used to obtain hemostasis. A 3.5 mm grooved incision was placed tangent to the limbus approximately 2 mm posterior to the surgical limbus, and a scleral tunnel was formed anteriorly toward clear cornea. A stab incision was made at the 2 o'clock position in the limbus with a #75 Beaver blade forming an irrigating peritomy site, and the anterior chamber was entered at the base of the scleral tunnel, using a #55 Keratome blade. Healon was instilled in the anterior chamber, and then an irrigating cystotome blade was used to perform a smooth capsulorrhexis opening of the anterior capsule. A balanced salt solution was used to perform hydrodissection, and the phacoemulsification tip was used to break up and remove the nucleus of the lens. The remaining cortical material was removed from the eye using the irrigation-aspiration tip. The posterior capsule of the lens was polished using a Kratz scratcher. The wound was extended very slightly, and then a 6 mm folding posterior chamber lens was placed in the eye with the lens within the capsular bag. Excess Healon was removed from the eye using the irrigation-aspiration tip.

The corneosclera was tested and found to be watertight and free of any iris incarceration. The conjunctiva was repositioned to its original site and tacked down using bipolar cautery. A collagen shield, which had been soaked in a suspension of Tobradex eyedrops, was then placed over the cornea and one drop of Timoptic was instilled on the conjunctiva. The blepharostat and the bridle suture were removed from the eye, and a dry dressing and Fox shield were placed over the eye. The patient tolerated the procedure well and left the OR in good condition. She was instructed to leave the eye dressing intact for the remainder of the day and to return to the office the following day for follow-up care and instructions.

1. Code(s): _____

   What index entries were used to find the code(s)?

   _____

   _____

Auditory System Subsection

The auditory system subsection includes codes for procedures to the inner, outer, and middle ear. Figure 4.13 depicts the structure of the ear.

Diagnostic services such as audiometry and vestibular testing are found in the medicine section of *Current Procedural Terminology*. Surgical procedures are found in the code range from 69000–69979 and have no specific coding guidelines designated that impact code assignment.

One of most commonly performed auditory surgical procedures is the tympanostomy for insertion of ventilating tubes for children with chronic ear infections. Under direct visualization with a microscope, the physician makes an incision in the eardrum (tympanum). The physician also may remove fluid from the middle ear. A ventilating tube is inserted through the opening in the tympanum. Coders may be confused by the terminology when the physicians

Figure 4.13. **The structure of the ear**

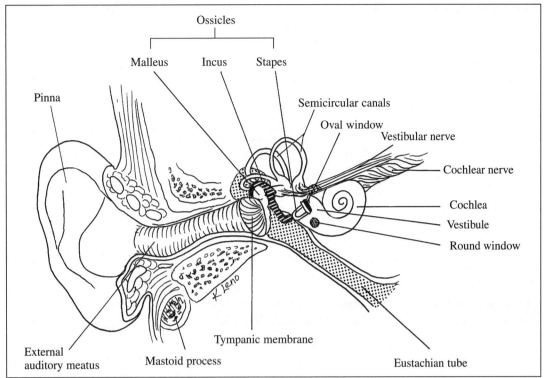

state that they performed a "myringotomy for insertion of ventilating tubes." For coding purposes, this describes a tympanostomy (code 69433 or 69436).

Exercise 4.48

Assign CPT codes and index entries for the following procedures. Append modifiers if applicable.

1. Labyrinthectomy with mastectomy   *mastoidectomy*

    Code(s) _____ *69910*

    Index entries: _*labyrinthectomy, with mastoidectomy*_

    _____

2. Under general anesthesia, the surgeon removes a pebble from the left external auditory canal of a one-year-old child.

    Code(s) _____

    Index entries: _____

    _____

3. Tympanoplasty with mastoidotomy and ossicular chain reconstruction

    Code(s) _____

    Index entries: _____

    _____

Exercise 4.49

Operative Report

Preoperative Diagnosis: Bilateral otitis media

Postoperative Diagnosis: Same   *tympanostomy*

Operation: Bilateral myringotomy with tubes

Procedure: The patient was brought to the operating room, placed in a supine position, and given a general anesthesia. Myringotomies were performed bilaterally in the anterior-superior quadrant of each tympanic membrane. The left middle ear cavity contained a mucopurulent material; the right middle ear cavity contained a thick mucoid material. Tympanostomy tubes were placed bilaterally without difficulty. The patient tolerated the procedure well and was discharged to the recovery area.

1. Code(s): _____

    What index entries were used to find the code(s)?

    _____

    _____

Exercise 4.50 Chapter Review

The following procedures were performed in the outpatient department or emergency department of Central Hospital. Assign the appropriate CPT codes the *hospital* should submit for payment, along with the index entries you used to find the codes. Assign modifiers when applicable.

1.   Incision and drainage of complicated parotid gland abscess   _____

2.   Bilateral tympanostomy with insertion of ventilating tube performed under general anesthesia   _____

3.   Colposcopy of cervix (upper vagina) with biopsy of the cervix   _____

4.   Cystourethroscopy with fulguration of small bladder tumor (1.0 cm)   _____

5.   Open incisional biopsy of left breast (Medicare patient)   _____

6.   Intermediate wound repair of a 2 cm laceration of the face   _____

7.   Closed treatment of distal phalangeal fracture of right thumb without manipulation (Medicare patient)   _____

8.   Direct laryngoscopy with biopsy and use of operating microscope   _____

9.   Percutaneous placement of central venous catheter in 50-year-old patient for hemodialysis

     _____

10. Flexible sigmoidoscopy with removal of polyp by hot biopsy forceps   _____

11. Repair of bilateral, initial inguinal hernia with strangulation in a 10-year-old   _____

12. Arthroscopy of the left elbow with removal of loose body   _____

13. Drainage of abscess of left thumb and second finger   _____

Exercise 4.51 Chapter Review

The following procedures were performed by physicians at the surgical clinic. Assign the appropriate CPT codes so that the *physicians* can receive payment for services rendered, along with the index entries you used to find the codes. Assign modifiers when applicable.

1. Craniectomy for excision of cerebellopontine angle tumor. Dr. Reynolds and Dr. Jones performed this complex surgery. Assign the appropriate codes and index entries for each physician.

   Dr. Jones:

   _____

   Dr. Reynolds:

   _____

2. Induced abortion by dilatation and curettage.

   Code(s) _____

   Index entries: _____

   _____

3. Diagnostic and surgical arthroscopy of the right shoulder with complete synovectomy.

   Code(s) _____

   Index entries: _____

   _____

4. Insertion of permanent cardiac pacemaker with insertion of atrial and ventricular transvenous electrodes. Dr. Reynolds provided only the postoperative management for this patient; another physician at a university hospital provided the preoperative management and the procedure. Assign the appropriate code to describe the service that Dr. Reynolds provided.

   Code(s) _____

   Index entries: _____

   _____

5. Endoscopic retrograde cholangiopancreatography (ERCP) with endoscopic retrograde insertion of tube into pancreatic duct.

   Code(s) _____

   Index entries: _____

   _____

6. Laparoscopy with removal of tubes and ovaries. The surgeon documents that the procedure was extremely difficult to perform therefore taking an additional two hours to complete.

   Code(s) _____

   Index entries: _____

   _____

(Continued on next page)

Exercise 4.51 (cont.)

7. Bilateral probing of lower nasolacrimal ducts with irrigation under general anesthesia.

   Code(s) _____

   Index entries: _____

   _____

8. Bilateral sinus endoscopy with maxillary antrostomy and removal of maxillary sinus tissue.

   Code(s) _____

   Index entries: _____

   _____

9. Total abdominal colectomy with continent ileostomy.

   Code(s) _____

   Index entries: _____

   _____

10. Closed treatment of distal fibular fracture without manipulation. This patient is in the post-operative period for an arthroscopy of the shoulder performed two weeks ago. Dr. Reynolds performed both surgeries.

    Code(s) _____

    Index entries: _____

    _____

11. Microdermabrasion of the epidermis to remove tattoo of arm.

    Code(s) _____

    Index entries: _____

    _____

Chapter 5

Radiology

The radiology section of CPT includes the following subsections:

Subsection	Code Range
Diagnostic Radiology (Diagnostic Imaging)	70010–76499
Diagnostic Ultrasound	76506–76999
Radiation Oncology	77261–77799
Nuclear Medicine	78000–79999

It is important to understand the differences between the subsections and not to assign codes based on the area of the body being treated or studied. Some of the subsections contain instructions that are unique to them, and notes are included throughout each subsection to explain important instructions, such as the definitions of A-mode, M-mode, or B-scan ultrasounds.

Many of the conventions and guidelines discussed in earlier chapters of *Basic CPT/ HCPCS Coding* also apply to this chapter. Specific conventions pertinent to the radiology section are included in this chapter.

Links to the Society of Interventional Radiology and MedLearn that are pertinent to the discussion in this chapter are located in the Web Resources at the back of this chapter.

Hospital Billing and Radiology Code Reporting

When reporting radiologic procedures, many hospitals use a computer program called a chargemaster. The chargemaster contains all the codes, abbreviated definition descriptions, charges, and sometimes other information used by any given hospital, physician office, or clinic. (See table 5.1 for an example excerpt from a radiology chargemaster.) Thus, whenever a radiologic procedure is ordered and performed, the computer automatically assigns the code and applies the charge from the requisition form the physician used to order the service. The chargemaster is known by several other names, including charge description master, standard charge file, service item master, or charge compendium. In most cases, each ancillary department is responsible for maintaining its codes in the chargemaster. Requests for input, however, often are made to health information management (HIM) departments.

Periodic review of these systems is mandatory for correct reimbursement and data quality control. The wrong code attached to a procedure can result in significant revenue loss or

Table 5.1.   Example excerpt from radiology chargemaster

In numeric order by department				
Charge Seq Number	**Revenue Center**		**Description**	**CPT Code**
DEPT 721 RADIOLOGY—DIAGNOSTIC				
1700004 999	320	X RAY	NO CHARGE	
1701101 999	320	X RAY	MANDIBLE	70110
1701309 999	320	X RAY	MASTOIDS STENVERS LAWS	70130
1701341 999	320	X RAY	INT AUD CANAL	70134
1701341 999	320	X RAY	FACIAL BONES	70150
1701606 999	320	X RAY	NASAL BONES	70160
1701903 999	320	X RAY	OPTIC FORAMINA	70190
1702000 999	320	X RAY	ORBITS	70200
1702208 999	320	X RAY	SINUSES	70220
1702406 999	320	X RAY	SELLA TURCICA	70240
1702604 910	320	X RAY	SKULL	70260
1703305 999	320	X RAY	TEMPMAND JT BI	70330
1703552 999	320	X RAY	DENTAL PANOREX	70355
1703602 999	320	X RAY	NECK FOR SOFT TISSUE	70360
1703800 999	320	X RAY	SALIVARY GLAND	70380
1710102 910	324	X RAY	CHEST PA	71010
73010320 = MDLAB, 910 = ER, 920 = OUTP, 921 = OUTP, 999 = INP				

overpayment for a hospital or large clinic. Inappropriate unbundling of codes can result in fraudulent charges to insurance companies, so the accuracy of any automated coding via a chargemaster program is an important data quality concern.

Physician Billing

Because many physicians do not have radiologic equipment in their offices, they usually refer patients who need radiologic procedures to the local hospital or a freestanding radiologic center. In such cases, coders and billers for referring physicians do not assign radiology codes unless the physicians or facilities provide supervision and interpretation. Usually, radiologic procedures are reported by radiologists associated with a hospital, clinic, or freestanding radiology center. Individuals providing billing services for radiologists and/or radiation oncologists must have a thorough understanding of radiologic procedures, ultrasound procedures, nuclear medicine procedures, and radiation therapy.

In some cases, hospitals may employ radiologists and report both technical and professional components of procedures or, when available, CPT codes representing complete procedures or CPT codes without modifiers. Revisions have been made to CPT that have created fewer complete procedures and more procedures where the professional and technical components are reported using separate codes.

Radiological Supervision and Interpretation

Many codes in the radiology section of CPT include the term *radiological supervision and interpretation* in their description. These codes are used to describe the radiologic portion of a procedure that two physicians often perform. In situations where one physician performs the procedure and also provides the supervision and interpretation, two codes are reported: a radiologic code and a code from another section of the CPT codebook, such as surgery. This is often referred to as a complete procedure.

Example: Unilateral lymphangiography of the extremity—complete procedure. The physician submits codes 75801 and 38790. Code 75801 identifies the radiologic procedure, including interpretation of the results, and code 38790 identifies the injection provided for the lymphangiography.

It should be noted that the radiological supervision and interpretation codes do not apply to the radiation oncology subsection.

Modifiers in the Radiology Section

A complete listing of modifiers is in appendix A of the CPT codebook. Some of the common modifiers used with the radiology section follow:

–22 **Unusual Procedural Services** *(for physician use only):* This modifier is intended for use when the service provided is greater than that usually required for the listed procedure. The CPT codebook states that modifier –22 may be reported with computerized tomography codes when additional slices are required or when a more detailed examination is necessary.

–26 **Professional Component** *(for physician use only):* In circumstances where a radiologic procedure includes both a physician (professional) component and a technical component, modifier –26 may be reported to identify the physician (professional) component. The professional component includes supervising the procedure, reading and interpreting the results, and documenting the interpretation in a report. This service can be provided by the physician who ordered the procedure or by the radiologist on staff at the hospital or freestanding radiology clinic. The technical component includes performance of the actual procedure and expenses for supplies and equipment. Usually, this service is provided by a radiologic technician at a hospital or a freestanding radiology clinic. The physician reports the professional component by attaching modifier –26 to the appropriate radiologic procedure. The freestanding radiology clinic reports the technical component by attaching modifier –TC (technical component) to the same procedure. Modifier –TC is a Level II HCPCS modifier that may not be recognized by all payers.

Example: Code 74220, Radiologic examination of the esophagus. The physician should report 74220–26, and the clinic should report 74220–TC.

When reporting a code that includes "radiologic supervision and interpretation" in the description, modifier –26 should not be appended to the procedure code. Because the radiologic supervision and interpretation code already describes the professional component, the modifier is unnecessary.

Example: Cervical myelography with the physician providing only the supervision and interpretation of this procedure. The physician should report as follows: 72240, Myelography, cervical, radiological supervision and interpretation.

In this example, modifier –26 is inappropriate because the descriptor for code 72240 already indicates that the physician provided only supervision and interpretation of the procedure.

–51 **Multiple Procedures** *(for physician use only):* Modifier –51 may be reported to identify that multiple radiologic procedures were performed on the same day or during the same radiologic episode. The first procedure listed should identify the major procedure or the one that is most resource intensive.

–52 **Reduced Services** *(for hospital and physician use):* Modifier –52 may be reported to indicate that a radiologic procedure has been partially reduced or eliminated at the discretion of the physician.

The CPT codebook states that modifier –52 may be reported with computerized tomography codes for a limited study or a follow-up study.

–53 **Discontinued Procedure** *(for physician use only):* Modifier –53 is appropriate in circumstances where the physician elected to terminate or discontinue a diagnostic procedure, usually because of risk to the patient's well-being. Modifier –73 or –74 would be used for hospital reporting.

> **Example:** A patient planned to have urography with KUB, which would be reported with code 74400. Because the patient fainted during the procedure, it was discontinued before completion. The physician should report 74400–53.

–59 **Distinct Procedural Service** *(for hospital and physician use):* Modifier –59 may be used to identify that a procedure or service was distinct or independent from other services provided on the same day. Modifier –59 is appropriate for procedures that have been performed together because of specific circumstances, although they usually are not integral to one another or not performed together.

–RT and –LT Modifiers: Modifiers –RT and –LT are Level II HCPCS modifiers that should be reported when bilateral radiologic procedures are performed. To report these modifiers to reflect a bilateral radiologic procedure, the procedure code should be assigned twice and –RT attached to one code and –LT to the other.

> **Example:** 73650–RT and 73650–LT, Radiologic examination of the calcaneus with a minimum of two views, bilateral

Both of these modifiers apply to Medicare claims, and their use varies according to the reporting requirements of Medicaid programs and other third-party payers. The CMS guidelines for hospitals state that –RT and –LT are not to be used to report bilateral surgical procedures. Instead, modifier –50 is to be used because of the effect on payment.

Diagnostic Radiology (Diagnostic Imaging)

Codes 70010–76499 describe diagnostic radiology services and are subdivided first by anatomic site and then by specific type of procedure performed: X ray, computed tomography (CT) scan, magnetic resonance imaging (MRI) scan, and magnetic resonance angiography (MRA) scan. These radiology procedures may be found in the alphabetic index of the CPT codebook by referencing the following main entries: "X ray," "CT scan," "Magnetic Resonance Imaging," and "Magnetic Resonance Angiography." They also may be referenced under the specific site with a subterm identifying the specific procedure.

The CPT codebook differentiates between radiologic procedures with and without contrast material. Contrast material consists of radiopaque substances that obstruct the passage of X rays and cause the areas containing the material to appear white on the X-ray film, thus outlining the contour of body structures and permitting the identification of abnormal growths. Contrast material may be administered orally or intravenously. Examples of contrast agents include barium or Gastrografin, iohexol, iopamidol, ioxaglate, Hypaque, and Renografin. Commonly performed radiologic examinations using contrast material include barium enema, angiography, cystogram, endoscopic retrograde cholangiopancreatogram, fistulogram, intravenous pyelogram, excretory urogram, lymphangiography, oral cholecystogram, retrograde pyelogram, and voiding cystourethrogram.

CT scans also may be performed with or without contrast material. Although this radiologic procedure can scan any body part, it is most helpful in evaluating the brain, lung, mediastinum, retroperitoneum, and liver.

When coverage requirements are met, reimbursement for the supply of contrast media may be obtained by reporting the appropriate HCPCS code.

MRI scans are almost equal to CT scans, although they are considered superior for scanning the brain, spinal cord, soft tissues, and adrenal and renal masses. This radiologic procedure is contraindicated for patients who have metallic objects in their bodies, such as pacemakers, shrapnel, cochlear implants, metallic eye fragments, and vascular clips in the central nervous system. Contrast material also can be used when performing MRI scans. Gadolinium (gadopentetate dimeglumine) is the contrast agent most often used.

Exercise 5.1

Assign the appropriate codes for the following procedure(s). Append modifiers if applicable.

1. MRI of abdomen with contrast

   Code(s): _____

2. CT scan of lumbar spine without contrast

   Code(s): _____

3. X ray of pelvis, AP

   Code(s): _____

4. Upper GI series with KUB

   Code(s): _____

5. Cystography, 3 views, supervision and interpretation only

   Code(s): _____

Interventional Radiology

Interventional radiology is the branch of medicine that diagnoses and/or treats diseases using percutaneous or minimally invasive techniques with the use of imaging guidance. Assigning codes from this section requires advanced study and thorough knowledge of anatomy and physiology. Suggested references are provided in this book.

Diagnostic Ultrasound

The subsection of diagnostic utrasound includes codes 76506–76999, which are subdivided by anatomic site. The diagnostic ultrasound codes can be found in the alphabetic index of the CPT codebook by referencing the main entries of "Ultrasound" or "Echography." Diagnostic ultrasound involves the use of ultrasonic waves, or high-frequency sound waves, to visualize internal structures of the body. Ultrasounds are commonly performed for evaluation of the abdomen, the pelvis (for both gynecologic and obstetric diagnoses), and the heart.

Four types of diagnostic ultrasounds are recognized:

- An A-mode ultrasound is a one-dimensional ultrasonic measurement procedure.

- An M-mode ultrasound is a one-dimensional ultrasonic measurement procedure with movement of the trace to record amplitude and velocity of moving echo-producing structures.

- A B-scan ultrasound is a two-dimensional ultrasonic scanning procedure with a two-dimensional display.

- A real-time scan is a two-dimensional ultrasonic scanning procedure with display of both two-dimensional structure and motion with time.

The medicine section of the CPT codebook includes ultrasounds involving the following areas:

- Cerebrovascular arterial studies (93875–93888)

- Arterial studies of the extremities (93922–93931)

- Venous studies of the extremities (93965–93971)

- Visceral and penile vascular studies (93975–93981)

- Ultrasounds of the heart (echocardiography) (93303–93350)

Exercise 5.2

Assign the appropriate codes for the following procedure(s). Append modifiers if applicable.

1. Saline infusion hysterosonography with color flow Doppler

   Code(s): _____

2. Limited ultrasound of pregnant uterus to determine fetal position

   Code(s): _____

3. Bilateral ultrasound of breasts

   Code(s): _____

Radiation Oncology

The radiation oncology codes (77261–77799) describe the therapeutic use of radiation to treat diseases, especially neoplastic tumors. Radiation therapy may be used as primary therapy to treat certain types of malignancies, such as early stages of Hodgkin's disease. It also may be used as adjuvant treatment in small-cell lung cancer and head and neck cancers, and as palliative treatment to alleviate pain caused by metastasis to bone, to control bleeding caused by gynecologic malignancies, and to relieve obstruction and compression from advanced lung cancer, brain lesions, and spinal cord lesions. The most common type of radiation used in the treatment is electromagnetic radiation with X rays and gamma rays. X rays are photons generated inside a machine; gamma rays are photons emitted from a radioactive source. Radiation is measured in units known as the radiation absorbed dose (rad) or the gray (Gy). The Gy is equal to 100 rad.

The delivery of radiation therapy may be external or internal. *External* radiation therapy involves delivery of a beam of ionizing radiation from an external source through the patient's skin toward the tumor region. *Internal* radiation therapy, also known as brachytherapy, involves applying a radioactive material inside the patient or in close proximity. This material may be contained in various types of devices, including tubes, needles, wires, seeds, and other small containers. Common radioactive materials used in brachytherapy include radium-226, cobalt-60, cesium-137, and iodine-125. Three types of brachytherapy are recognized in the CPT codebook:

- Interstitial brachytherapy involves placing a radiation source directly into tissues.

- Intracavitary brachytherapy utilizes radiation source(s) placed in special devices and then implanted in body cavities.

- Surface application brachytherapy uses radioactive material that is contained on the surface of a plaque or mold and applied directly or close to the surface of the patient.

Consultation: Clinical Management

Consultative services that the radiation oncologist provides before making a decision to treat the patient should be reported with the appropriate E/M, medicine, or surgery code.

Radiation Treatment Management

Radiation treatment management is reported in units of five fractions or treatment sessions, regardless of the actual time period in which the services are furnished. The services need not be furnished on consecutive days. Multiple fractions representing two or more treatment sessions furnished on the same day may be counted as long as there has been a distinct break in therapy sessions and the fractions are of the character usually furnished on different days.

Radiation Treatment Delivery

Codes 77401 through 77418 describe the technical component of delivering the radiation treatment, as well as the various energy levels administered. To assign the appropriate code, the following information is needed:

- Number of treatment areas involved

- Number of ports involved

- Number of shielding blocks used

- Total million electron volts (MeV) administered

Hyperthermia

Hyperthermia involves the use of heat to raise the temperature of a specific area of the body to increase cell metabolism and destroy cancer cells. Usually, it is performed as an adjunct to radiation therapy or chemotherapy. The hyperthermia codes (77600–77615) in the CPT codebook include external, interstitial, and intracavitary treatment. If administered at the same time, radiation therapy should be reported separately.

Codes 77600–77615 include management during the hyperthermia treatment and follow-up care for three months after completion.

Clinical Brachytherapy

Clinical brachytherapy uses natural or man-made radioactive elements that are applied in or around a particular treatment field. A therapeutic radiologist supervises the radioactive elements and interprets appropriate dosage. When the services of a surgeon are needed, modifier –66 or –62 may be reported to ensure that both physicians are reimbursed.

Codes 77750–77799 include admission to the hospital and daily visits by the physician. The codes differentiate between interstitial and intracavitary brachytherapy, and are subdivided further to identify the number of sources/ribbons applied: simple, intermediate, or complex. The CPT codebook includes definitions for each of these levels.

Note: Above, the term sources refers to intracavitary or permanent interstitial placement of radioactive material. The term ribbons refers to temporary interstitial placement of radioactive material.

Nuclear Medicine

Nuclear medicine involves the administration of radioisotopes, which are radioactive elements that diagnose diseases. The radioactive isotope deteriorates spontaneously and emits gamma rays from inside the body that enable the physician to view internal abnormalities. Some radioisotopes are selectively absorbed by tumors or specific organs in the body, making them visible on the scan.

Nuclear medicine procedures are organized in codes 78000 through 79999 according to body systems, such as the cardiovascular system. The provision of radium or other radio-elements is not included in the services listed in this section. Additional codes may be reported if the physician provides these supplies: 78990, Diagnostic radiopharmaceuticals; and 79900, Therapeutic radiopharmaceuticals. These procedures may be found in the alphabetic index of the CPT codebook by referencing "Nuclear Imaging" or "Nuclear Medicine."

Some of the more common diagnostic nuclear medicine scans are described below:

- Bone scans are performed as part of metastatic workups to identify infections such as osteomyelitis, to evaluate hip prosthesis, to distinguish pathologic fractures from traumatic fractures, and to evaluate delayed union of fractures.

- Cardiac scans are performed for diagnosis of myocardial infarction, stress testing, ejection fractures, measurement of cardiac output, and diagnosis of ventricular aneurysms.

  —The thallium 201 scan examines myocardial perfusion, with normal myocardium appearing as "hot" and ischemic or infarcted areas appearing as "cold."

  —The technetium 99m pyrophosphate scan identifies recently damaged myocardial tissue and is most sensitive 24 to 72 hours after an acute myocardial infarction.

  —The technetium 99m ventriculogram scan identifies abnormal wall motion, cardiac shunts, size and function of heart chambers, cardiac output, and ejection fraction. The multigated acquisition (MUGA) scan is another form of this type of study.

When the following tests are performed during exercise and/or pharmacologic stress, the appropriate stress-testing code from the 93015–93018 range should be reported in addition to the appropriate code from the nuclear medicine subsection:

- Hepatobiliary scans (HIDA scans) are performed for diagnosis of biliary obstruction, acute cholecystitis, or biliary atresia.

- Lung scans (ventilation-perfusion [V/Q] scans) can reveal pulmonary disease, chronic obstructive pulmonary disease, and emphysema. When performed along with chest X rays, these scans are important tools in evaluating pulmonary emboli.

- Renal scans are performed to evaluate the overall function of the kidneys.

- Thyroid scans are most commonly performed with technetium 99m pertechnetate and are useful in detecting nodules.

Exercise 5.3 Chapter Review

Assign the appropriate codes for the following procedure(s). Include CPT modifiers and Level II modifiers when applicable.

1. Radiologic examination (X ray) of the forearm, anteroposterior (A/P) and lateral views. What code(s) should be submitted on the claim form if the physician provided only the supervision and interpretation (professional component) for this procedure? _____

2. MRI of the cervical spine with contrast material. What code(s) should be submitted on the claim form for the radiologist to receive payment? _____

3. Physician performed the radiologic supervision and interpretation for cystography (minimum of three views). _____

4. Myocardial perfusion imaging (nuclear medicine) single study performed at rest; myocardial perfusion study with ejection fraction. _____

5. Bilateral screening mammogram. _____

6. Radiologic supervision and interpretation for transluminal atherectomy of renal artery. _____

7. CT scan of the head with contrast material. Identify the appropriate code(s) and modifier that the radiology clinic should report on the claim it submits. _____

8. Pelvic ultrasound, pregnant uterus. Real time with image documentation, transvaginal. _____

9. Radiologist provided radiologic supervision and interpretation for ultrasonic guidance needle biopsy. _____

10. Whole-body bone scan (nuclear medicine). _____

11. Barium enema with KUB. _____

12. Percutaneous placement of IVC filter. Dr. Jones provided radiologic supervision and interpretation, and Dr. Williams performed the actual procedure. Identify the codes the physicians should report on their individual claims.

    Dr. Jones: _____

    Dr. Williams: _____

13. Delivery of radiation therapy to single area with single port and simple blocks–13 MeV. _____

14. Renal scan with vascular flow and function study (nuclear medicine) without pharmacological intervention. _____

15. Chest X ray, two views. _____

16. Intracavitary placement of four radioelement sources. _____

17. Radiopharmaceutical therapy for hyperthyroidism, subsequent therapy. Assign the appropriate code(s) to report provision of both the radiopharmaceutical and the actual therapy. _____

18. Retroperitoneal ultrasound, limited study. _____

19. X ray of the hips and pelvis in a five-year-old, with minimum of two views. _____

20. Gastroesophageal reflux study. _____

Chapter 6

Pathology and Laboratory

The pathology and laboratory section of the CPT codebook includes services provided by physicians, including pathologists and technologists under the supervision of a pathologist or other physician. It includes codes for services and procedures such as organ or disease panel tests, automated multichannel tests, urinalysis, hematologic and immunologic studies, and surgical and anatomic pathologic examinations. This chapter discusses specific subsections of the pathology and laboratory section.

Subsection	Code Range
Organ or Disease Oriented Panels	80048–80076
Drug Testing	80100–80103
Therapeutic Drug Assays	80150–80299
Evocative/Suppression Testing	80400–80440
Consultations (Clinical Pathology)	80500–80502
Urinalysis	81000–81099
Chemistry	82000–84999
Hematology and Coagulation	85002–85999
Immunology	86000–86849
Transfusion Medicine	86850–86999
Microbiology	87001–87999
Anatomic Pathology	88000–88099
Cytopathology	88104–88199
Cytogenetic Studies	88230–88299
Surgical Pathology	88300–88399
Transcutaneous Procedures	88400
Other Procedures	89050–89399

Alphabetic Index

Laboratory and pathology procedures/services are listed in the alphabetic index of the CPT codebook under the following main terms:

- Specific name of the test, such as urinalysis, evocative/suppression test, and fertility test

- Specific substance/specimen/sample, such as glucose, CPK, cyanide, enterovirus, bone marrow, and nasal smear

- Specific method used, such as culture, fine needle aspiration, and microbiology

Hospital Billing for Laboratory and Pathology Procedures

In the hospital setting, the chargemaster is used to automate the billing of laboratory and pathology services. (See table 6.1 for an example excerpt from a laboratory chargemaster.) As mentioned in chapter 5, the chargemaster is a computer program containing codes, abbreviated definition descriptions, charges, and possibly other information used by a given hospital. Therefore, when patients visit the outpatient department with a requisition from their physician for laboratory work, the computer automatically assigns the appropriate code and charge for that particular service. Although coders are not really involved in the actual coding of these services, the health information management (HIM) department may be asked to help the laboratory and pathology department update its portion of the chargemaster.

Physician Billing

When reporting laboratory services provided by a physician, the coder must determine whether the physician performed the complete procedure or only a component of it. Some physician offices and physician-owned clinics have sophisticated laboratory equipment on the premises that enables the physicians to provide complete laboratory testing. A complete test would involve ordering the test, obtaining the sample (for example, blood or urine), handling the specimen, performing the actual test or procedure, and analyzing and interpreting the results. However, most physicians typically send the sample to a freestanding or hospital-based laboratory for testing and analysis. In this instance, the physician may report only the collection and handling of the blood sample or specimen.

Physicians also may send the patient for laboratory testing to a local hospital, where the sample or specimen is taken, the test or procedure is performed, and the results are analyzed and interpreted. The physician may seek reimbursement for these tests from some insurance plans when the tests are purchased from a reference laboratory or a hospital acting as a reference lab. Medicare, however, does not allow any provider who does not perform the test to bill

Table 6.1.   Example excerpt from laboratory chargemaster

In numeric order by department			
Charge Seq Number	**Revenue Center**	**Description**	**CPT Code**
		DEPT 703 CHEMISTRY	
2026250 910	302	LIPTHOPROTEIN ELECTROPHOR	83715
2120053 320	301	HEPATITIS B CORE AB IGG	86289
2120053 910	301	HEPATITIS B CORE AB IGG	86289
2120103 320	301	ELECTROLYTES PROFILE I	80012
2120111 999	301	LYTES 4	80004
2120129 320	301	GLUCOSE FASTING	82947
2120137 320	301	ACETONE SERUM	82009
2120145 320	301	GLUCOSE 1HR PP	82950
2120152 999	301	HDL CHOLESTEROL	83718
2120160 320	301	GLUCOSE 2HR PP	82950
2120186 999	301	UREA NITROGEN	84540
320 = MDLAB, 999 = INP			

for it. The reporting of laboratory tests depends on the organizations involved and the health plan guidelines applicable to the patient.

> **Example:** Dr. Reynolds performed a bone marrow needle biopsy in an oncology clinic and sent the specimen to a pathologist for review and interpretation. Dr. Reynolds reports 38221 for the actual biopsy of the bone marrow, and the pathologist reports 88305 for the review and interpretation of the specimen. If Dr. Reynolds pays the pathologist for the interpretation, he may report both codes, depending on the guidelines of the health plan involved.

Quantitative and Qualitative Studies

Throughout the laboratory and pathology section of the CPT codebook, code descriptions state whether the test performed is quantitative or qualitative in nature. *Qualitative* screening refers to tests that detect the presence of a particular analyte, constituent, or condition. Typically, qualitative studies are performed to determine whether a particular substance is present in the sample being evaluated. In contrast, *quantitative* studies provide results expressing specific numerical amounts of an analyte in a specimen. Usually, these tests are performed after a qualitative study to identify the specific amount of a particular substance in the sample.

Modifiers in the Laboratory Section

Because most of the commonly used modifiers in the pathology and laboratory section have been discussed in earlier chapters, only a brief summary of each is offered here.

-22 **Unusual Procedural Services:** This modifier is intended for use when the service provided is greater than the one usually required for the listed procedure.

-26 **Professional Component:** In circumstances where a laboratory or pathology procedure includes both a physician (professional) component and a technical component, modifier -26 can be reported to identify the physician component.

-32 **Mandated Services:** Modifier -32 may be reported when a group such as a third-party payer or a PRO mandates a service.

-52 **Reduced Services:** Modifier -52 may be reported to indicate that a laboratory or pathology procedure is partially reduced or eliminated at the discretion of the physician.

-53 **Discontinued Procedure:** Modifier -53 may be reported to indicate that the physician elected to terminate a procedure due to circumstances that put the patient's well-being at risk.

-59 **Distinct Procedural Service:** Modifier -59 may be used to identify that a procedure or service was distinct or independent from other services provided on the same day. This modifier may be used when procedures are performed together because of specific circumstances, even though they usually are not.

-90 **Reference (Outside) Laboratory:** Modifier -90 may be reported to indicate performance of the test by a party other than the treating or reporting physician.

-91 **Repeat Clinical Diagnostic Laboratory Test:** Modifier -91 shows the need to repeat the same laboratory test on the same day to obtain multiple test results. It is not to be used to confirm initial results due to testing problems with specimens or equipment or for any reason when a normal one-time reportable result is all that is required. In addition, it is inappropriate for tests where codes describe a series of test results, such as with glucose tolerance or evocative suppression testing.

Example: Dr. Reynolds performed a venipuncture to obtain a blood sample for a lipid panel. He prepared the sample for transport and had it sent to an outside laboratory for testing, analysis, and interpretation. Dr. Reynolds should report 80061–90 to describe the laboratory test with the interpretation and analysis being performed at an off-site laboratory, along with code 36415 for the venipuncture. If this were a Medicare patient, HCPCS code G0001 would be used to report the venipuncture and the off-site laboratory would report code 80061 for the lipid panel.

Organ- or Disease-Oriented Panels

The organ- or disease-oriented panels describe the laboratory procedures performed most commonly for specific diseases, such as hepatitis and arthritis, or for specific organs, such as thyroid and hepatic function. All the tests listed in a panel must be performed for that code to be reported. When additional tests are performed that are not part of that particular panel, the codes describing those tests also must be reported. When some, but not all, of the tests in the panel are performed, the individual CPT codes should be reported, rather than the panel code. In the index, reference the main term "Organ" for a list of the panels.

Example: Code 80051 describes an electrolyte panel and includes the following tests: carbon dioxide, chloride, potassium, and sodium. For code 80051 to be reported, all four tests must be performed. If the carbon dioxide test is omitted, separate codes must be assigned for the remaining tests: chloride (82435), potassium (84132), and sodium (84295). Code 80051 should not be reported.

If a glucose test is performed in addition to the electrolyte panel, a separate code is reported for the glucose test (82947), along with the electrolyte panel (80051).

Evocative/Suppression Testing

The codes used for evocative/suppression testing (80400–80440) allow the physician to determine a baseline and the effects on the body after evocative or suppressive agents are administered. In reviewing the codes in this series, it should be noted that the description for each panel identifies the type of test(s) included in that panel and the number of times a specific test must be performed.

Example: Code 80420, Dexamethasone suppression panel, 48-hour. This panel must include:

- Free cortisol, urine (82530 x 2)

- Cortisol (82533 x 2)

- Volume measurement for timed collection (81050 x 2)

Physician attendance and monitoring during the test should be reported with the appropriate E/M services code, as well as the prolonged physician care codes, if they apply.

Chemistry

This series of codes (82000–84999) is used to report individual chemistry tests that are not performed as part of the automated organ- or disease-oriented panels (80048–80076). Unless otherwise noted in the code description, these tests are quantitative in nature.

> **Example:** Patient was seen in the laboratory department and the following test was performed:
>
> Total calcium: 82310

Hematology and Coagulation

The codes in the hematology and coagulation subsection (85002–85999) are used to report hematologic procedures, such as complete blood count (CBC), and coagulation procedures, such as clotting factor and prothrombin time.

To assign the appropriate code, careful attention must be paid to the specific type of procedure performed. Collaboration with the medical laboratory director or technician is helpful in ensuring that CPT codes are correct and consistent with the equipment available and the actual test performed.

Surgical Pathology

In surgical pathology coding (88300–88399), the unit of service is known as the specimen. The CPT codebook defines a specimen as tissue or tissues submitted for individual and separate attention, requiring individual examination and pathologic diagnosis. Codes are differentiated by six levels: level I (88300) identifies the gross examination of tissue only; levels II–VI (88302–88309) refer to the gross and microscopic examination of tissue. Selection of a level between II and VI is made on the basis of the type of specimen submitted. When two or more specimens are obtained from one patient, separate codes identifying the appropriate level for each should be reported.

> **Example:** Gross examination of a gallstone. The pathologist reports code 88300.
>
> **Example:** Gross and microscopic examination of a pituitary adenoma. The pathologist reports code 88305.
>
> **Example:** Gross and microscopic examination of two separate colon polyps. The pathologist reports codes 88305 and 88305 to identify examination of two separate specimens.

It should be noted that codes 88300–88309 include the accession or acquisition, examination, and reporting of a specimen. When performed by the pathologist, services identified in codes 88311–88365 and 88399 may be reported.

Exercise 6.1 Chapter Review

Assign the appropriate codes for the following pathology and laboratory procedures.

1. Gross and pathologic examination of transurethral resection of the prostate _____

2. Natriuretic peptide _____

3. ACTH stimulation panel for 21-hydroxylase deficiency _____

4. Automated urinalysis, without microscopy _____

5. Reticulated platelet assay _____

6. Gross and microscopic examination of left mastectomy with regional lymph nodes _____

7. Candida skin test _____

8. Confirmatory test for HTLV-1 antibody _____

9. The following tests were performed as a group from one blood sample: (lipid panel) total serum cholesterol, HDL and triglycerides; (electrolyte panel) carbon dioxide, chloride, potassium, and sodium. _____

10. Quantitative testing (therapeutic drug assay) of theophylline level _____

11. Evaluation of blood gases—pH, pCO_2, pO_2, CO_2, and HCO_3 _____

12. Hepatitis B surface antibody (HBsAb) _____

13. Partial thromboplastin time of whole blood (PTT) and prothrombin time (PT) _____

14. Gross and microscopic autopsy, including brain and spinal cord _____

15. Pathology consultation provided during surgery with frozen section of single specimen _____

Chapter 7

Evaluation and Management Services

In 1992, the evaluation and management (E/M) services section was added to the CPT codebook. The new E/M codes were designed to classify cognitive services provided by physicians, including skilled nursing facility (SNF) visits, consultations, and hospital and office visits. The various levels of the E/M codes describe the wide variations in skill, effort, time, responsibility, and medical knowledge required for the prevention, diagnosis, and treatment of illness or injury and the promotion of optimal health.

When processing insurance claims for physicians, E/M codes are reported for payment of professional services rendered. Because medical decision making is a key component in selecting a level of service and sometimes difficult to quantify in documentation, it is recommended that physicians select the codes, rather than having coding professionals assign them based on review of the health record. Nonphysicians may perform validation and verification of code selection using documentation guidelines developed jointly by the American Medical Association (AMA) and the Centers for Medicare and Medicaid Services (CMS). Healthcare facilities such as hospitals report E/M codes to designate encounters or visits for outpatient services.

Assignment of an E/M code for hospital services is required in most of the prospective payment systems developed by third-party payers, such as ambulatory payment group (APG) or ambulatory payment classification (APC) systems. E/M code assignment helps distinguish medical services from surgical services when assigning patients to a particular payment group. It also facilitates data collection by counting patients rather than services for outpatient reporting because one patient may have a number of outpatient services during a single visit. Under the prospective payment system, the CMS instructed hospitals to develop their own method for assignment of the facility E/M codes.

Links to the CMS and the American Academy of Family Physicians that are pertinent to the discussion in this chapter are located in the Web Resources at the back of this book.

Classification of E/M Services

The E/M services section is divided into broad categories, which are further divided into subcategories. The categories and their subcategories are as follows:

Office or Other Outpatient Services
    New Patient   99201–99205
    Established Patient   99211–99215

Hospital Observation Services	
Observation Care Discharge Services	99217
Initial Observation Care	99218–99220
Observation or Inpatient Care Services (Including Admission and Discharge Services)	
Observation or Inpatient Hospital Care	99234–99236
Hospital Inpatient Services	
Initial Hospital Care	99221–99223
Subsequent Hospital Care	99231–99233
Hospital Discharge Services	99238–99239
Consultations	
Office or Other Outpatient Consultations	99241–99245
Initial Inpatient Consultations	99251–99255
Follow-up Inpatient Consultations	99261–99263
Confirmatory Consultations	99271–99275
Emergency Department Services	
New or Established Patient	99281–99285
Other Emergency Services	99288
Pediatric Critical Care Patient Transport	99289–99290
Critical Care Services	99291–99296
Inpatient Pediatric Critical Care	99293–99294
Inpatient Neonatal Critical Care	99295–99296
Intensive (Non-Critical) Low Birth Weight Services	99298–99299
Nursing Facility Services	
Comprehensive Nursing Facility Assessments	99301–99303
Subsequent Nursing Facility Care	99311–99313
Nursing Facility Discharge Services	99315–99316
Domiciliary, Rest Home, or Custodial Care Services	
New Patient	99321–99323
Established Patient	99331–99333
Home Services	
New Patient	99341–99345
Established Patient	99347–99350
Prolonged Services	
With Direct Patient Contact	99354–99357
Without Direct Patient Contact	99358–99359
Standby Services	99360
Case Management Services	
Team Conferences	99361–99362
Telephone Calls	99371–99373
Care Plan Oversight Services	99374–99380

Preventive Medicine Services
New Patient	99381–99387
Established Patient	99391–99397
Individual Counseling	99401–99404
Group Counseling	99411–99412
Other	99420–99429

Newborn Care	99431–99440

Special Evaluation and Management Services
Basic Life/Disability Evaluation Services	99450
Work-Related or Medical Disability Evaluation Services	99455–99456

Other E/M Services	99499

The basic format of the E/M services codes, which remains the same for most of the categories, consists of five elements. E/M services codes:

1. Are composed of a unique code number beginning with 99

2. Generally identify the place or type of service (for example, office or other outpatient service or initial or subsequent hospital care)

3. Define the extent or level of the service (for example, detailed history and detailed examination)

4. Describe the nature of the presenting problem (for example, moderate severity)

5. Identify the time typically required to provide a service

Before an E/M services code can be assigned, three groups of questions must be answered. These questions are:

1. What type of service is the patient receiving? Is this an initial or subsequent episode of care? Is this an initial, follow-up, or confirmatory consultative service? Is this a critical care service?

2. What is the place of service? A physician's office or clinic? A hospital inpatient or outpatient department? An emergency department? A nursing facility or rehabilitation unit?

3. Is the patient new or established to the physician?

E/M Documentation Guidelines

Documentation is the basis for all coding, including E/M services. In the fall of 1994, the AMA and the CMS developed documentation guidelines for E/M reporting in an effort to clarify code assignment for both physicians and claim reviewers. These guidelines were implemented in 1995.

In 1997, the CMS and the AMA collaborated again on a revised edition of the guidelines to include specific elements that should be performed and documented for general multisystem and selected single-specialty exams. However, the 1997 revised version did not replace the 1995 documentation guidelines. Physicians can elect to use either set of guidelines.

Appendix A of this workbook provides an excerpt from the 1997 documentation guidelines for E/M. However, it should be emphasized that providers can use either the 1995 or 1997 documentation guidelines, whichever is most advantageous to the physician. The 1995 and 1997 E/M Documentation Guidelines may be found at http://cms.hhs.gov/medlearn/emdoc.asp.

Terms Commonly Used in E/M Services Code Assignment

The following sections offer definitions of terms that are commonly used when determining E/M services code assignments.

New or Established Patient

A new patient is a patient who has not received any professional services from a physician or another physician of the same specialty belonging to the same group practice within the past three years. Professional services are those face-to-face services rendered by a physician and reported by a specific CPT code or codes. An established patient is a patient who has received these services under the identical conditions and circumstances as those of a new patient.

Coders should note that the following E/M services categories are the only ones that provide separate code ranges to identify new and established patients:

Office or Other Outpatient Services	99201–99215
Domiciliary, Rest Home, or Custodial Services	99321–99333
Home Services	99341–99350
Preventive Medicine Services	99381–99429

Concurrent Care

The CPT codebook defines concurrent care as the circumstance in which two or more physicians provide similar services (for example, hospital visits or consultations) to the same patient on the same day. Health plans often limit reimbursement to one physician per day unless the physicians have different specialties and the services of more than one physician are medically necessary. The CMS assigns a specialty number that is used for this purpose.

Correct assignment of ICD-9-CM codes also plays an important role in billing and receiving payment for concurrent care services. The physicians involved in the concurrent care episode must identify the appropriate ICD-9-CM code for each service provided. Assigning the same ICD-9-CM code could result in one of the physicians being denied payment, usually the one who submitted the claim last.

> **Example:** Patient is admitted to the hospital complaining of unstable angina and uncontrolled Type II diabetes mellitus. Dr. Smith treats the patient's angina, and Dr. Reynolds follows the patient's diabetes. The following codes should be reported:
>
> Dr. Smith: 411.1, Intermediate coronary syndrome, and the appropriate E/M level of service code from the hospital inpatient services category
>
> Dr. Reynolds: 250.02, Diabetes mellitus, uncontrolled, and the appropriate E/M level of service code from the hospital inpatient services category

Levels of Service

The E/M services categories and subcategories include three to five levels of service codes. Seven components, applicable to all E/M services, must be considered before selecting a code and ought to be available in the associated documentation:

History
Examination   } Key Components
Medical decision making

Counseling
Coordination of care   } Contributing Components
Nature of presenting problem
Time

The first three components—history, examination, and medical decision making—are essential factors when considering what E/M services code to select because they represent the amount of resources expended by the provider to render the service. When applicable, the remaining four components are factored in. For example, when counseling and coordination dominates, or comprises more than 50 percent of, the physician–patient or physician–family encounter, time is considered the controlling fact for determining the correct code. Documentation in the health record must support code-level selection by describing the key components and the pertinent contributing factors. Physician selection of E/M codes is recommended to ensure clinical validity for service levels. Coders may validate code selection with documentation and assist physicians in meeting the current guidelines for code selection. Facility use of E/M coding is usually assigned via a chargemaster, which is a computerized program that contains codes, abbreviated definition descriptions, and charges. (Chargemaster programs are discussed further in chapters 5 and 6.)

Appendix C of the CPT codebook includes a supplement of clinical examples illustrating the appropriate selection of E/M services codes for specific medical specialties. However, these examples are only guidelines and the documentation in the health record remains the most authoritative and final source when assigning a code for a particular level of service.

The CPT codebook defines each level of E/M services by basing it on a unique combination of the three essential components. The key elements that define E/M services, and the variation within these elements, are reflected in table 7.1.

The following sections discuss the seven components related to E/M services. Sample documentation guidelines (based on guidance from the CMS and the AMA) for the key elements also are discussed. For Medicare purposes, the guidelines (1995 or 1997 version) that are most advantageous to the physician may be used.

Table 7.1.   Key elements that define E/M services

History	Examination	Medical Decision Making
Problem focused	Problem focused	Straightforward
Expanded problem focused	Expanded problem focused	Low complexity
Detailed	Detailed	Moderate complexity
Comprehensive	Comprehensive	High complexity

History

The following types of histories are recognized. The level of complexity is based on the amount of information (number of elements) obtained by the physician:

- Problem focused: Limited to a chief complaint and a brief history of the present illness or condition

- Expanded problem focused: A chief complaint, brief history, and a problem-pertinent system review

- Detailed: A chief complaint, expanded history of the present illness, a system review, and one item from any of the following: past, family, or social history

- Comprehensive: A chief complaint, extended history of present illness, extended system review, and one item from at least two (or in some cases three, depending on the E/M category) of the following: past, family, and/or social history

Each type of history includes some or all of the following elements:

- Chief complaint

- History of present illness

- Review of systems

- Past, family, and/or social history

Chief Complaint

The chief complaint (CC) is a concise statement describing the symptom, problem, condition, diagnosis, a return visit recommended by the physician, or other factor as the reason for the visit.

History of Present Illness

The history of present illness (HPI) describes the patient's developing condition/problem from the first sign and/or symptom in chronological order, starting from the initial visit to the present. Table 7.2 reflects the elements included in the HPI.

Table 7.2.   Elements included in the HPI

HPI Element	Examples
Location	Abdomen, chest, leg, head
Severity	Bad, intolerable, minimal, slight
Timing	Two hours after eating, one hour after waking
Quality	Burning, dull, puffy, pus-filled, red
Duration	For two months, since prescription began
Associated signs/manifestations	Rash with blistering, nausea and vomiting, abdominal pain
Context	When walking in company of smokers
Modifying factors	Improves when lying down, worse after eating

There are two types of HPI: a brief HPI and an extended HPI. A *brief HPI* refers to the documentation of no more than one to three HPI elements. It may involve a single problem without any complicating factors or symptoms. An *extended HPI* refers to the documentation of four or more HPI elements. It may be appropriate when multiple, confusing, or complex symptoms are present; when the symptoms are prolonged in development; when the history is obtained from an individual other than the patient; and when other complicating factors are present.

> **Example:** A patient is seen in the physician's office with flu-like symptoms (chief complaint). For the past two days (duration), she has had chills, fever, and muscle aches (associated signs). She feels worse in the evening (timing).

In the above example, three HPI elements are documented (duration, associated signs, and timing). Therefore, this would be considered a brief HPI.

Review of Systems

A review of systems (ROS) is an inventory of body systems obtained by the physician through a series of questions seeking to identify signs and/or symptoms the patient may be experiencing or has experienced. An ROS includes the following fourteen systems:

1. Constitutional symptoms (fever, weight loss, and so on)

2. Eyes

3. Ears, nose, mouth, throat

4. Cardiovascular

5. Respiratory

6. Gastrointestinal

7. Genitourinary

8. Musculoskeletal

9. Integumentary (skin and/or breast)

10. Neurological

11. Psychiatric

12. Endocrine

13. Hematologic/lymphatic

14. Allergic/immunologic

Three types of ROS are recognized:

1. Problem-pertinent ROS: The system is directly related to the problem(s) identified in the HPI.

   Documentation guideline: The patient's positive responses and pertinent negatives for the system related to the problem should be documented.

2. Extended ROS: The system is directly related to the problem(s) identified in the HPI and a limited number of additional systems.

   Documentation guideline: The patient's positive responses and pertinent negatives for two to nine systems should be documented.

3. Complete ROS: The system is directly related to the problem(s) identified in the HPI and all additional body systems.

   Documentation guideline: At least ten organ systems must be reviewed. Those systems with positive or pertinent negative responses should be documented individually. For the remaining systems, a notation indicating that all other systems are negative is permissible. In the absence of such a notation, at least ten systems must be documented individually.

   > **Example:** A patient presents with nausea (chief complaint). She has lost 7 pounds in the past month (constitutional). She denies abdominal pain, diarrhea, and vomiting (gastrointestinal).

   According to documentation guidelines, the above example would demonstrate an extended ROS because two systems are documented.

Past, Family, and/or Social History

The past, family, and/or social history (PFSH) element is broken down as follows:

- A past history consists of the patient's past experiences with illnesses, operations, injuries, and treatments (including medications). For pediatric populations, the past history also should include prenatal and birth history, feedings, food intolerance, and immunization history.

- A family history consists of a review of medical events in the patient's family, including diseases that may be hereditary or may place the patient at risk, as well as the age and status (alive or dead) of blood relatives.

- A social history consists of an age-appropriate review of past and current social activities. It also may include the patient's marital status and number of children, present and past employment, exposure to environmental agents, religion, hobbies, living conditions, water supply, and daily habits such as alcohol, tobacco, drug, and caffeine use. For veterans, it includes military service history. For pediatric populations, it may include school grades, sleep, and play habits.

There are two types of PFSH: a pertinent PFSH and a complete PFSH. A *pertinent PFSH* refers to the documentation of at least one specific item from any of the three history areas. A *complete PFSH* refers to the documentation of at least one specific item from two of the three history areas for the following E/M categories: office or other outpatient services, established patient; emergency department; subsequent nursing facility care; domiciliary care, established patient; and home care, established patient.

At least one specific item from *each of the three history areas* must be documented for a complete PFSH for the following E/M categories: office or other outpatient services, new patient; hospital observation services; hospital inpatient services, initial care; consultations;

comprehensive nursing facility assessments; domiciliary care, new patient; and home care, new patient.

Table 7.3 incorporates all the elements of a history. All three levels must be met to qualify for a specific level. A CC is required for all levels.

Following are some history documentation guidelines:

- The CC, ROS, and PFSH may be listed as separate elements of the history or included in the description of the HPI.

- An ROS and/or PFSH obtained during an earlier encounter does not need to be redocumented if there is evidence that the physician has reviewed and updated the previous information. The review and update may be documented by:

  —Describing any new ROS and/or PFSH information or noting that no change in the previous information has occurred

  —Noting the date and location of the earlier ROS and/or PFSH

- The ROS and/or PFSH may be recorded by ancillary staff or the patient on a completed form.

  Note: To indicate that the physician has reviewed the information, a notation must supplement or confirm the documentation recorded by the other parties.

- If the physician is unable to obtain a history from the patient or other source, the documentation in the record should describe the patient's condition or other circumstance that precludes obtaining a history.

Table 7.3.   Elements of a history

History Component (equal to lowest category documented)	Problem Focused	Exp Problem Focused	Detailed	Comprehensive
Chief Complaint _____ HPI—History of Present Illness __ Location __ Duration __ Severity __ Quality __ Context __ Timing __ Modifying factors __ Associated signs and symptoms	Brief 1–3 HPI elements documented	Brief 1–3 HPI elements documented	Extended ≥ 4 HPI or status of ≥ 3 chronic conditions documented	Extended ≥ 4 HPI or status of ≥ 3 chronic conditions documented
ROS—Review of System(s) __ Constitutional __ Integumentary (wt loss, etc.) __ Endocrine __ Eyes __ GI __ Hem/Lymph __ ENT, mouth __ GU __ Allergy/ __ Respiratory __ MS Immun __ Cardiovascular __ Neuro __ Psychiatric	None	Problem Specific (1 system)	Extended (2–9 systems)	Complete (Greater than 10 systems or some with all others negative)
PFSH (past medical, family and social histories) __Previous medical (past experience with illness, injury, surgery, medical treatments, and so on) __Family medical history (diseases, which may be hereditary or with increased risk of occurrence) __Social (relationships, diet, exercise, occupation, and so on)	None	None	Pertinent At least 1 item from at least 1 history	Complete Specifics of at least 2 history areas documented

Note: A chief complaint (CC) is required for all history types.

Examination

The physical examination is the objective description of the patient's chief complaint, illness, or injury. Four types of examination are recognized:

1. Problem focused: Exam limited to the affected body area or organ system

2. Expanded problem focused: Exam of affected body area or organ system, as well as symptomatic or related organ systems

3. Detailed: Extended exam of affected body area(s) and other symptomatic or related organ system(s)

4. Comprehensive: A general multisystem examination or complete examination of a single-organ system and other symptomatic or related body area(s) or organ system(s)

The types of examination have been defined by the revised guidelines for general multisystem and the following single-organ systems:

- Cardiovascular

- Ears, nose, mouth, and throat

- Eyes

- Genitourinary (female)

- Genitourinary (male)

- Hematologic/lymphatic/immunologic

- Musculoskeletal

- Neurological

- Psychiatric

- Respiratory

- Skin

For purposes of examination, the following body areas are recognized:

- Head, including the face

- Genitalia, groin, buttocks

- Neck

- Back, including spine

- Chest, including breasts and axillae

- Each extremity

- Abdomen

For purposes of examination, the following organ systems are recognized:

- Constitutional (vital signs, general appearance)
- Genitourinary
- Eyes
- Musculoskeletal
- Ears, nose, mouth, and throat
- Skin
- Cardiovascular
- Neurologic
- Respiratory
- Psychiatric
- Hematologic/lymphatic/immunologic
- Gastrointestinal

Table 7.4 displays the components of the examination.

Medical Decision Making

Medical decision making involves the complexity of establishing a diagnosis and/or selecting a management opinion or treatment plan as measured by the following:

- The number of possible diagnoses and/or management options or treatment plans to be considered
- The amount and/or complexity of the data (health records, diagnostic tests, and/or other information) to be obtained, reviewed, and analyzed
- The risk of significant complications, morbidity, and/or mortality associated with the patient's presenting condition, the diagnostic procedure(s), and/or the possible management options or treatment plans

These items are discussed in more detail in the paragraphs that follow.

Table 7.4.   Components of an examination

Exam Component			Problem Focused	Expanded Problem Focused	Detailed	Comprehensive
Body Areas	**Organ Systems**		1 body area or system	2–4 body systems or 2–7 basic systems, including affected area	5–7 body systems or 2–7 detailed systems, including affected area	8 or more systems
__ Head, face	__ Const. (Vitals, general appearance)					
__ Neck	__ Eyes	__ GU				
__ Chest, breasts	__ ENT, mouth	__ Skin				
__ Abdomen	__ Respiratory	__ Integumentary				
__ Genit, groin	__ Cardiovascular	__ MS				
__ Back, spine	__ Gastrointestinal	__ Neurological				
__ Each extremity	__ Lymph/Hem/Immun	__ Psychiatric				

Note: Some texts use 2–4 body systems for expanded problem-focused and 5–7 body systems for detailed. Both of these methods have been published in CMS publications. This is a controversy in the industry and CMS will not give an opinion on whether they find one method more acceptable over the other. Physicians frequently find the 2–4 and 5–7 distinction to be easier to understand and follow.

Number of Possible Diagnoses and/or Management Options

The number of possible diagnoses and/or management options is based on the number and types of problems addressed during the encounter, the complexity of establishing a diagnosis, and the management decisions made by the physician.

The following documentation guidelines apply:

- For each encounter, an assessment, clinical impression, or diagnosis should be documented. It may be stated explicitly or implied in documented decisions regarding management plans and/or further evaluation.

- For a presenting problem with an established diagnosis, the record should reflect whether the problem is improving, well controlled, resolving, or resolved; or inadequately controlled, worsening, or failing to change as expected.

- For a presenting problem without an established diagnosis, the assessment or clinical impression may be stated in the form of a differential diagnosis, or as a possible, probable, or rule-out diagnosis.

- The initiation of, or changes in, treatment should be documented clearly. Treatment involves a wide range of management options, including patient instructions, nursing instructions, therapies, and medications.

- The record should indicate whether referrals are made and where, whether consultations are requested and with whom, and whether advice is sought and from whom.

Amount and/or Complexity of Data for Review

The amount and/or complexity of data for review is based on the types of diagnostic testing ordered or reviewed. A decision to obtain and review old health records and/or to obtain history from sources other than the patient increases the amount and complexity of data to be reviewed.

The following documentation guidelines apply:

- When a diagnostic service (test or procedure) is ordered, planned, scheduled, or performed at the time of the E/M encounter, the type of diagnostic service should be documented.

- The review of laboratory, radiology, and/or other diagnostic tests should be documented. An entry in a progress note (for example, "WBC elevated" or "chest X ray unremarkable") is acceptable. Alternatively, the review may be documented by initialing and dating the report containing the test results.

- Relevant findings from any review of old records and/or the receipt of additional history from the family, caretaker, or other sources should be documented. If nothing exists beyond the relevant information that already has been obtained, that fact should be documented. A notation of "old records reviewed" or "additional history obtained from family" without further specification is insufficient.

- Documentation of discussions with the physician(s) who performed or interpreted laboratory, radiology, or other diagnostic tests should be included.

- The direct visualization and independent interpretation of an image, tracing, or specimen previously or subsequently interpreted by another physician should be documented.

Risk of Significant Complications, Morbidity, and/or Mortality

The risk of significant complications, morbidity, and/or mortality is based on the risks associated with the presenting problem(s), the diagnostic procedure(s), and the possible management options. The determination of risk is complex and not readily quantifiable.

The risk assessment of the presenting problem(s) is based on the risk related to the disease process anticipated between the present and the next encounter. The risk assessment of selecting diagnostic procedures and management options is based on the risk during and immediately following any procedures or treatment. The highest level of risk in any one category (presenting problem, diagnostic procedure, or management option) determines the overall risk. Table 7.5 outlines the factors that determine medical decision making.

Two of the three elements in table 7.6 must be met or exceeded before selecting a type of medical decision making.

Counseling and Coordination of Care

Both counseling and coordination of care are contributing factors in the selection of an E/M level of service. Counseling involves discussion of the patient's care with the patient and/or his or her family. Coordination of care is a contributing factor in the majority of encounters for E/M services. When coordination of care with other providers or agencies occurs without a patient encounter on the same day, the case management codes (99361–99373) should be reported.

When counseling and/or coordination of care dominates, or comprises more than 50 percent of, the physician–patient and/or physician–family encounter (face-to-face time in the office or other outpatient setting or floor/unit time in the hospital or nursing facility), time is considered the key or controlling factor to qualify for a particular level of E/M services. Typical times are listed in the descriptions of each code. These times are used in code selection based on counseling and/or coordination of care, including time spent with parties who have assumed responsibility for the care of the patient or decision making, whether or not they are family members (for example, foster parents, person acting in loco parentis, legal guardian).

Documentation guideline: If the physician elects to report the level of service based on counseling and/or coordination of care, the total length of time of the encounter (face-to-face or floor time, as appropriate) should be documented and the record should describe the counseling and/or activities to coordinate care.

Nature of Presenting Problem

CPT defines presenting problems as diseases, conditions, illnesses, injuries, symptoms, signs, findings, complaints, or other reasons for an encounter, regardless of whether a diagnosis is established at the time of the encounter.

Five types of presenting problems are identified:

1. Minimal: A problem that does not require the presence of a physician, although care is provided under a physician's supervision (for example, a blood pressure check).

2. Self-limited, or minor: A temporary problem with a definite and prescribed course and good prognosis (for example, an upper respiratory infection). The conditions are typically transient in nature.

3. Low severity: With no treatment, this problem carries a low risk of morbidity and little or no risk of mortality (for example, a teenager with acne that does not respond to over-the-counter medications). A patient with this type of problem can expect full recovery without impairments.

Table 7.5.   Decision-making process

Number of Diagnosis or Treatment Options			
	$A \times B = C$		
Problem Status	**Number**	**Point**	**Result**
Self-limited or minor	(max 2)	1	
Established problem; stable, improving		1	
Established problem; worsening		2	
New problem; no additional workup planned	(max 1)	3	
New problem; additional workup planned		4	
	Total _____		

Amount and/or Complexity of Data Reviewed	
Reviewed Data	**Points**
Review and/or order clinical lab tests	1
Review and/or order of tests in the radiology section of CPT	1
Review and/or order tests in the medicine section of CPT	1
Discussion of test results with performing provider	1
Decision to obtain old records/obtain history from other than patient/discuss case with other provider	2
Independent visualization of image, tracing, or specimen itself (not simply review of report)	2
Total _____	

Risk Factors

Level of Risk	Presenting Problem	Dx Procedures Ordered	Mgmt. Options
Minimal	One self-limited or minor problem	Lab tests, x-rays, EKG, EEG	Rest, superficial dressings, none required
Low	• Two or more self-limited or minor problems • One stable chronic illness • Acute uncomplicated illness or injury	• Physiologic tests w/o stress • Imaging studies w/contrast • Superficial needle biopsy • Skin biopsy • Arterial blood draw	• Over-the-counter remedy • Minor surgery w/o risk factor • Physical, occupational therapy • IV fluids w/o additive
Moderate	• One or more chronic illness with exacerbation, progression, or treatment side effects • Undiagnosed new problem with uncertain prognosis • Acute complicated injury • Acute illness with systemic symptoms	• Stress tests • Endoscopies w/o risk factor • Cardiovascular imaging study w/o identified risk factors • Deep needle or incisional biopsy • Centesis of body cavity fluid	• Minor surgery with identifiable risk factors • Elective major surgery without identifiable risk factors • Prescription drug management • Therapeutic radiology • IV fluids with additives • Closed treatment of skeletal injury
High	• One or more chronic illness with severe exacerbation, progression, or Tx side effects • Acute or chronic illness or injury that may pose a threat to life or bodily function • An abrupt change to mental status	• Cardiovascular imaging studies with identifiable risk factors • Cardiac electrophysiological tests • Endoscopy with identifiable risk factors	• Elective major surgery with identifiable risk factors • Emergency major surgery • Parenteral-controlled substances • Drug therapy requiring intensive monitoring • DNR status

Tabulation of Medical Decision-Making Elements: Highest 2 of 3				
Diagnosis/Management Options	Minimal ≤ 1	Limited 2	Multiple 3	Extensive ≥ 4
Amount/Complexity of Data	Min./Low ≤ 1	Limited 2	Moderate 3	Extensive ≥ 4
Highest Risk (from any category)	Minimal	Low	Moderate	High
Medical Decision Making	**Straightforward**	**Low Complexity**	**Moderate Complexity**	**High Complexity**

Table 7.6.   Selection of level of E/M service

All three of the key components must meet or exceed the stated requirements to qualify for a particular level of E/M services code.	Two of the three components must meet or exceed the stated requirements to qualify for a particular level of E/M services code.	Time
Office or other outpatient services, new patient Initial observation care Initial hospital care Office or other outpatient consultations Initial inpatient consultations Confirmatory consultations ED services Comprehensive nursing facility assessments Domiciliary, rest home, or custodial care, new patient Home services, new patient	Office or other outpatient services, established patient Subsequent hospital care Follow-up inpatient consultations Subsequent nursing facility care Domiciliary, rest home, or custodial care, established patient Home services, established patient	When counseling and/or coordination of care dominates, or is more than 50 percent of, the face-to-face physician–patient encounter, time is considered the key factor to qualify for a particular level of E/M services code.

4. Moderate severity: With no treatment, this problem carries a moderate risk of morbidity and mortality (for example, Dupuytren's contracture of the hand involving several fingers). The patient's prognosis may be uncertain, or the probability of prolonged functional impairment is increased.

5. High severity: With no treatment, the risk of morbidity is high and a high probability exists for severe, prolonged functional impairment or moderate to high risk of mortality (for example, Type I diabetes mellitus, uncontrolled, with chronic renal failure requiring dialysis).

Time

The 1992 edition of *Current Procedural Terminology* introduced the notion of including time as a separate contributing factor in selecting the appropriate E/M level of service code. Prior editions reflected the belief that time was an implicit factor in the definition of each level of service.

Note: The specific times included within the level of service codes are averages and, as such, may vary depending on the actual clinical circumstances.

Face-to-Face Time

Face-to-face time is defined as only the time the physician spends face-to-face with the patient and/or his or her family. This includes the period during which the physician obtains a history, performs an examination, and counsels the patient.

Face-to-face time applies to the following categories and subcategories:

- Office and other outpatient visits

- Office consultations

Unit/Floor Time

Unit/floor time is defined as the time the physician is present on the patient's hospital unit and rendering services for the patient at the bedside. This includes the period when the physician establishes and/or reviews the patient's health record, examines the patient, writes notes, and communicates about the patient with other professionals and the patient's family.

Unit/floor time applies to the following categories and subcategories:

- Hospital observation services

- Inpatient hospital care

- Initial and follow-up hospital consultations

- Nursing facility

Instructions for Selection and/or Validation of a Level of E/M Services

The following steps should be taken when selecting and/or validating a level of E/M services:

1. Identify the category and subcategory of service. Is this an office visit with an established patient? Initial inpatient consultation? Comprehensive nursing facility assessment? New patient home services? Individual counseling for preventive medicine services? Visit to the emergency department? Hospital outpatient service?

2. Review specific notes and instructions for the selected category and subcategory.

3. Review the narrative descriptors within the category and subcategory of the E/M services. The seven components should be reviewed in selecting the appropriate level of service code.

4. Using the definitions provided under each level of service, determine the extent of history obtained.

5. Determine the extent of examination performed using the definitions provided under each level of service.

6. Determine the complexity of medical decision making.

7. Select or verify the appropriate level of E/M services based on the information provided in table 7.6.

Modifiers

Under certain circumstances, a listed service may be modified slightly without changing its basic definition. In these situations, several modifiers are available for use with E/M services codes. Modifiers are reported as two-digit numbers attached to the main code.

Following is a list of modifiers available for use with E/M codes:

–21 **Prolonged Evaluation and Management Services** *(for physician use only):* Modifier –21 may be reported only with the highest level of E/M service within a specified category. Use of this modifier informs the third-party payer that the physician's service surpassed the one described in the highest level of service.

> **Example:** Office consultation when the physician's care exceeded the criteria listed under code 99245. The physician may submit 99245–21 on the claim.

Note: Most third-party payers may require submission of a written report to support the use of modifier –21. In selected circumstances, the prolonged services codes 99354–99359 may be more accurate than using a modified code.

–24 **Unrelated Evaluation and Management Service by the Same Physician During a Post-operative Period** *(for physician use only):* Modifier –24 can be reported with an E/M service provided during the postoperative period by the same physician who performed the original procedure. The E/M service must be unrelated to the condition for which the original procedure was performed.

> **Example:** Office visit provided to a patient who is in the postoperative period for a cholecystectomy performed three weeks earlier. The patient's current complaint is a possible infection of a finger that was lacerated four days ago. The physician may report the appropriate office visit code and attach modifier –24 to identify this activity as an unrelated service provided during the postoperative period of the cholecystectomy.

–25 **Significant, Separately Identifiable Evaluation and Management Service by the Same Physician on the Day of a Procedure or Other Service** *(for hospital and physician use):* Modifier –25 may be reported to indicate that the patient's condition required a separate E/M service on the day a procedure or other service was performed because the care provided went beyond the usual procedures associated with the activity. Modifier –25 is appropriate with procedures that Medicare designates as minor, which are generally those with a 10-day global fee period or 0-day global fee.

> **Example:** Office visit is provided to a patient for evaluation of diabetes and associated chronic renal failure, as well as a mole on the arm that has increased in size. Suspecting the mole is malignant, the physician excises it. The pathology report confirms a 1.1 cm malignant lesion. The physician can bill for the malignant lesion removal and use the office visit code accompanied by modifier –25 to identify that, during the visit, a separate condition was addressed (in this example, the diabetes and the renal failure). Generally, two diagnosis codes are required to explain the reporting of two separate services during the same encounter, although CPT guidelines do not require it.

Hospitals are instructed by the CMS to use modifier -25 when E/M services (from only the following CPT/HCPCS codes: 92002-92014, 99201-99499, G0101, and G0175) are performed with diagnostic and/or therapeutic medical or surgical procedures.

> **Example:** A patient is seen in the emergency department for chest pains. An EKG is performed. The hospital would report the emergency department E/M code of 99283-25 with 93005 (EKG).

–27 **Multiple Outpatient Hospital E/M Encounters on the Same Date** *(for hospital use only):* Modifier –27 was developed to allow hospitals to report multiple outpatient hospital E/M encounters on the same date. The modifier is appended to the second encounter and each subsequent E/M code.

> **Example:** Patient is seen in the dermatology clinic in the morning and the orthopedic clinic in the afternoon. A Level III clinic visit is performed at both visits. The hospital would report 99213 with 99213–27.

Note: The CMS has instructed hospitals to assign E/M codes for facility billing based on their own system, which reflects the facility's resources to give care to the patient.

–32 **Mandated Services** *(for physician use only):* Modifier –32 is reported when an entity such as a third-party payer or a quality improvement organization mandates a service. Most often, this modifier is reported with the consultation codes.

–52 **Reduced Services** *(for hospital and physician use):* Modifier –52 is reported when a physician decides to partially reduce or eliminate a service. Although its purpose is to identify a reduction in the service provided, modifier –52 is used by some physicians to report a reduction in the charges for a particular service because the complete service was not carried out.

> **Example:** Patient is seen in the ophthalmologist's office for an eye exam (92002). The patient only has one eye; thus, the correct code assignment would be 92002–52.

Hospitals have been instructed by the CMS to append modifier -52 to an incomplete procedure when the procedure does not involve anesthesia (local, regional, or general).

Note: Coders should reference current directives from the CMS for use of modifiers. It is not unusual for guidelines to be changed.

> **Example:** Patient is taken to the endoscopy suite for a flexible sigmoidoscopy, but the scope could not be passed because of poor preparation. The patient is given conscious sedation (not considered anesthesia). For the surgeon's services, the correct code assignment would be 45330–52.

–57 **Decision for Surgery** *(for physician use only):* Modifier –57 is reported along with the appropriate E/M services code when an E/M service was the result of an initial decision to perform surgery on a patient. Modifier –57 is appropriate with procedures that Medicare designates as major, which typically are those with a 90-day global fee period assigned. Generally, it is not required when the decision for surgery occurs at a time earlier than the day of or before surgery. Some insurance plans include consultation and/or visit codes where the decision is made in the global fee for surgery and do not provide separate payment.

> **Example:** An office visit is provided to a Medicare patient complaining of acute right, upper-quadrant pain and tenderness referred to the right scapula, nausea and vomiting, and anorexia. A low-grade fever and an elevated white blood count are noted. An ultrasound confirms the diagnosis of acute cholecystitis with cholelithiasis. The physician recommends that surgery be performed later that day. The physician can report the appropriate office visit code along with modifier –57 to identify that, during this office visit, it was decided to perform a cholecystectomy.

Exercise 7.1

Circle the correct answer for each of the following statements.

1. The AMA and the CMS developed documentation guidelines for use with the CPT codebook.

    (True)   False

2. All seven of the following are considered key components in selecting an E/M level of service: history, examination, medical decision making, (coordination of care, counseling, nature of presenting problem, and time.)

    True   (False)

    — Key
    ( ) contributing

3. The CMS mandates the use of the E/M documentation guidelines.

    (True)   False

4. The review of systems is a chronological description of the development of the patient's presenting symptoms.

    True   (False)

    — inventory

5. The element of time is never considered a factor in selecting an E/M level of service.

    True   (False)

Based on 1995 Documentation Guidelines, write the answer to each of the following questions in the space provided:

6. Based on the following information, is this history of present illness (HPI) brief or extended?

    An 86-year-old patient presents with a CC of vomiting and dizziness. Yesterday, she became dizzy while getting ready to go to church. In addition, she vomited bile several times and complained of deafness in her left ear at the start of the dizziness.

    _____ Extended _____

    1 Sign & Symp
    2 Timing   3 Context
    vomiting
    dizziness 4 Duration
    deafness

7. Based on the following information, what is the level of examination?

    The CC is chest pain. The examination determined: respiration quiet and unlabored; skin with good color, warm and dry, and no rashes; mucous membranes moist; ears and throat clear; lungs with good breath sounds in all fields; rare expiratory wheeze, no rales, no rhonchi; heart regular rate and rhythm with normal heart sounds, no murmur; abdomen soft with no liver or spleen enlargement; and bowel sounds active.

    _____ expanded _____

    Sys/ Body
    5/2 Areas

8. Based on the following information, is this past, family, and/or social history (PFSH) pertinent or complete?

    New patient presents to the office with a CC of nasal congestion and headache. ROS: Denies shortness of breath or fever, stiffness of neck, or visual disturbances. Past history: No drug allergies or other allergies were noted, nor any history of TB, COPD, or asthma. Last physical exam one year ago was unremarkable.

    _____ pertinent _____

Categories of E/M Services

The following sections discuss the various categories of E/M services.

Office or Other Outpatient Services (99201–99215)

The office or other outpatient services category may be used to describe services provided in the physician's office, the outpatient clinic, or some other ambulatory facility. This category is divided into two subcategories: new patient and established patient. It is important to remember that the basic difference between a new and established patient is whether the patient received professional services within the past three years from the same physician or another physician within the same group practice. Whereas the new patient level of services requires meeting all three of the key components prior to assigning a code, the established patient level of services requires meeting only two of the three key components.

Note: Reporting an office visit code is inappropriate if, during the course of events within a specific encounter, the physician admits the patient into the hospital as an inpatient or observation patient or into a nursing care facility. Only the resulting admission service should be reported in such a situation, which should incorporate the level of care provided in the office. There may be a rare circumstance where the patient receives office services early in the day and then returns later and must be admitted to the hospital from the office. Such a situation would merit use of modifier –25 to show that the services were separately identifiable.

Hospital Observation Services (99217–99220) and Hospital Observation or Inpatient Care Services (Including Admission and Discharge Services) (99234–99236)

The hospital observation services category identifies patients who are admitted into a hospital or are placed in observation status in a hospital and the services span more than one calendar date. For observation and inpatient care where admission and discharge occur on the same date, codes 99234–99236 would be used.

Consulting physicians providing services while patients are in observation status would use either outpatient consultation (99241–99245) or inpatient consultation codes (99251–99255), depending on the patient's status at the time of service. Only attending physicians should use the observation codes. When a patient is admitted to the hospital (and not discharged on the same date), the initial hospital or inpatient consultation codes will be used, as appropriate.

The initial encounter with a patient in observation status is reported with a code from 99218 to 99220. Coders should note that all three key components must be met to assign a particular level of service. In the rare circumstance that a patient remains in observation status after the date of admission, but is removed before the date of discharge, codes 99211–99215 may be used to report a physician visit on the intervening dates between removal from observation status and discharge.

Code 99217 (Observation care discharge services) is used to describe the services provided to a patient on discharge from observation status, but only if the discharge was not on the same date as the initial care. These services include a final examination of the patient, discussion of the hospital stay, instructions for continuing care, and completion of the health record.

Hospital Inpatient Services (99221–99239)

The hospital inpatient services category includes codes for initial hospital care (99221–99223), subsequent hospital care (99231–99233), and hospital discharge services (99238–99239). These codes also may be used to describe services provided to patients in a so-called partial hospital setting. Partial hospitalization is used for crisis stabilization, intensive short-term daily treatment, or intermediate-term treatment of psychiatric disorders.

The initial hospital care codes (99221–99223) are used to report the physician's first inpatient hospital visit with a new or established patient. Coders should note that all three of the key components must be met to assign a particular level of service.

Codes 99231–99233 are reported for subsequent hospital services provided by the physician. Changes in the patient's medical status and the related documentation in the health record allow the physician to report various levels of service for the subsequent hospital care. It should be noted that only two of the three key components must be met to assign a specific level of service for subsequent hospital care services.

Codes 99238–99239 are used to report the services related to discharging a patient from the hospital. This reflects the added work the physician must perform, such as final examination of patient, discussion of hospital stay, instructions for home care, and completion of the health record. Code selection is based on time. For example, code 99238 describes discharge services requiring 30 minutes or less, and code 99239 identifies those services requiring more than 30 minutes.

Note: Patients receiving inpatient or observation services when admission and discharge occur on the same date are reported using codes 99234–99236.

Consultations (99241–99275)

The CPT codebook defines a consultation as a type of service provided by a physician when his or her opinion or advice on a specific problem is requested by another physician or other appropriate source. Although consulting physicians may initiate diagnostic and/or therapeutic services, they cannot assume responsibility for any portion of that patient's care. If responsibility is assumed, the service is no longer considered a consultation and the appropriate code should be assigned for hospital care or office or other outpatient services.

Documentation to support a consultation is essential and should include the request and need for a consultation, the opinion of the consultant, and any services ordered and/or performed. All of this information should be documented in the health record and communicated by written report to the requesting physician or other appropriate source.

Note: When a consultation is requested by the patient and/or his or her family, but not by another physician, the consulting physician should report the service using the office visit or confirmatory consultation codes. Reporting the initial consultation codes would be inappropriate in this case because the consultation was not performed at the request of another physician.

CPT identifies four types of consultations: office or other outpatient, initial inpatient, follow-up inpatient, and confirmatory.

Office or Other Outpatient Consultations (99241–99245)

Codes 99241–99245 describe office or other outpatient consultation services provided to new or established patients. These services may be provided in an office, outpatient or other ambulatory facility, hospital observation services program, home services program, domiciliary, rest home, custodial care program, or emergency department. Subsequent visits to the consulting physician's office are reported using the office visit codes for established patient (99211–99215). All three key components must be met in the selection of a level of service code from 99241 to 99245.

Initial Inpatient Consultations (99251–99255)

Initial inpatient consultation codes (99251–99255) are used to report consulting services provided to hospital inpatients, residents of nursing facilities, or patients in a partial hospital setting. All three key components must be met in the selection of a level of service code from 99251 to 99255. In addition, a consultant can report only one initial consultation code per admission.

Follow-up Inpatient Consultations (99261–99263)

Follow-up consultative visits (99261–99263) may be used to report a subsequent visit to complete the initial consultation or a subsequent visit requested by the attending physician. Follow-up consultations include monitoring the patient's progress, recommending changes to management, or suggesting a new plan of care because of changes in the patient's medical status. Only two of the three key components must be met before selecting follow-up inpatient consultation codes.

Confirmatory Consultations (99271–99275)

Confirmatory consultation codes 99271–99275 may be reported when the consulting physician answers a request to provide a confirmatory opinion and/or advice on the patient's condition and/or treatment plan. This service may be provided in any setting (office, hospital, or nursing home). All three key components must be met in the selection of a level of service from codes 99271–99275. Modifier –32 also may be reported when, for example, a third-party payer mandates a confirmatory consultation.

Emergency Department Services (99281–99288)

Emergency department services category codes are used to report E/M services that a physician provides when treating a patient in the emergency department. The CPT codebook defines the emergency department as an organized hospital-based facility for the provision of unscheduled episodic services to patients who present for immediate medical attention. Moreover, the facility must be available twenty-four hours a day. All three of the key components, as stated within each level, must be met prior to selection of an emergency services code.

Special attention should be given to the description of code 99285, "which requires these three key components within the constraints imposed by the urgency of the patient's clinical condition and mental status." This description allows the code to be assigned, even when all the documentation does not meet the criteria so stated. For example, when the patient is unconscious, it may be impossible to document a comprehensive history.

Again, code selection by physicians rather than coders or billing services is important because a physician is the only one in a position to determine clinical condition and mental status. Nonphysicians may verify compliance of the code selection to the current guidelines, but the provider of service best determines the level of code selection.

When a patient receives critical care services in the emergency department, codes 99291–99292 may be reported for these services, provided the requirements for critical care are met.

Pediatric Critical Care Patient Transport (99289–99290)

The pediatric critical care patient transport services codes are used to report face-to-face critical care services delivered by a physician during the interfacility transport of a critically ill or injured pediatric patient, 24 months of age or less.

Code 99289 is used to report the first 30 to 74 minutes, and code 99290 is an add-on code for each additional 30 minutes. Transport time less than 30 minutes is not reported. Guidelines direct the coder to report only these codes once on any given date.

A physician's attendance during the transport of critically ill or injured patients *over the age of 24 months* should be reported with codes 99291–99292.

Critical Care Services (99291–99296)

The critical care services category involves the care of critically ill patients in a medical emergency that requires the constant attention of the physician. However, the physician's constant attendance/monitoring does not have to be continuous on a given date. Types of medical emergencies can include cardiac arrest, shock, bleeding, respiratory failure, and postoperative complications. Although usually provided in critical care areas such as a coronary care unit, intensive care unit (ICU), or emergency department, this type of care may be offered in other settings as well.

Critical care provided to neonatal and pediatric inpatients is reported with codes 99293–99296. (See the definitions for neonatal and pediatric in the table provided in the next section.)

Critical care services include the following procedures, which should not be reported separately:

- Interpretation of cardiac output measurements (93561, 93562)

- Chest X rays (71010, 71015, 71020)

- Pulse oximetry (94760, 94761, 94762)

- Blood gases and information data stored in computers (99090)

- Gastric intubation (43752, 91105)

- Temporary transcutaneous pacing (92953)

- Ventilator management (94656, 94657, 94660, 94662)

- Vascular access procedures (36000, 36410, 36415, 36540, 36600)

Other services performed that are not included in the preceding list may be reported separately.

Time is a key factor when selecting a critical care code. Code 99291 is reported for the first 30 to 74 minutes of critical care on a given date and may be reported only once per date. Code 99292 is reported for each additional 30 minutes of care beyond the first 74 minutes. As mentioned above, coders should note that the constant attention the physician provides need not be continuous on a given date. Critical care of less than 30 minutes on a given date should be reported with an appropriate E/M services code, such as subsequent hospital inpatient services, rather than a critical care code. A comprehensive explanation of time as an element in code selection can be found in the note under the critical care services subcategory.

Neonatal and Pediatric Critical Care Services (Inpatient) (99293–99296)

These codes are used to report services by a physician directing the care of a critically ill neonate or infant. The following table provides guidance on using the codes in this category:

Definition	Initial Critical Care (Date of Admission)	Subsequent Critical Care
Neonatal (birth to 30 days of age)	99295	99296
Pediatric (31 days to 2 years of age)	99293	99294

Coding guidelines dictate that these codes may be reported only once by a single physician per patient per day. The same definitions for critical care services apply for adult, pediatric, and neonatal patients.

Intensive (Non-Critical) Low Birth Weight Services (99298–99299)

Codes in this category are used by physicians to report intensive (non-critical) care given to infants of low birth weight. These infants require intensive services that do not meet the definition of critical care. The following table outlines the appropriate use of these codes:

Definition	Initial Care	Subsequent Intensive Care
Very low birth weight (less than 1,500 grams)	Code selected from initial hospital care (99221–99223)	99298
Low birth weight (between 1,500–2,600 grams)	Code selected from initial hospital care (99221–99223)	99299

Physicians may report these codes only once per patient per day.

Nursing Facility Services (99301–99316)

The codes in the nursing facility services category are used to report services in the following facilities:

- Skilled nursing facilities, including hospital-based skilled care or swing beds in rural hospitals

- Intermediate care facilities

- Long-term care facilities

Nursing facilities (NFs) are required by law to perform a comprehensive assessment of each resident's functional capacity upon admission. Additional assessments must be conducted immediately after significant changes in a resident's condition, or at least every twelve months. The assessments are documented in a form called the resident assessment instrument (RAI), which is composed of a uniform Minimum Data Set (MDS) and resident assessment protocols (RAPs). The MDS includes a minimum set of assessment elements to evaluate SNF and NF residents. SNFs and NFs are responsible for completing the RAI, although specific portions of the form must be completed by a physician only.

CPT recognizes two types of NF services: comprehensive nursing facility assessments and subsequent nursing facility care. Both of these subcategories apply to new or established patients.

The comprehensive nursing facility assessments (99301–99303) may be performed at one or more sites in the assessment process: the hospital, observation unit, office, NF, domiciliary/non-NF, or patient's home. All three of the key components must be met in these cases before code selection.

Subsequent NF care (99311–99313) includes reviewing the health record, noting changes in the resident's status since the last visit, and reviewing and signing orders. Subsequent NF care requires that only two of the three key components be met before assigning a specific level of service code.

NF discharge day management codes are used to report the total duration of time spent by a physician for the final NF discharge of a patient. These include final examination of the patient and discussion of the NF stay, even when the time spent on that date is not continuous. Instructions are given for continuing care to all relevant caregivers and for preparation of discharge records, prescriptions, and referral forms. These codes are 99315 for services of 30 minutes or less and 99316 for services of more than 30 minutes.

Domiciliary, Rest Home, or Custodial Care Services (99321–99333)

Physician visits to patients being provided room, board, and other personal assistance services (usually on a long-term basis) are reported using codes 99321–99333. A medical component is not part of the facility's services. Such facilities may include group homes or correctional facilities. All three key components, as defined in the levels of service, must be met before code assignment in the new patient subcategory (99321–99323). However, only two of the three key components must be met in the established patient subcategory (99331–99333).

Home Services (99341–99350)

Home services codes 99341–99350 are used to report E/M services provided in a private residence. As stated in the levels of service, all three key components are required prior to code assignment in the new patient subcategory (99341–99345). However, only two of the three key components must be met in the established patient subcategory (99347–99350).

Prolonged Services/Standby Services (99354–99360)

The first set of codes (99354–99357) is used when a physician provides prolonged service involving direct, face-to-face contact with the patient that is beyond the usual service. The time the physician spends providing prolonged service on a given date need not be continuous. Coders should note that these codes may be reported in addition to other services, including E/M services at any level. Moreover, other procedures or supplies provided during the same encounter should be reported according to payer directions or guidelines.

The codes are further subdivided to identify prolonged services provided in the outpatient setting (99354–99355) and the inpatient setting (99356–99357). Codes 99354 and 99356 describe the first hour of prolonged service and should be reported only once per any given date. Codes 99355 and 99357 describe each additional 30 minutes of prolonged service. Coders should note that prolonged service of less than 30 minutes should not be reported separately.

Codes 99358–99359 describe prolonged physician service without direct or face-to-face contact with the patient that is beyond the usual service. This type of service can involve prolonged communication with other healthcare professionals, prolonged review of extensive health record and diagnostic tests, and prolonged communication with the patient and/or family regarding the patient's prognosis. These codes may be reported along with other services, including E/M services at any level. Code 99358 is used to report the first hour of prolonged service, and code 99359 describes each additional 30 minutes of service. Prolonged service of less than 30 minutes should not be reported separately.

Code 99360 is used to report physician standby services requested by another physician that require prolonged physician attendance without direct or face-to-face contact. This type of service may involve a physician who stands by for assistance in surgery or high-risk delivery for care of a newborn. Code 99360 may be reported for each full 30-minute period the physician stands by. Less than 30 minutes of standby service may not be reported separately.

Case Management Services (99361–99373)

The case management services category includes services when a physician is responsible for providing direct care for a patient, as well as coordinating and controlling access to other healthcare services or initiating and/or supervising them. This category includes two subcategories: team conferences and telephone calls.

Codes 99361–99362 describe a team conference that includes a physician, an interdisciplinary health team, or representatives of community agencies for the purpose of coordinating the activities of the patient. Codes 99371–99373 describe telephone calls a physician makes to consult with a patient or to coordinate medical management with other healthcare professionals. The content of the call determines the code assignment: simple/brief, intermediate, or complex/lengthy. Many health plans consider telephone communication bundled with other E/M services and do not provide additional reimbursement for this service.

Care Plan Oversight Services (99374–99380)

The care plan oversight services category describes the services a physician provides when supervising and coordinating the patient's care within a 30-day period, but not actually seeing the patient face-to-face. These codes are appropriate when a physician provides recurrent supervision of therapy for patients in NFs, home health agencies, or hospice beds.

Code 99374 (home health), code 99377 (hospice), or code 99379 (NF) is reported for services lasting between 15 and 29 minutes, whereas codes 99375, 99378, and 99380 cover services lasting longer than 30 minutes. Only one physician may report this type of service within a 30-day period.

Work involved in providing very low-intensity services or infrequent supervision is included in the pre- and postencounter work for the home, office/outpatient, and NF or domiciliary visit codes and should not be reported with care plan oversight codes.

Preventive Medicine Services (99381–99429)

The preventive medicine services category codes are used to report the preventive medicine evaluation and management of infants, children, adolescents, and adults.

When an abnormality is discovered or a preexisting condition is addressed during this service, the appropriate office visit code also should be reported if the condition/abnormality proves significant enough to require additional workup. Moreover, modifier –25 should be added to the office visit code to indicate that the same physician provided a significant and separate E/M service and on the same date as the preventive medicine service. Any insignificant conditions/abnormalities discovered during the preventive medicine services that do not require additional workup should not be reported separately.

Ancillary procedures (such as laboratory or radiological procedures), screening tests identified with a specific CPT code, and immunizations provided during the preventive medicine encounter should be coded and reported separately.

The subcategories of preventive medicine services distinguish between new and established patients, with the individual codes identifying specified age ranges.

Codes 99401–99412 are used to report services provided to individuals at a separate encounter for the purpose of promoting health and preventing illness or injury. Counseling and/or risk factor reduction intervention vary with age and should address issues such as family problems, diet and exercise, substance abuse, sexual practices, injury prevention, dental health, and diagnostic and laboratory test results available at the time of visit.

A separate code is not needed for counseling (99401–99412) when provided as part of preventive medicine services (99381–99397) or during an E/M service. The preventive medicine codes (99381–99397) include counseling, anticipatory guidance, and risk factor reductions in the service provided. An additional code is not required to identify them. The E/M services codes also include counseling in the care provided.

Newborn Care (99431–99440)

The newborn care codes are used to report services provided to normal or high-risk newborns in different settings. Code 99431 is reported for history and examination of the normal newborn, initiation of diagnostic and treatment programs, and preparation of hospital records. This code is appropriate for birthing room deliveries. Code 99433 is reported to indicate subsequent hospital care for the evaluation and management of a normal newborn on a per day basis. Code 99435 should be reported for discharge services provided to the newborn admitted and discharged on the same date. Code 99436 is used to report attendance at a delivery at the request of the delivering physician for initial stabilization of the newborn. Newborn resuscitative services are reported with code 99440, which includes the provision of positive pressure ventilation and/or chest compressions in the presence of acute inadequate ventilation and/or cardiac output. Code 99440 cannot be reported with 99436. When other procedures are performed in addition to the resuscitative services, additional codes should be reported.

Special Evaluation and Management Services (99450–99456)

The special evaluation and management services category codes were developed to report services that can be performed in the office setting or other setting to establish baseline information before life or disability insurance certificates are issued. Coders should note that no active management of the patient's problem is performed during this visit. If other E/M services and/or procedures are performed on the same date, the appropriate E/M services codes also should be reported, with modifier –25 appending them.

Other Evaluation and Management Services (99499)

The other evaluation and management services category code is used to report an unlisted E/M service that does not fit into the previous categories.

Exercise 7.2

Assign only the appropriate E/M services code(s) for the following situations:

1. An established patient with hypertension visits a physician's office for a blood pressure check. The nurse performs the service under the physician's supervision. _____

2. A new patient was seen in the physician's office for abdominal pain. The physician performs a detailed history and comprehensive examination. Medical decision making is of moderate complexity. _____

3. A patient with rectal bleeding was seen in the office of a gastroenterologist. The patient's primary care physician requested that the gastroenterologist provide advice about this case. The specialist conducted a comprehensive history and exam, and medical decision making was high. The consultant documented his findings and communicated them via written report to the primary care physician. _____

4. A new patient is seen in the physician's office for a cough, sore throat, and fever. The physician performs an expanded problem-focused history and a detailed exam, and medical decision making was of low complexity. _____

5. Dr. Jones asks Dr. Matthews to confirm his diagnosis and treatment plan for a five-day-old patient with a congenital heart defect of tetralogy of Fallot. The patient's insurance company requires this service before authorizing payment for an operation. Dr. Matthews obtains a comprehensive history and reviews the medical records from Dr. Jones, including diagnostic test results. He performs a comprehensive examination, including a complete organ system evaluation, and provides medical decision making of high complexity by evaluating all treatment options and considering the high risk of mortality with this type of defect. _____

6. Dr. Jones provides critical care services in the emergency department for a patient in respiratory failure and with congestive heart failure. Ventilator management is initiated. Dr. Jones spends an hour and 10 minutes providing critical care for this patient.

   _____

7. Dr. Michaels provides E/M services for a patient in acute hysteria who has been admitted to the emergency department. After performing a problem-focused history and examination with straightforward medical decision making, he determines that the patient is suffering from acute grief reaction secondary to the death of her granddaughter due to sudden infant death syndrome. At discharge, the patient is in complete control of her actions and is referred to a SIDS organization. _____

8. Dr. Gerald provides preventive medicine services to an established 45-year-old patient who is in good health and has no complaints. Dr. Gerald obtains a comprehensive history, performs a comprehensive examination, and counsels the patient on proper diet and exercise.

   _____

9. Dr. Hawthorne sees an established patient in his office for evaluation of insulin-dependent diabetes mellitus with nephropathy. In addition to a problem-focused history, he performs an expanded problem-focused examination that includes a limited exam of the genitourinary, immunologic, skin, and musculoskeletal systems, and documents all positive and negative findings. The patient's status does not seem to have changed, and medical decision making is of low complexity. Dr. Hawthorne discusses the patient's insulin dosage, diet, and exercise, and plans to see the patient in six months. _____

Exercise 7.2 (cont.)

10. An established patient sees Dr. Ryan in his office with complaints of chest pain. Dr. Ryan decides to admit the patient to Central Hospital on March 2 under observation status. He obtains a comprehensive history that includes a complete review of body systems and complete past, family, and social histories. The patient reveals that he has been under emotional stress the past month due to his recent divorce and that this is the first time he has experienced chest pain. Dr. Ryan performs a comprehensive examination that includes a complete evaluation of the respiratory and cardiovascular systems. Pertinent diagnostic tests reveal no coronary artery disease. Dr. Ryan performs medical decision making of moderate complexity and determines the origin of the pain to be musculoskeletal secondary to stress. He discharges the patient on March 2 and recommends that he join a stress management group. _____

11. In her office, Dr. Childers sees an established patient who complains of abdominal pain. She provides a problem-focused history and examination, which reveals the onset of abdominal pain beginning early that morning and characterized by a sharp, crampy feeling with some radiation to the back. Nausea and dry heaves are present, but no vomiting. The patient had a normal bowel movement in the morning. No fever or chills are noted, and bowel sounds are active. A rectal examination reveals hard stool in the rectal vault, guaiac negative. An X ray of the abdomen is negative except for extensive gas. Dr. Childers tells the patient to take an enema and return if the pain is not relieved. A change in diet would involve increasing the intake of fiber. The impression is that the patient's pain is the result of impacted feces. _____

12. A new patient sees Dr. Reynolds in his office complaining of diarrhea and watery stool the previous night, as well as nausea, vomiting, and crampy, lower abdominal pain. Dr. Reynolds provides a detailed history and examination, and medical decision making of moderate complexity. _____

Chapter 8

Medicine

The medicine section of the CPT codebook comprises a wide variety of specialty services and procedures such as psychiatric therapy, chemotherapy administration, rehabilitative procedures, and immunizations.

The medicine section includes the following subsections:

Subsection	Code Range
Immune Globulins	90281–90399
Immunization Administration for Vaccines/Toxoids	90471–90474
Vaccines and Toxoids	90476–90749
Therapeutic or Diagnostic Infusions	90780–90781
Therapeutic, Prophylactic, or Diagnostic Injections	90782–90799
Psychiatry	90801–90899
Biofeedback	90901–90911
Dialysis	90918–90999
Gastroenterology	91000–91299
Ophthalmology	92002–92499
Special Otorhinolaryngologic Services	92502–92700
Cardiovascular	92950–93799
Non-Invasive Vascular Diagnostic Studies	93875–93990
Pulmonary	94010–94799
Allergy and Clinical Immunology	95004–95199
Endocrinology	95250
Neurology and Neuromuscular Procedures	95805–96004
Central Nervous System Assessments/Tests	96100–96117
Health and Behavior Assessment/Intervention	96150–96155
Chemotherapy Administration	96400–96549
Photodynamic Therapy	96567–96571
Special Dermatological Procedures	96900–96999
Physical Medicine and Rehabilitation	97001–97799
Medical Nutrition Therapy	97802–97804
Osteopathic Manipulative Therapy	98925–98929
Chiropractic Manipulative Treatment	98940–98943
Special Services, Procedures, and Reports	99000–99091
Qualifying Circumstances for Anesthesia	99100–99140
Sedation With or Without Analgesia (Conscious Sedation)	99141–99142
Other Services and Procedures	99170–99199
Home Health Procedures/Services	99500–99600
Home Infusion Procedures	99601–99602

Specific subsections are discussed later in this chapter. In some cases, the services listed in the medicine section may be performed in conjunction with services or procedures listed elsewhere in the CPT codebook. It may be appropriate to use multiple codes from different sections of the codebook to identify the particular circumstances.

Example: An established patient was seen in the physician's office for DTP immunization injection. In addition to the immunization, the physician provides documentation for a minimal-level office visit. The following codes are reported: 90701, 90471, and 99211–25 (E/M code).

Modifier Use in the Medicine Section

Modifiers are discussed extensively in earlier chapters of this workbook.

Immunization Injections

Separate codes exist for the administration (immunization procedure) of vaccines and toxoids and for the toxoid products themselves. Codes 90471–90474 are used to report the administration of a toxoid substance, and a code or codes from the 90476–90749 range identify the type of immunization or vaccine (measles, polio, DTP, and so on).

When a significant, separately identifiable E/M service (for example, office or other outpatient services or preventive medicine services) is performed, the appropriate E/M services code appended with modifier –25 should be reported in addition to the immunization administration and toxoid substance codes. For some health plans, other types of injections, including immunization administration, are bundled with E/M services and not reported separately.

Therapeutic or Diagnostic Infusions (Excludes Chemotherapy)

The two codes listed under therapeutic or diagnostic infusions are used to report procedures involving prolonged intravenous injections. These codes require that the physician be present during the entire procedure. Code 90780 is reported for the first hour of infusion, and code 90781 is reported for each additional hour, up to eight hours. These codes are inappropriate for antineoplastic drugs for the treatment of malignancies or for therapeutic, prophylactic, or diagnostic injections.

Note: The prolonged service codes (99354–99357) may not be reported with this series of codes.

Therapeutic, Prophylactic, or Diagnostic Injections

Codes 90782–90799 are used to describe subcutaneous, intramuscular, intradermal, intravenous, and intra-arterial injections for diagnostic, prophylactic, and therapeutic purposes. As with immunization injections, the specific substance injected must be reported with another code. For Medicare cases, a Level II HCPCS code (J series) is reported with the identification of the specific substance or drug; for non-Medicare cases, code 99070 may be reported. Because Medicare considers the administration of injections bundled into E/M services at the same encounter, it does not reimburse separately for the visit and the injection. However, when the injection is the only service, these codes are used. The HCPCS J code can always be reported, even when the injection administration code is not. HCPCS Level II codes (J codes) are discussed in chapter 10.

This series of codes is not used for allergy injections or immunizations; specific CPT codes are available for these services.

The payment policies of individual payers (including Medicare) differ and should be reviewed carefully to ensure appropriate payment. For example, some payers reimburse for an office visit code only when an injection was performed during that visit; others reimburse only for the drug administered (J code), as well as the method of administration (for example, intravenous injection). If there is a need for data collection, most health plans do not object to a nonpayable code being reported with a zero or no-charge amount.

Exercise 8.1

Assign the appropriate codes for the following procedures/services:

1. Immunization injection of Cholera vaccine   _____

2. IV infusion for one hour   _____

3. IM injection of hepatitis B and Hemophilus influenza b vaccine   _____

Psychiatry

The psychiatric services included in codes 90801–90899 may be provided in an outpatient or inpatient setting or in a partial hospital setting. The Centers for Medicare and Medicaid Services (CMS) defines psychiatric facility partial hospitalization as a facility for the diagnosis and treatment of mental illness that provides a planned therapeutic program for patients who do not require full-time hospitalization, but who need broader programs than are possible from outpatient visits in a hospital-based or hospital-affiliated facility. Partial hospitalization may be used for crisis stabilization, intensive short-term daily treatment, or intermediate-term treatment of psychiatric disorders.

When E/M services such as hospital or office visits are provided along with services from the psychiatry subsection, a code from the E/M section and a code from the psychiatry subsection are usually reported. However, some codes in the psychiatry subsection combine the psychiatric services and the E/M services into one code. In this situation, only the code from the psychiatry subsection is reported.

> **Example:** A psychiatrist provided psychoanalysis along with E/M services to an established patient in the office setting. The office visit included an expanded, problem-focused history and an examination and medical decision making of low complexity. The following codes should be reported: 90845 and 99213-25.

Example: A patient in a clinic receives individual insight-oriented psychotherapy for more than 25 minutes. The physician also provides E/M services that include a problem-focused history, a problem-focused examination, and a straightforward level of medical decision making. Code 90805 should be reported.

Note: Some third-party payers (such as Medicare) do not reimburse for an E/M service and psychotherapy when both are performed on the same day.

The psychiatry subsection is further divided to identify consultative and therapeutic services such as psychotherapy, electroconvulsive therapy, and hypnotherapy. Following are discussions of specific categories of the psychiatry subsection.

General Clinical Psychiatric Diagnostic or Evaluative Interview Procedures

Code 90801, Psychiatric diagnostic interview examination, typically is reported during the initial phases of psychiatric treatment. This service includes:

- Complete medical and psychiatric history that may be obtained from the patient and/or the patient's family

- Complete mental status examination that focuses on the patient's condition during the examination

When provided in the inpatient hospital setting, this service may be reported only once during the hospitalization.

Psychiatric Therapeutic Procedures

Codes 90804–90899 describe specific psychotherapeutic procedures in the treatment of mental disorders and behavioral disturbances, including interactive psychotherapy, supportive psychotherapy, psychoanalysis, narcosynthesis, electroconvulsive therapy, and so on. Interactive psychotherapy (90810–90815 and 90823–90829) uses physical aids and nonverbal communication as a way for physicians to communicate with patients who are unable to interact verbally. Narcosynthesis (90865) involves administration of a medication that frees patients of their inhibitions and allows them to reveal information they might otherwise have found difficult to discuss.

It should be noted that some of the psychotherapy codes reflect time spent with the patient. When the time is less or greater than the time specified in the code description, modifiers –22, Unusual Procedural Services, or –52, Reduced Services, may be reported to reflect the change.

Exercise 8.2

Assign the appropriate codes for the following procedures/services:

1. Psychiatric evaluation of patient's health records, psychiatric reports, and tests in order to make a diagnosis _____

2. Psychotherapy involving patient and family members _____

3. Individual behavior modification and insight-oriented psychotherapy in office for 45 minutes _____

Dialysis

Codes 90918–90999 describe services related to end-stage renal disease (ESRD), hemodialysis, and peritoneal dialysis. The CPT codebook indicates that all E/M services related to the patient's ESRD that are provided on the same day as the dialysis should be included in the dialysis procedure code (90935–90947) and should not be reported separately. However, E/M services unrelated to ESRD services that cannot be performed during the dialysis session may be reported separately.

The first series of codes (90918–90925) describes the physician services provided to patients with ESRD, including outpatient visits, phone calls, and general management. Codes 90918–90921 describe services provided for a full month and are divided further by age.

The second series of codes (90922–90925) also is subdivided by age and is reported for ESRD services for less than one full month. A code from this series is assigned each day the physician provides the service.

Hemodialysis is defined as the process of removing metabolic waste products, toxins, and excess fluid from the blood. Codes 90935 and 90937 are reported to identify the physician service(s) provided on the day of hemodialysis. Code 90935 is reported when the physician provides a single evaluation of the patient during the hemodialysis, and code 90937 is reported when the physician is required to evaluate the patient more than once during the procedure. If the physician is required to provide prolonged services, codes 99354–99360 may be reported along with the hemodialysis code.

Note: Codes describing development of a shunt, cannula, or fistula for hemodialysis can be found in the surgery section of the CPT codebook.

Peritoneal dialysis involves insertion of a catheter into the abdominal cavity and infusion of a fluid (dialysate) into the peritoneum that allows for diffusion between the dialyzing fluid and the body fluids containing the waste products. The fluid containing the waste products then is removed from the peritoneum through the catheter. Codes 90945 and 90947 are reported to identify the physician service(s) provided on the day of peritoneal dialysis. Code 90945 is reported when the physician provides a single evaluation of the patient during the peritoneal dialysis, and code 90947 is reported when the physician is required to evaluate the patient more than once during the dialysis procedure. If the physician is required to provide prolonged services, codes 99354–99360 may be reported along with the dialysis code.

Note: The codes describing insertion of the peritoneal dialysis catheter are found in the surgery section of the CPT codebook.

Exercise 8.3

Assign the appropriate codes for the following physician procedures/services:

1. Fifty-year-old patient with end-stage renal disease treated in the outpatient dialysis unit for the past month _____

2. Peritoneal dialysis with a single physician evaluation _____

Ophthalmology

The ophthalmology subsection includes codes (92002–92499) describing ophthalmologic medical services provided to both new and established patients. The definitions for new and established patient are the same as those mentioned for E/M services:

- A new patient is one who has not received any professional services (face-to-face) within the past three years from the physician or another physician of the same specialty who belongs to the same group practice.

- An established patient is one who has received professional services (face-to-face) within the past three years from the physician or another physician of the same specialty who belongs to the same group practice.

The complete definitions and examples provided in the CPT codebook should be noted for intermediate and comprehensive ophthalmological services. Following is a summary of each:

- Intermediate services involve the evaluation of a new or existing condition complicated with a new diagnostic or management problem and include a history, general medical observation, external ocular and adnexal examination, and other diagnostic procedures as indicated.

- Comprehensive services involve a general evaluation of the complete visual system and include a history, general medical observation, an external and ophthalmoscopic examination, gross visual fields, and a basic sensorimotor examination. Initiation of diagnostic and treatment programs is always part of a comprehensive service.

An ophthalmologic examination and evaluation performed under general anesthesia is reported with codes 92018–92019.

Contact Lens Services

The prescription of contact lenses is not part of the general ophthalmological service and should be reported separately with the code series 92310–92326. When supplying contact lenses is part of the service of fitting them (92310–92317), a separate code should not be reported.

Spectacles Services

The prescription of glasses is considered part of a general ophthalmological service and thus should not be reported separately. Because the actual fitting of the glasses is considered a separate procedure, it should be reported with codes 92340–92371. In addition, the supply of materials (glasses) is reported separately with either code 92390 or 92395.

Exercise 8.4

Assign the appropriate codes for the following procedures/services:

1. Gonioscopy is performed under general anesthesia. _____

2. New patient has a comprehensive ophthalmological exam and evaluation. _____

Special Otorhinolaryngologic Services

Special otorhinolaryngologic services include diagnostic and therapeutic services usually employed by ear, nose, and throat specialists. Vestibular function tests and audiologic function tests are found in this section. No specific coding guidelines apply to these codes other than to use modifier –52, Reduced Services, in the audiologic function tests when a test is applied to only one ear.

Cardiovascular

The cardiovascular subsection includes codes describing diagnostic and therapeutic services such as electrocardiogram, cardiac catheterization, atrial septostomy, and percutaneous transluminal coronary atherectomy. The first series of codes (92950–92998) describes therapeutic services such as cardiopulmonary resuscitation, percutaneous transluminal coronary angioplasty (PTCA), percutaneous valvuloplasty, and coronary thrombolysis. When coding coronary thrombolysis (92975–92977), the coder must identify the type of infusion: intracoronary or intravenous.

It should be noted that the codes describing PTCA (92982–92984), atherectomy (92995–92996), and transcatheter placement of stent(s) (92980–92981) require the assignment of additional codes when more than one vessel is involved.

Procedure	Single Vessel	Each Additional Vessel
Stent placement	92980	92981
Coronary angioplasty	92982	92984
Coronary atherectomy	92995	92996

Example: Percutaneous transluminal coronary balloon angioplasty involving three vessels. The following codes should be reported: 92982 (first vessel), 92984 (second vessel), and 92984 (third vessel).

Codes 92995 and 92996 describe percutaneous transluminal coronary atherectomy that may or may not be accompanied by balloon angioplasty of the same vessel.

When percutaneous coronary atherectomy and balloon angioplasty are performed during the same episode on different vessels, the two treatment modes should be reported with multiple codes to describe them.

Example: Percutaneous transluminal coronary balloon angioplasty of the left anterior descending artery and percutaneous transluminal coronary atherectomy of the right anterior descending artery. The following codes should be reported: 92995 and 92982.

The next two series of codes involve diagnostic cardiography (93000–93278), which includes EKGs and stress tests, and echocardiography (93303–93350), which includes echocardiograms (ultrasounds of the heart).

Cardiac catheterization is a diagnostic procedure that can identify diseases in the coronary arteries. According to the CPT definition, a cardiac catheterization includes the following procedures/services:

- Introduction, positioning, and repositioning of catheter(s)

- Recording of intracardiac and intravascular pressure

- Obtaining blood samples for measurement of blood gases or dilution curves

- Cardiac output measurements (Fick or other method) with or without electrode catheter placement

- Final evaluation and report of procedure

Codes 93501–93562 describe cardiac catheterizations and associated procedures. Intracardiac electrophysiological procedures, which may be diagnostic or therapeutic, are reported with codes 93600–93662. Electrophysiologic testing is performed on patients with cardiac arrhythmias causing palpitations, near syncope, or syncope with cardiac arrest.

Codes 93600–93612 include diagnostic electrophysiologic procedures that provide only recording and pacing from a single site. Codes 93619–93622 describe a comprehensive electrophysiologic evaluation that may be reported when recording and pacing are performed from multiple sites.

The services described in codes 93600–93652 include the insertion and repositioning of catheters.

Pulmonary

Pulmonologists and hospitals use codes from the pulmonary subsection for pulmonary testing. When E/M services are provided separately, a code from the E/M section also should be assigned. Codes 94010–94799 include the performance of lab procedures and the interpretation of the test results.

Allergy and Clinical Immunology

The allergy and clinical immunology subsection includes the categories of allergy testing and allergen immunotherapy. The complete definitions provided in the CPT codebook for allergy sensitivity tests and immunotherapy should be noted. A brief summary of each follows:

- Allergy sensitivity tests refer to the performance and evaluation of selective skin and mucous tests in association with the patient's history and physical examination.

- Immunotherapy (desensitization, hyposensitization) involves the parenteral administration of allergenic extracts as antigens at periodic intervals, usually on an increasing dosage scale to one that is maintained as maintenance therapy.

Codes from the E/M services section should be used to report visits with the patient involving the use of mechanical and electronic devices such as air conditioners, air filters, and humidifiers; climatotherapy; and physical, occupational, and recreational therapy.

Allergy testing (95004–95078) is further divided by type of test: percutaneous, intracutaneous, patch or application, and so on. It should be noted that with most of the codes in this series, the number of tests performed should be reported on the CMS-1500 form under item 24G. (See figure 1.1 on page 5.)

> **Example:** Ten percutaneous tests with allergenic extracts were performed. The following should be reported: 95004 with 10 (to identify the number of tests) in item 24G of the CMS-1500 form.

Allergen immunotherapy (95115–95199), more commonly referred to as allergy shots, includes the professional services related to the immunotherapy. A separate office visit code(s) should not be reported unless some other identifiable service was provided during the visit.

Neurology and Neuromuscular Procedures, and Central Nervous System Assessments/Tests

Consulting neurologists and hospitals generally use the range of codes in the subsections classifying neurology and neuromuscular procedures and central nervous system tests to report such procedures, assessments, and tests. Sleep testing, nerve conduction studies, and developmental testing are found in this area of the medicine section of the CPT codebook.

Health and Behavior Assessment/Intervention

The focus of these services (codes 96150–96155) is not on mental health but, rather, on the biopsychosocial factors affecting physical health problems and treatments (that is, patients with chronic illnesses). The codes can be reported by clinical social workers, advanced practice nurses, psychologists, and other healthcare professionals who have training with health and behavior assessment/intervention procedures. Physicians performing these services are directed to report E/M or preventive medicine codes.

Chemotherapy Administration

The administration of chemotherapy is reported with codes 94600–96549. The codes further identify the mode of administration: subcutaneous or intramuscular, intralesional, intravenous, or intra-arterial. The codes describing intravenous and intra-arterial administration are further subdivided to identify the technique—infusion or push—and length of time. Codes 96440–96450 describe the administration of chemotherapy to specific body sites: pleural or peritoneal cavity, or central nervous system. Codes 96520 and 96530 describe the maintenance and refilling of portable or implantable pumps or reservoirs.

Although preparation of the chemotherapy agent is included in the administration, provision of the chemotherapy drug is not. For Medicare claims, a code from the J series of the Level II HCPCS should be reported to identify the specific drug administered. For non-Medicare claims, code 96545, Provision of chemotherapy agent, may be reported. The individual payer should be contacted for further directions.

When additional services are provided on the same day as the chemotherapy and are independent of the chemotherapy, the physician may bill separately for that service (for example, an E/M office visit).

Note: Codes describing the placement of pumps, catheters, or reservoirs may be found in the surgery section of the CPT codebook.

Special Dermatological Procedures

Services such as actinotherapy and photochemotherapy are found in the special dermatological procedures subsection of CPT. Generally, these codes are used by consulting dermatologists.

Physical Medicine and Rehabilitation

The area of physical medicine and rehabilitation continues to expand as new modalities and therapeutic procedures are implemented within this specialty. These codes are used by physiatrists and physical therapists who provide a variety of physical therapy services to patients with a need to improve physical functioning. Tests and measurement codes are included to provide coding for prosthetic checkout and use, and physical performance testing. No special guidelines are applicable to this section. Physiatrists use the E/M section for professional service billing.

Active wound care management (97601–97602) codes are provided for reporting active wound care performed by *nonphysician healthcare professionals* (for example, nurses, physician assistants, physical therapists, occupational therapists). According to CPT guidelines, codes 97601 and 97602 should not be reported in addition to the debridement codes 11040–11044 located in the integumentary section of CPT.

The debridement codes (11040-11044) are considered surgical debridement, whereas codes 97601–97602 are considered nonsurgical. The two techniques of nonsurgical debridement are *selective* and *nonselective* debridement.

Code 97601 is assigned for the selective technique, which includes use of scalpels, scissors, and forceps to cut and remove the necrotic tissue. Other selective debridement includes the use of high-pressure water jets, enzyme applications, or autolysis.

Code 97602 is assigned for nonselective techniques that include the gradual removal of loosely adherent areas of necrotic tissue achieved by irrigating the wound using various hydrotherapies.

CPT codes 97601 and 97602 include the application and removal of any protective or bulk dressings and should not be reported when a dressing change is performed without any active wound procedure described by 97601–97602. Do not report both selective and nonselective debridement codes for techniques performed on the same devitalized tissue area(s) of a wound on the same date of service.

Osteopathic Manipulative Treatment and Chiropractic Manipulative Treatment

Osteopathic-trained physicians and chiropractic physicians or other physicians trained in these techniques use the codes found in the osteopathic manipulative treatment and chiropractic manipulative treatment subsections. E/M service codes are to be reported separately only when they are significant and separate from the manipulative treatments. In these cases, modifier –25, Significant, Separately Identifiable Evaluation and Management Service by the Same Physician on the Same Day of the Procedure or Other Service, may be appended to the E/M code to communicate this circumstance on a claim form.

Special Services, Procedures, and Reports

The special services and reports subsection (99000–99091) describes certain procedures/services or reports the physician may add to the basic service provided. Codes 99050–99058 describe special services provided to a patient beyond the basic service, such as those requested between 10 p.m. and 8 a.m. (code 99052). Because a third-party payer may or may not reimburse these services, a review of each payer's policies would be advantageous to the coder and assignment of the codes without charges may be important from a data-tracking or management perspective.

CPT code 99070 may be reported when the physician submits claims for supplies and other materials to an insurance plan that does not recognize Level II HCPCS codes.

When submitting Medicare claims, it is important to remember that, in most cases, a more specific code describing a particular supply may exist in Level II of HCPCS and routine supplies associated with professional services are not separately reimbursed.

Qualifying Circumstances for Anesthesia

Four CPT codes (99100–99140) may be used to report qualifying circumstances or additional information on patients undergoing anesthesia who show greater risk of complications. For example, codes describing patients of an extreme age (elderly or newborn), with total body hypothermia or controlled hypotension, or with possible emergency conditions may need to be reported in addition to the code describing the anesthesia service.

Sedation with or without Analgesia

The sedation with or without analgesia codes are available to report conscious sedation used in a number of endoscopic procedures. Use of these codes requires the presence of an independent, trained observer to assist the operating physician in monitoring the patient's level of consciousness and physiological status. The codes represent performance and documentation of pre- and postsedation evaluations of the patient, administration of the sedation, and monitoring of cardiorespiratory functions.

Other Services and Procedures

Certain miscellaneous procedures performed by physicians do not fit into the other sections of *Current Procedural Terminology*. One example is hyperbaric oxygen therapy supervision. Another is the administration of Ipecac and observation of the patient until the stomach is emptied of poison. Such codes are located in the other services and procedures subsection.

Home Health Procedures/Services

Codes from the section on home health procedures/services (99500–99512) are used by nonphysician healthcare professionals when providing services in the patient's residence. Physicians are directed to use codes from the E/M section. Healthcare professionals who are authorized to use E/M home visit codes (99341–99350) may report 99500–99512 with the E/M code if the patient's condition requires a significant identifiable E/M service above and beyond the home health service/procedure. In this case, modifier –25 would be appended to the E/M code.

Home Infusion Procedures

Codes from the home infusion procedures section (99601-99602) include a home visit by nonphysician healthcare professionals and all necessary solutions, equipment, and supplies (except drugs) required to deliver a therapy, per visit. All drugs are excluded and should be reported separately.

Exercise 8.5 Chapter Review

Assign the appropriate medicine section codes and modifiers when appropriate. These exercises should be considered non-Medicare cases.

1. Hemodialysis with the physician evaluating the patient twice during the service _____

2. Active immunization with live measles, mumps, and rubella virus vaccine _____

3. Routine ECG with 15 leads, with the physician providing only the interpretation and report of the test _____

4. Intra-arterial chemotherapy administration via infusion technique for 30 minutes (the chemotherapy agent administered was Cisplatin). Assign CPT codes only. _____

5. Intermittent positive pressure breathing (IPPB) therapy _____

6. Speech audiometry with threshold and recognition, both ears _____

7. Intramuscular steroid injection _____

8. Individual interactive psychotherapy for 45 minutes provided in the outpatient setting _____

9. Percutaneous transluminal coronary atherectomy of left posterior descending and left obtuse marginal arteries _____

10. Comprehensive ophthalmological services provided to an established patient with extended color vision examination _____

11. Evaluation of oral and pharyngeal swallowing function _____

12. Leg prosthetic training for 45 minutes by a physical therapist _____

13. What code, in addition to the basic E/M services code, is assigned if the physician provided service on July 4 per the request of the patient? _____

14. Complete duplex scan of the lower extremity arteries _____

15. EMG of three extremities and related paraspinal areas _____

16. Acupuncture treatment using electrical stimulation _____

17. Osteopathic manipulation; head, cervical, thoracic, and lumbar spine _____

18. Nurse makes a home visit for newborn care/assessment _____

Chapter 9

Anesthesia

The anesthesia section of the CPT codebook includes codes that describe general, regional, and local anesthesia services. These services should be reported by the physician who provides or supervises the anesthesia. The anesthesia services (00100–01999) in this section include:

- Usual pre- and postoperative visits

- Anesthesia provided during the procedure

- Administration of fluids and/or blood

- Usual monitoring services, such as ECG, temperature, blood pressure, oximetry, capnography, and mass spectrometry (Unusual monitoring, such as intra-arterial, central venous, or Swan-Ganz, is not included and should be reported separately.)

Some health plans require the reporting of anesthesia services by the code for the procedure performed rather than by the anesthesia code. Coders must be aware of and follow the guidelines required for specific cases.

The codes in this section are arranged first by body site and then by specific surgical procedure performed. They may be found in the alphabetic index of the CPT codebook by referencing the main entries of "Anesthesia" or "Analgesia."

Reporting of Time

Time may be reported for reimbursement of services, if preferred, by local carrier. Counting anesthesia time should begin with preparation of the patient by the anesthesiologist for induction of anesthesia (usually in the OR) and end when the anesthesiologist no longer is in attendance.

The American Society of Anesthesiologists (ASA) publishes the *Relative Value Guide* each year to provide a resource for establishing basic values for anesthesia used in most surgical procedures. The basic value unit includes usual pre- and postoperative visits by the anesthesiologist, and may be added to the time units and the modifying units for physical status to establish the charge for anesthesia services. It should be noted that the ASA guide is a relative value study and not a fee schedule, although it is widely accepted as a method of establishing fees for anesthesia services.

Anesthesia Modifiers

When reporting anesthesia services, a physical status modifier code should be used to distinguish between various levels of complexity of the anesthesia service provided. The anesthesiologist usually provides physical status modifiers on the anesthesia record. The ranking of patient physical status by the ASA is consistent with the following modifiers:

P1   A normal, healthy patient
P2   A patient with mild systemic disease
P3   A patient with severe systemic disease
P4   A patient with severe systemic disease that is a constant threat to life
P5   A moribund patient who is not expected to survive without the operation
P6   A declared brain-dead patient whose organs are being removed for donor purposes

Under certain circumstances, other modifiers may be assigned. The following modifiers are commonly used in the anesthesia section.

−22   **Unusual Procedural Services:** Modifier −22 may be reported to identify that the service provided was greater than that usually required for a particular service. Supportive documentation may need to be submitted to the third-party payer to justify use of modifier −22.

−23   **Unusual Anesthesia:** Modifier −23 may be reported when anesthesia is administered for a procedure that usually requires local anesthesia or none at all. This modifier would be reported along with the appropriate code describing the anesthesia service.

−32   **Mandated Services:** Modifier −32 may be reported when a group such as a third-party payer or a quality improvement organization (QIO) mandates a service.

−51   **Multiple Procedures:** Modifier −51 may be reported to identify that multiple anesthesia services were provided on the same day or during the same operative episode. The first procedure listed should identify the major or most resource-intensive service provided. Subsequent or secondary services should be appended with modifier −51.

−53   **Discontinued Procedure:** Modifier −53 is appropriate for circumstances when the physician elects to terminate or discontinue a procedure, usually because of risk to the patient's well-being. However, this modifier is not meant to report the elective cancellation of a procedure before the patient's surgical preparation or induction of anesthesia. Also, the appropriate ICD-9-CM code should be assigned to identify the reason for the procedure's termination or discontinuation.

−59   **Distinct Procedural Service:** Modifier −59 may be used to identify that a procedure/service was distinct or independent from other services provided on the same day.

Note: Modifier −47, Anesthesia by Surgeon, is never used as a modifier for the anesthesia procedures in the CPT codebook (00100–01999).

Anesthesia Codes versus Surgery Codes

The codes in the anesthesia section are reported exclusively for Medicare claims, along with the appropriate physical status modifier. Selected third-party payers require anesthesiologists to report their services with the appropriate code from the surgery section that describes the procedure performed. The surgery code should be appended with the appropriate physical status modifier.

Example: Anesthesia services provided to a normal, healthy patient for transurethral resection of the prostate

        Medicare Claim: 00914–P1

        Non-Medicare Claim: 52601–P1

Qualifying Circumstances

When anesthesia services are provided under difficult circumstances because of the patient's condition, operative conditions, or unusual risk factors, an additional code may be reported along with the code describing the basic anesthesia service. Codes 99100–99140 can never be reported alone. Located in the medicine section of the CPT codebook, these codes (99100–99140) are described as follows:

- 99100, Anesthesia for patient of extreme age, under one year and over seventy

- 99116, Anesthesia complicated by utilization of total body hypothermia

- 99135, Anesthesia complicated by utilization of controlled hypotension

- 99140, Anesthesia complicated by emergency conditions

When reporting code 99140, a separate report must be submitted describing the type of emergency. According to the CPT codebook, an emergency exists when delay in treatment of the patient would significantly increase the threat to life or body part.

Application of Anesthesia Codes in the Hospital Setting

Because they were developed for professional services for anesthesiologists, the anesthesia codes are not reported by hospitals unless the hospitals perform billing services for the anesthesiologists.

Exercise 9.1 Chapter Review

Assign the appropriate codes and physical status modifiers to describe anesthesia services for the following *Medicare* claims. The anesthesia codes should be assigned from the anesthesia section, when applicable.

1. Anesthesia services for radical mastectomy with internal mammary node dissection. Patient has diabetes mellitus well controlled with American Dietetic Association (ADA) diet.
    _____

2. Anesthesia services for closed treatment of fracture of humerus. Patient is 85 years old, but otherwise healthy.   _____

3. Anesthesia services for CABG surgery of five vessels with pump oxygenator. The patient has severe coronary artery disease, as well as hypertensive end-stage renal disease requiring hemodialysis.   _____

4. Anesthesia services for left lobectomy due to lung carcinoma. The patient also has severe chronic obstructive pulmonary disease and emphysema treated with bronchodilators.
    _____

5. Anesthesia services for left carotid endarterectomy. Patient is otherwise healthy.
    _____

Assign the appropriate codes and physical status modifiers to describe anesthesia services for the following *non-Medicare* claims. The anesthesia codes should be assigned from the surgery section.

6. Anesthesia services for partial nephrectomy in a patient with renal cell carcinoma. The 45-year-old patient also has mild coronary artery disease and hypertension treated with medication.   _____

7. Anesthesia services for heart transplant secondary to congenital heart defect. The patient is three weeks old and requires the transplant for survival.   _____

8. Anesthesia services for carotid thromboendarterectomy with patch graft for severe carotid artery stenosis. The patient is 75 years old and has had recurrent carotid artery stenosis. The patient also has a pacemaker for control of atrial fibrillation.   _____

9. Anesthesia services for laparoscopic cholecystectomy with cholangiography for acute cholecystitis. The patient is 35 years old and in good health.   _____

10. Anesthesia services for extracapsular cataract extraction with insertion of intraocular lens prosthesis. The patient is 79 years old, with mild diabetes mellitus and hypertension.
    _____

Chapter 10

HCPCS Level II

Developed by the Centers for Medicare and Medicaid Services (CMS), Level II HCPCS also is referred to as the National Codes. The National Codes were designed to report physician and nonphysician services such as drugs, chiropractic services, dental procedures, durable medical equipment, and other selected procedures.

Although the National Codes were developed for Medicare, they also are used by commercial payers. Coders should note that some Medicare carriers mandate the use of Level II codes rather than specific CPT codes. For example, there is a CPT code for removal of impacted cerumen (69210), but CMS will deny payment for this code. HCPCS Level II code G0268 should be reported for the earwax removal procedure. Bulletins from Medicare carriers announce such mandates. Some Medicaid programs and private insurance carriers also may accept or mandate the use of National Codes.

As mentioned in chapter 1, a listing of these codes may be purchased from the U.S. Government Printing Office or any local Medicare carrier (which provides them as a computer-generated list). In addition, several publishing firms offer the National Codes in book format, which can offer better indexing and cross-references. Finally, a file containing the most current versions of the HCPCS Level II codes can be found under the "Utilities/Miscellaneous" heading at the following CMS Web site page: www.cms.gov/providers/pufdownload/.

The HCPCS Level II codes included in this publication are current as of October 1, 2003.

As mentioned in earlier chapters, the third level of HCPCS, Local Codes, was eliminated on December 31, 2003. Local Codes described services and procedures required by individual Medicare carriers or state agencies that process Medicare and/or Medicaid claims.

Structure of the HCPCS Level II Codes

Level II HCPCS consists of five-digit alphanumeric codes beginning with an alphabetic character (A through V, excluding S) followed by four numeric digits.

Example:	A4625	Tracheostomy care kit for new tracheostomy
	D5730	Reline complete maxillary denture (chairside)
	J2360	Injection, orphenadrine, citrate, up to 60 mg
	V2500	Contact lens, PMMA, spherical, per lens

The National Codes are divided into the following sections:

Codes	Section
A codes	Transportation Services, Including Ambulance
	Medical and Surgical Supplies
	Administrative, Miscellaneous, and Investigational
B codes	Enteral and Parenteral Therapy
C codes	Temporary Codes for Use with Outpatient PPS
D codes	Dental Procedures
E codes	Durable Medical Equipment (DME)
G codes	Procedures/Professional Services (Temporary)
H codes	Alcohol and Drug Abuse Treatment Services
J codes	Drugs Administered, Other Than Oral Method,
	Chemotherapy Drugs
K codes	Temporary (assigned to Durable Medical Equipment Regional Carriers [DMERC]).
L codes	Orthotic Procedures, Prosthetic Procedures
M codes	Medical Services
P codes	Pathology and Laboratory Services
Q codes	Miscellaneous Services (Temporary Codes)
R codes	Diagnostic Radiology Services
S codes	Temporary National Codes (Non-Medicare)
T codes	Established for State Medicaid Agencies
V0000–V2999	Vision Services, Hearing Services

General Guidelines for HCPCS Level II Coding

HCPCS rules, like CPT rules, instruct coders to:

1. Never code directly from the index
2. Search for main terms and any applicable subterms
3. Note the reference codes as given in the index
4. Verify the codes by reading the entire description

Table of Drugs

HCPCS National Codes identify drugs administered with the codes beginning with the letter *J*. J codes identify drugs by the generic name, amount, and route of administration. The following abbreviations are used in the route of administration column:

IA:	Intra-arterial
IT:	Intrathecal

IV: Intravenous
IM: Intramuscular
SC: Subcutaneous
INH: Inhalant solution
INJ: Injection, not otherwise specified
VAR: Various routes
ORAL: Oral
OTH: Other routes

Note: VAR is used for drugs that are commonly administered into cavities, joints, tissues, or as topical applications. OTH refers to other administration methods such as suppositories or catheter injections.

Modifiers

Modifiers were developed to serve the same purpose they do in the CPT codebook. They may indicate that a service/procedure was modified in some way, but with no change to its basic definition. HCPCS modifiers can be used to indicate that:

- The service was supervised by an anesthesiologist.

- The service was performed by a specific healthcare professional, such as a clinical psychologist, a nurse practitioner, or a physician assistant.

- The service was provided as part of a specific government program.

- The service was provided to a specific site of the body.

- Equipment was purchased or rented.

- Single or multiple patients were seen during nursing home visits.

Note: In the coding of Medicare claims, the Level II HCPCS modifiers may be used with the National Codes or with codes from the CPT codebook.

The HCPCS modifiers may consist of one or two digits and are appended to the appropriate Level II HCPCS or CPT code. Following is a partial listing of HCPCS modifiers:

–AA   Anesthesia services personally furnished by the anesthesiologist

–AD   Medical supervision by a physician: more than four concurrent anesthesia procedures

–AH   Clinical psychologist

–AJ   Clinical social worker

–AM   Physician, team member service

–AP   Determination of refractive state not performed in the course of diagnostic ophthalmological examination

–AS   Physician assistant, nurse practitioner, or clinical nurse specialist services for assistant at surgery

–AT   Acute treatment (should be used when reporting service 98940, 98941, 98942)

–CC   Procedure code change (use –CC when the procedure code submitted was changed either for administrative reasons or because an incorrect code was initially filed)

–GA   Waiver of liability statement on file

–KP   First drug of a multiple-drug unit dose formulation

–LR   Laboratory round trip

–NU   New equipment

–QS   Monitored anesthesia care service

–TD   RN

The following modifiers are documented in field items 12 and 13 on CMS form 1491 (figure 10.1) and are used to identify ambulance place of origin and destination. The first modifier listed identifies the origin and the second, the destination.

–D   Diagnostic or therapeutic site other than –P or –H when these are used as origin codes

–E   Residential, domiciliary, custodial facility (other than an 1819 [SNF] facility)

-G   Hospital-based dialysis facility (hospital or hospital related)

–H   Hospital

–I   Site of transfer (for example, airport or helicopter pad) between types of ambulance vehicles

–J   Non-hospital-based dialysis facility

–N   Skilled nursing facility (SNF) (1819 facility)

–P   Physician's office (includes HMO nonhospital facility, clinic, and so on)

–R   Residence

–S   Scene of accident or acute event

–X   (Destination code only) Intermediate stop at physician's office on the way to the hospital (includes HMO nonhospital facility, clinic, and so on)

Figure 10.1.   CMS-1491 form

REQUEST FOR MEDICARE PAYMENT – AMBULANCE
MEDICAL INSURANCE BENEFITS - SOCIAL SECURITY ACT
(SEE INSTRUCTIONS ON BACK - TYPE OR PRINT INFORMATION)

FORM APPROVED
OMB NO 0938-0042

PART 1 – PATIENT TO FILL IN ITEMS 1 THROUGH 6 ONLY

No Part B Medicare Benefits may be paid unless a completed application form has been received as required by existing law and regulations (20 C.F.R. 405-251).
NOTICE – Anyone who misrepresents or falsifies essential information requested by this form may upon conviction be subject to fine and imprisonment under Federal law.

COPY FROM YOUR OWN HEALTH INSURANCE CARD *(See Example on Back)*

1 Name of Patient (First Name, Middle Initial, Last Name)

2 Health Insurance Claim No.   ☐ Male   ☐ Female

3 Patient's complete mailing address *(including Apt. No.)* City, State, ZIP code   Telephone Number ( )

4 Was your illness or injury: | Yes | No
a. Connected with your employment? | |
b. Result of an auto accident? | |
c. Result of other type accident? | |

5 If any of your medical expenses will be or could be paid by another insurance organization or government agency, show below
Name and address of organization or agency   Policy or Identification Number

Note: If you **Do Not** want information about this Medicare claim released to the above upon request, check (X) the following block ☐

6 I authorize any holder of medical or other information about me to release to the Social Security Administration and Centers for Medicare & Medicaid Services or its intermediaries or carriers any information needed for this or a related Medicare claim. I permit a copy of this authorization to be used in place of the original, and request payment of medical insurance benefits either to myself or to the party who accepts assignment below.

Signature of patient *(See instructions on reverse where patient is unable to sign)*   Date signed
SIGN HERE ►

PART II – AMBULANCE SUPPLIER TO FILL IN 7 THROUGH 25

7. Date of Service   ☐ Emergency ☐ Admission ☐ Discharge ☐ Outpatient visit   8. Ordered By

9. Description of Illness or Injury *(Describe factors which made ambulance transportation necessary)*

10. Name of Treating Doctor   11. Address and Telephone Number of Doctor

12. Origin of Service   13. Destination of Service

14. Number of Miles   15. Cost per Mile   16. Mileage Charge

22. Describe special service *(no none leave blank)*   17. Base Rate

18. Spec. Serv. Chg. *(Desc. Item 22)*

23. Name and Address of Supplier *(Number and Street, City, State, ZIP Code)*   Supplier Code   19. Total Charges

20. Amount Paid

Telephone Number ( )   21. Any Unpaid Balance Due

24. Assignment of Patient's Bill   ☐ I accept assignment *(See reverse)*   ☐ I do not accept assignment

25. Signature of Supplier   Date Signed

CMS-1491 (SC) (1/89)   Department of Health and Human Services
Centers for Medicare & Medicaid Services

Exercise 10.1 Chapter Review

Use the HCPCS Level II codebook to answer the following questions:

1. What is the code for a gel mattress? _____

2. What code would be assigned if the surgeon provided a surgical tray for a procedure? _____

3. If a patient was given a B12 injection in the office, what HCPCS code would be assigned for the actual substance? _____

4. What Level II code would indicate that the patient received an above-the-knee surgical stocking? _____

5. If a patient was given an IM injection of 400,000 units of penicillin G benzathine, what HCPCS code would be assigned for this drug? _____

Assign CPT code(s) and HCPCS Level II code(s) to the following procedures:

6. The physician implanted the contraceptive capsules in a 23-year-old female patient.

   CPT code for procedure: _____

   HCPCS code for contraceptive supply: _____

7. Patient was treated for a sprained ankle. Strapping was applied, and the patient was given crutches (pair of adjustable, underarm, wood with pads, tips, and handgrips).

   CPT code for procedure: _____

   HCPCS code for crutches: _____

In addition to CPT codes, assign HCPCS Level II modifiers to the following procedures.

8. Patient is seen in the emergency department for a 1.5 cm laceration of the lower right eyelid. Physician performs a simple wound repair. _____

9. Avulsion of nail bed of left great toe and left second toe _____

10. Release of trigger finger, right ring finger _____

Chapter 11

Reimbursement in the Ambulatory Setting

Coding professionals must be aware of, and apply skills to, the reimbursement systems used by government payers and other health plans. Because these systems utilize codes as the basis for calculating payment amounts, complete and accurate coding is a key element in the financial performance of healthcare organizations.

Because CPT coding is the method used to communicate patient services rendered to third-party payers, a number of health plans use it as the basis for determining the reimbursement allowed for each service. Managed care organizations often contract with physicians and facilities for a fee schedule that lists CPT codes with the corresponding amount of payment. When they participate in these plans, physicians and/or healthcare facilities agree that they will not expect or require more than this amount in compensation for the services provided to patients covered by the plan. Paying attention to reporting requirements for codes, as well as to rules on bundling of services, is essential for optimizing reimbursement in a managed care environment or within a government-mandated prospective payment system (PPS). Complete knowledge and application of coding guidelines is the responsibility of all coding professionals. The following sections discuss reimbursement systems currently in use or expected to be in use in the near future.

Reimbursement for Ambulatory Services Provided to Medicare Patients

Reimbursement for ambulatory services provided to Medicare patients changed significantly in 2000 with implementation of ambulatory payment classifications (APCs) in hospital settings.

Hospital Outpatient Prospective Payment System

In 2000, the Centers for Medicare and Medicaid Services (CMS) issued its final rule on an outpatient prospective payment system (OPPS). This payment system is based on groups of services called ambulatory payment classifications (APCs), which divide outpatient services into fixed payment groups. Each APC may include multiple CPT/HCPCS codes but is clinically similar and requires comparable resources. National payment rates were established with an adjustment for geographical factors. Table 11.1 contains an excerpt from the list of ambulatory payment classes.

Table 11.1.   Excerpt from the list of APCs

APC	Group Title	Status Indicator	Relative Weight	Payment Rate
0001	Level I Photochemotherapy	S	0.3779	$19.71
0002	Fine Needle Biopsy/Aspiration	T	0.5911	$30.83
0003	Bone Marrow Biopsy/Aspiration	T	1.2306	$64.18
0004	Level I Needle Biopsy/Aspiration Except Bone Marrow	T	1.7441	$90.96

Key to Status Indicators   S: Payment discount does not apply   T: Multiple-procedure payment discount applies

The following example displays a selection of CPT procedure codes for APC 0004:

APC 0004
    19000   Puncture aspiration of cyst of breast
    19001   each additional cyst

Case Study

Using table 11.1 and APC 0004 as a reference, follow this simulated case study. Assume a patient with Medicare insurance was seen in the outpatient surgery suite for a puncture aspiration of a cyst of the breast. CPT code 19000 was assigned for the procedure. Note that from the reference above, CPT code 19000 is assigned to APC 0004. According to table 11.1, the hospital will be reimbursed $90.96 for providing the services applicable to this procedure. The APC payment will include "packaged" items such as room charges, medical/surgical equipment, surgical dressing supplies, and pharmaceuticals. The APC payment methodology is only applicable to the hospital; the physician will be reimbursed under another method. On table 11.1, note that each APC in the "Status Indicator" column has a status indicator code. Code "T" for APC 0004 designates that the APC payment is subject to payment reduction when multiple procedures are performed during the same visit. A complete reference for status indicators is found in table 11.2.

Not all outpatient facility services are paid under OPPS. Medicare has a variety of payment methods for a range of outpatient services. Every HCPCS code is assigned a status indicator as shown in table 11.2. For example, ambulance services are reimbursed by the ambulance fee schedule.

Drug and Device Pass-through Payments

Under the APC system, additional reimbursement may be made for certain drugs and devices. Certain high-cost drugs are not packaged into the APC groups. Additional information can be found on the CMS's Web site at http://cms.hhs.gov.

Reimbursement for Ambulatory Surgery Centers

An ambulatory surgery center (ASC) is a state-licensed supplier of surgical healthcare services. It is a separate entity from any other facility, such as a hospital. ASCs are reimbursed at fixed prices according to one of nine payment groups. Medicare maintains a list showing the

Table 11.2.   APC status indicators

Indicator	Service	Status
A	Pulmonary rehabilitation clinical trial	Not paid under OPPS
A	Durable medical equipment, prosthetics, and orthotics (DMEPOS) (excluding implanted DME and prosthetics)	DMEPOS fee schedule
A	Physical, occupational, and speech therapy	Physician fee schedule
A	Ambulance	Ambulance fee schedule
A	EPO for end-stage renal disease (ESRD) patients	National rate
A	Clinical diagnostic laboratory services	Laboratory fee schedule
A	Physician services for ESRD patients	Physician fee schedule
A	Screening mammography	Physician fee schedule
C	Inpatient procedures	Not payable under OPPS; admit patient; bill as inpatient
D	Deleted code	Deleted effective beginning of calendar year
E	Noncovered items and services; codes not reportable in hospital outpatient setting	Not paid under Medicare or when performed in a hospital outpatient setting
F	Corneal tissue or orphan drug	Paid at reasonable cost
G	Drug/biological pass-through	Paid under OPPS; separate APC payment includes pass-through amount
H	Device category pass-through	Paid under OPPS; separate cost-based pass-through payment
K	Non-pass-through drug/biological, certain brachytherapy seeds	Paid under OPPS; separate APC
L	Influenza vaccine; Pneumococcal pneumonia vaccine	Paid reasonable cost; not subject to deductible or coinsurance
N	Items and services packaged into APC rate	Paid under OPPS; payment packaged into payment for other services
P	Partial hospitalization	Paid under OPPS, per diem APC
S	Significant procedure, not discounted when multiple	Paid under OPPS; separate APC
T	Significant procedure; multiple-procedure reduction applies	Paid under OPPS; separate APC
V	Visit to clinic or emergency department	Paid under OPPS; separate APC
X	Ancillary service	Paid under OPPS; separate APC

appropriate CPT code for each procedure and the payment group to which each procedure is assigned. The ASC list and its payment methodology apply only to Medicare claims.

The procedures mentioned in the ASC list are classified on the basis of complexity and resource intensity. The fixed rate covers the cost of nursing services, supplies, equipment, and use of the facility. The physician's fee for performing the procedure is reported separately. More information about ASCs can be found at the following CMS Web site page: http://cms.hhs.gov/suppliers/asc/.

Reimbursement for Ambulatory Services Provided to Non-Medicare Patients

Ambulatory services provided to non-Medicare patients may be reimbursed based on ambulatory payment groups (APGs). APGs are used by many third-party payers, including Blue Cross/Blue Shield plans and state Medicaid agencies. They use CPT codes to place procedures in specified groups with an assigned relative weight. Because APG system rules may vary by health plan, no general rules currently apply. Packaging and discounting depend on the plan or version of the APG grouper used.

Reimbursement for Physician Services Provided to Medicare Patients

In 1985, the Health Care Financing Administration (now the CMS) awarded a contract to W. C. Hsiao and his colleagues at the Harvard School of Public Health to develop a resource-based relative value scale (RBRVS). The goals were to:

- Provide a systematic, rational approach for establishing physician fees

- Establish a fair, equitable approach to compensating physicians

- Remove distortions in current fees

- Enhance cost-effective medical care

In September 1990, the *Federal Register* published the initial RBRVS values. With payment reforms implemented through the Omnibus Reconciliation Acts of 1989 and 1990 (OBRA 89 and OBRA 90), the RBRVS fee schedule was phased in over a five-year period. RBRVS was implemented on January 1, 1992, along with the newly developed E/M services codes in the CPT codebook. Before this time, physicians were paid for Medicare claims on the basis of customary, prevailing, and reasonable charges.

The standard relative values per procedure include:

- Physician work: The technical skill, physical and mental effort, risk, and related stress

- Practice expense: The cost of supplies and equipment, wages for employees, and other overhead expenses, such as rent and utilities (There are currently values for facility and nonfacility physician practice expense in the RBRVS system; services rendered at a facility have a lower RVU associated with them than nonfacility or office-based services do.)

- Malpractice expense: The average cost of malpractice insurance

For determining payment, the geographic practice cost index value allows for consideration of the following factors:

- Physician work: Percentage of difference between the physician's work effort in a geographic area and the national average for the work effort

- Practice expense: Relative cost of the mix of goods and services in a geographic area

- Malpractice expense: Relative cost of malpractice insurance in a geographic area

To determine the RBRVS for a specific CPT code, this formula is followed:

$$(RVU_w \times GPCI_w) + (RVU_{pe} \times GPCI_{pe}) + (RVU_m \times GPCI_m) = RBRVS$$
$$\text{Total RBRVs} \times CF = \text{fee}$$

Explanation: RVU = relative value for the procedure; w = physician work; GPCI = geographic practice cost index value; pe = practice expense; m = malpractice expense; CF = conversion factor (variable)

To determine the RVU for each CPT code, reference the Federal Register for the current year. Using CPT code 19000 as an example, the following table represents the RVUs for 2003:

Work	Practice Expense	Malpractice
.84	1.20	.07

Using a simulated geographic practice expense of (.67), malpractice expense of (.15), and work of (.88) with a conversion factor of $63.00, one can calculate the payment for this procedure:

$$(.84 \times .88) + (1.20 \times .67) + (.07 \times .15) \times \$63.00 = \$97.84$$

Medicare Outpatient Code Editor

For the evaluation of procedural and diagnostic data submitted with ambulatory claims, the CMS requires each Medicare carrier and fiscal intermediary (FI) to use the Medicare Outpatient Code Editor (OCE). With implementation of the Medicare OPPS, the OCE has been greatly expanded. The OCE performs four basic functions:

- Editing the data on the claim for accuracy

- Specifying the action the FI should take when specific edits occur

- Assigning APCs to the claim (for hospital outpatient services)

- Determining payment-related conditions that require direct reference to HCPCS codes or modifiers

Routine edits for age and sex inconsistencies are performed on all claim forms. In addition to editing HCPCS codes, the hospital billing form (UB-92) is checked for revenue codes, modifier use, and service units. All claims are subject to the National Correct Coding Initiative

(NCCI) edits. The NCCI edits identify combinations of procedures that are mutually exclusive. (See chapter 4.) If an NCCI edit occurs, the component code is denied payment. When an OCE edit occurs, the FI can take one of six different actions:

- Claim rejections: Can correct and resubmit but cannot appeal

- Claim denial: Cannot resubmit but can appeal

- Claim returned to provider (RTP): Can correct and resubmit

- Claim suspension: Payment delayed for FI determination; may need additional information

- Line item rejection: Claim paid, but line item is rejected; can correct and resubmit but cannot be appealed

- Line item denial: Claim paid, but some line items denied; cannot be resubmitted but can be appealed

Reimbursement and record-processing efficiency are seriously compromised when incomplete or error-ridden claims are returned to the provider for correction and resubmission. Most insurance carriers accept only so-called clean claims, which means they have passed OCE scrutiny.

Quality Controls

Every healthcare facility, clinic, hospital, physician practice, and ambulatory service should implement quality controls to limit coding and claim errors so as to ensure that no fraudulent or abusive coding practices occur. ICD-9-CM and CPT coding books must be updated annually to ensure that the most current and complete codes are available for reporting purposes. Coding professionals should receive routine training to promote skill development and increase knowledge of new payment guidelines and rules. A regular coding review is a key element in any Medicare compliance program.

Updated CPT codebooks are available late in the year (usually November or December), with the implementation date sometime early in the new year (date varies depending on the third-party payer). The updated ICD-9-CM codebooks are available in late summer or early fall, with the changes implemented on October 1 of each year.

Summary

The reimbursement systems used by the government and private health plans use codes as the basis for calculating payment amounts to healthcare providers for services to patients who participate in those plans. Thus, coding professionals must understand the coding guidelines currently in use and how to apply them to ensure that their facilities receive appropriate reimbursement for their services.

Although all the reimbursement systems use codes, the ways in which payments to healthcare facilities are determined can vary greatly. For example, guidelines for reimbursement for ambulatory services provided to Medicare patients changed with implementation of ambulatory payment classifications, which divide outpatient services into fixed payment groups. On the other hand, ambulatory surgery centers receive reimbursement for their services at fixed prices determined by nine different payment groups. Fees for services provided to Medicare patients by physicians are determined by a fee schedule based on the resource-based relative value scale designed to provide a systematic and more equitable approach to compensation.

One tool required by the Centers for Medicare and Medicaid Services for evaluating procedural and diagnostic data submitted with ambulatory claims is the Medicare Outpatient Code Editor. The purpose of the OCE is to weed out incomplete or incorrect claims. Use of the quality controls is another way to reduce coding and claim errors.

With the CMS's emphasis on detecting fraud and abuse, coding professionals are expected to exhibit a high degree of competency in CPT coding. The CMS also is particularly interested in the correct application of coding guidelines.

Exercise 11.1

Review the individual scenario and the coding portion of the CMS-1500 billing form. Determine whether the CPT codes are correct. If incorrect, identify the coding error. The ICD-9-CM codes are provided for reference only.

1. The patient was seen in the emergency department for facial lacerations. Simple repairs of a 3.0 cm laceration on the forehead, a 2.8 cm laceration of the left upper eyelid, and a 1.0 cm laceration of the right upper eyelid were performed.

   Correct?   Yes   No

   Coding error: _____

21. DIAGNOSIS OR NATURE OF ILLNESS OR INJURY, (RELATE ITEMS 1,2,3 OR 4 TO ITEM 24E BY LINE)

1. 873.42   3. L_____

2. 870.0   4. L_____

24. A DATE(S) OF SERVICE From MM DD YY	To MM DD YY	B Place of Service	C Type of Service	D PROCEDURES, SERVICES, OR SUPPLIES (Explain Unusual Circumstances) CPT/HCPCS	MODIFIER	E DIAGNOSIS CODE
1 01-19-03				12013		1
2 01-19-03				12013	LT	2
3 01-19-03				12011	RT	2
4						
5						
6						

(Continued on next page)

Exercise 11.1 (cont.)

2. The patient was seen in the dermatologist's office where seven skin tags were destroyed.

    Correct?   Yes   No

    Coding error: _____

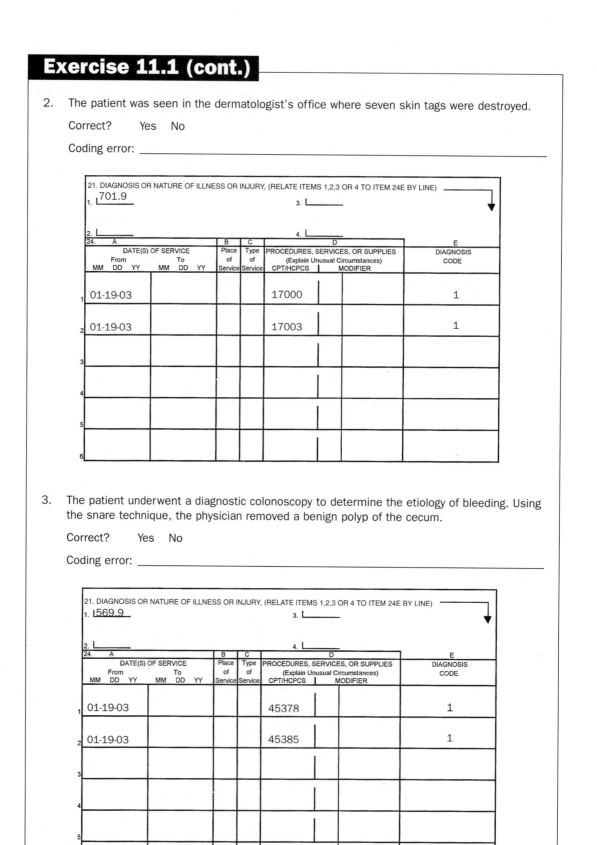

21. DIAGNOSIS OR NATURE OF ILLNESS OR INJURY, (RELATE ITEMS 1,2,3 OR 4 TO ITEM 24E BY LINE)					
1. 701.9		3.			
2.		4.			

24. A DATE(S) OF SERVICE From / To		B Place of Service	C Type of Service	D PROCEDURES, SERVICES, OR SUPPLIES (Explain Unusual Circumstances) CPT/HCPCS / MODIFIER	E DIAGNOSIS CODE
MM DD YY	MM DD YY				
1	01-19-03				17000	1
2	01-19-03				17003	1
3					
4					
5					
6					

3. The patient underwent a diagnostic colonoscopy to determine the etiology of bleeding. Using the snare technique, the physician removed a benign polyp of the cecum.

    Correct?   Yes   No

    Coding error: _____

21. DIAGNOSIS OR NATURE OF ILLNESS OR INJURY, (RELATE ITEMS 1,2,3 OR 4 TO ITEM 24E BY LINE)					
1. 569.9		3.			
2.		4.			

24. A DATE(S) OF SERVICE From / To		B Place of Service	C Type of Service	D PROCEDURES, SERVICES, OR SUPPLIES (Explain Unusual Circumstances) CPT/HCPCS / MODIFIER	E DIAGNOSIS CODE
MM DD YY	MM DD YY				
1	01-19-03				45378	1
2	01-19-03				45385	1
3					
4					
5					
6					

Exercise 11.1 (cont.)

4. The patient's chief complaint is dysuria. The physician performs a cystourethroscopy, ureteroscopy, and fulguration of ureteral polyp.

   Correct?   Yes   No

   Coding error: _____

21. DIAGNOSIS OR NATURE OF ILLNESS OR INJURY, (RELATE ITEMS 1,2,3 OR 4 TO ITEM 24E BY LINE)					
1. 593.89			3.		
2.			4.		

24. A DATE(S) OF SERVICE		B Place of Service	C Type of Service	D PROCEDURES, SERVICES, OR SUPPLIES (Explain Unusual Circumstances)	E DIAGNOSIS CODE
From MM DD YY	To MM DD YY			CPT/HCPCS | MODIFIER	
1 01-19-03				52214	1
2					
3					
4					
5					
6					

5. A gynecologist performs a total abdominal hysterectomy with bilateral salpingo-oophorectomy. The pathological diagnosis is submucous leiomyoma of the uterus.

   Correct?   Yes   No

   Coding error: _____

21. DIAGNOSIS OR NATURE OF ILLNESS OR INJURY, (RELATE ITEMS 1,2,3 OR 4 TO ITEM 24E BY LINE)					
1. 218.0			3.		
2.			4.		

24. A DATE(S) OF SERVICE		B Place of Service	C Type of Service	D PROCEDURES, SERVICES, OR SUPPLIES (Explain Unusual Circumstances)	E DIAGNOSIS CODE
From MM DD YY	To MM DD YY			CPT/HCPCS | MODIFIER	
1 01-19-03				58150	1
2 01-19-03				58720	1
3					
4					
5					
6					

(Continued on next page)

Exercise 11.1 (cont.)

6. A lab performs a hepatic function test, including albumin, total bilirubin, direct bilirubin, Alkaline phosphatase, and SGOT for a patient with jaundice.

   Correct?   Yes   No

   Coding error: _____

21. DIAGNOSIS OR NATURE OF ILLNESS OR INJURY, (RELATE ITEMS 1,2,3 OR 4 TO ITEM 24E BY LINE)

1. 782.4   3. L_____

2. L_____   4. L_____

24. A							B	C	D		E
DATE(S) OF SERVICE							Place of Service	Type of Service	PROCEDURES, SERVICES, OR SUPPLIES (Explain Unusual Circumstances)		DIAGNOSIS CODE
From			To						CPT/HCPCS	MODIFIER	
MM	DD	YY	MM	DD	YY						
1 01-19-03									80076		1
2											
3											
4											
5											
6											

7. A gynecologist performs a hysteroscopy with biopsy of endometrium and dilatation and curettage (D&C).

   Correct?   Yes   No

   Coding error: _____

21. DIAGNOSIS OR NATURE OF ILLNESS OR INJURY, (RELATE ITEMS 1,2,3 OR 4 TO ITEM 24E BY LINE)

1. 626.8   3. L_____

2. L_____   4. L_____

24. A							B	C	D		E
DATE(S) OF SERVICE							Place of Service	Type of Service	PROCEDURES, SERVICES, OR SUPPLIES (Explain Unusual Circumstances)		DIAGNOSIS CODE
From			To						CPT/HCPCS	MODIFIER	
MM	DD	YY	MM	DD	YY						
1 01-09-03									58558		1
2 01-09-03									58120		1
3											
4											
5											
6											

Exercise 11.1 (cont.)

8. A physician performs an excision of breast mass.

   Correct?   Yes   No

   Coding error: _____

21. DIAGNOSIS OR NATURE OF ILLNESS OR INJURY, (RELATE ITEMS 1,2,3 OR 4 TO ITEM 24E BY LINE)					
1. 611.72			3.		
2.			4.		

24. A DATE(S) OF SERVICE			B Place of Service	C Type of Service	D PROCEDURES, SERVICES, OR SUPPLIES (Explain Unusual Circumstances) CPT/HCPCS | MODIFIER	E DIAGNOSIS CODE
From MM DD YY	To MM DD YY					
1 01-09-03					19120	1
2						
3						
4						
5						
6						

9. A surgeon reports that he removed a 1.0 cm lesion of the chin with 0.5 cm margins around the diameter. Pathology report reveals basal cell carcinoma.

   Correct?   Yes   No

   Coding error: _____

21. DIAGNOSIS OR NATURE OF ILLNESS OR INJURY, (RELATE ITEMS 1,2,3 OR 4 TO ITEM 24E BY LINE)					
1. 173.3			3.		
2.			4.		

24. A DATE(S) OF SERVICE			B Place of Service	C Type of Service	D PROCEDURES, SERVICES, OR SUPPLIES (Explain Unusual Circumstances) CPT/HCPCS | MODIFIER	E DIAGNOSIS CODE
From MM DD YY	To MM DD YY					
1 01-09-03					11442	1
2						
3						
4						
5						
6						

(Continued on next page)

Exercise 11.1 (cont.)

10. Surgeon performs a flexible bronchoscopy with cell washings and brushings for a patient with acute bronchitis.

    Correct?   Yes   No

    Coding error: _____

21. DIAGNOSIS OR NATURE OF ILLNESS OR INJURY, (RELATE ITEMS 1,2,3 OR 4 TO ITEM 24E BY LINE)

1. 466.0   3. L_____

2. L_____   4. L_____

24.	DATE(S) OF SERVICE				B Place of Service	C Type of Service	D PROCEDURES, SERVICES, OR SUPPLIES (Explain Unusual Circumstances) CPT/HCPCS | MODIFIER	E DIAGNOSIS CODE
	From MM DD YY		To MM DD YY					
1	01-09-03						31622	1
2	01-09-03						31623	1
3								
4								
5								
6								

References and Bibliography

AdminiStar Federal. 1995. *National Correct Coding Policy Manual for Part B Carriers.* Indianapolis: AdminiStar Federal.

American Health Information Management Association. Accessed online at www.ahima.org.

——. 1990 to present. Coding Notes and Clinical Notes. *Journal of the American Health Information Management Association.* Chicago: American Health Information Management Association.

American Medical Association. Accessed online at www.ama-assn.org.

——. 2003. *Current Procedural Terminology 2004.* Chicago: American Medical Association.

——. 1989 to present. *CPT Assistant.* Chicago: American Medical Association.

Anand, Vijay, and William Panje, eds. 1993. *Practical Endoscopic Sinus Surgery.* New York: McGraw-Hill, Inc.

Baillie, John. 1992. *Gastrointestinal Endoscopy: Basic Principles and Practice.* Boston: Butterworth-Heinemann.

Benjamin, Bruce. 1998. *Endolaryngeal Surgery.* St. Louis: Mosby.

Centers for Medicare and Medicaid Services. Accessed online at www.cms.gov.

Church, James. 1995. *Endoscopy of the Colon, Rectum and Anus.* New York: Igaku-Shoin Medical Publishers, Inc.

Cotton, Peter, and Christopher Williams. 1996. *Practical Gastrointestinal Endoscopy,* 4th ed. Cambridge, Mass.: Blackwell Science, Ltd.

Feinsilver, Stephen A., and Alan Fein, eds. 1995. *Textbook of Bronchoscopy.* Baltimore: Williams & Wilkins.

Fordney, Marilyn Takahashi. 1998. *Insurance Handbook for the Medical Office,* 5th ed. Philadelphia: W. B. Saunders.

Kavic, Michael. 1997. *Laparascopic Hernia Repair.* Amsterdam: Harwood Academic Publishers.

Local Medical Review Policies. Accessed online at www.cms.hhs.gov/mcd.

Medicode. 1998. *CPT Billing Guide: Medicare Billing and Compliance Handbook.* Salt Lake City: Medicode.

Nyhus, Lloyd, and Robert Condon, eds. 1995. *Hernia,* 3rd ed. Philadelphia: Lippincott.

Rakel, Robert. 2000. *Saunders Manual of Medical Practice,* 2nd ed. Philadelphia: W. B. Saunders.

Raskin, Jeffrey, and H. Juergen Nord, eds. 1995. *Colonoscopy: Principles and Techniques.* New York: Igaku-Shoin Medical Publishers, Inc.

Rogers, Vickie L. 2001. *Applying Inpatient Coding Skills under Prospective Payment.* Chicago: American Health Information Management Association.

Schraffenberger, Lou Ann. 2003. *Basic ICD-9-CM Coding.* Chicago: American Health Information Management Association.

Society of Cardiovascular and Interventional Radiology, et al. 1999. *Interventional Radiology Coding User's Guide,* 5th ed. Fairfax, Va.: Society of Cardiovascular and Interventional Radiology, American College of Radiology, Radiology Business Management Association, American Health Radiology Administrators.

St. Anthony Publishing. 2002. *St. Anthony's Modifiers Made Easy.* Alexandria, Va.: St. Anthony Publishing.

——. 2002. *HCPCS Level II Code Book.* 2003 ed. Alexandria, VA.: St. Anthony Publishing.

——. 1998. *St. Anthony's Guide to APC and ASC Groups: A Clinical Coding and Reimbursement Reference for Hospitals and ASCs.* Alexandria, Va.: St. Anthony Publishing.

——. 1998a. *St. Anthony's Guide to Evaluation and Management Coding and Documentation,* 3rd ed. Alexandria, Va.: St. Anthony Publishing.

——. 1998b. *St. Anthony's Medicare Billing Compliance Guide.* Alexandria, Va.: St. Anthony Publishing.

Stradling, Peter. 1986. *Diagnostic Bronchoscopy: A Teaching Manual.* New York: Churchill Livingstone.

Web Resources

Aetna IntelliHealth

http://www.intelihealth.com

Aetna IntelliHealth is a partnership between Harvard Medical School and Aetna. It includes search tests/procedures, a medical dictionary, lists of drugs, and so on. It also is simple to navigate.

American Academy of Dermatology

http://www.aad.org

Click "Public Resources" for links to sites about diseases of skin.

American Academy of Facial Plastic and Reconstructive Surgery

http://www.facial-plastic-surgery.org

Click "Procedures" for links. A glossary and a page featuring common surgeries are included.

American Academy of Family Physicians

http://www.aafp.org

This Web resource includes articles on documentation guidelines.

American Academy of Orthopaedic Surgeons

http://www.aaos.org

Click on "Patient Information" to find fact sheets on many diseases and procedures.

American College of Gastroenterology

http://www.acg.gi.org

Click on "Patient Information" for links of interest.

American College of Obstetricians and Gynecologists

http://www.acog.org

This site has information on patient education and provides links to coding/nomenclature.

American Health Information Management Association

http://www.ahima.org

This site provides coding products and an educational forum for coders called Communities of Practice (members only).

American Medical Association

http://www.ama-assn.org

This site contains information about coding products, *CPT Assistant,* and CPT updates and errata.

American Society of Plastic Surgery

http://www.plasticsurgery.org

Click link to "Learn about Procedures."

Anatomy

http://www.innerbody.com

The site contains diagrams and definitions.

http://www.medtropolis.com

This site uses audio and visual effects. Visit the "Virtual Body."

Cancer

http://www.cancer.gov

Click on "Cancer Information" and then choose from the various types.

Cardiology

http://www.hgcardio.com

This site offers diagrams and descriptions of cardiac procedures.

Centers for Medicare and Medicaid Services (CMS)

http://cms.hhs.gov

http://www.cms.hhs.gov/paymentsystems/

This site discusses Medicare payment systems and coding files.

http://www.cms.hhs.gov/providers/hopps/

This site offers an explanation of the hospital outpatient prospective payment system.

http://cms.gov/providers/pufdownload/

Link to this page for downloads pertaining to Medicare payment systems.

http://cms.hhs.gov/medlearn/

This site provides reference guides and training modules.

http://cms.hhs.gov/manuals/transmittals/comm_date_dsc.asp

Link to this site for Medicare transmittals.

http://cms.hhs.gov/manuals/memos/comm_date_dsc.asp

Link to this site for Medicare program memorandums.

http://cms.hhs.gov/medlearn/emdoc.asp

This site discusses 1995 and 1997 E/M documentation guidelines.

Discovery Health

http://www.discoveryhealth.com

This site has numerous links and is very searchable.

Encyclopedia of Medicine

http://www.findarticles.com

This site offers a variety of links. Click "Health."

Gastroenterology

http://www.gastromd.com

This site has a patient education focus.

Health Central

http://www.healthcentral.com

Health Central is a consumer-friendly site and is easy to navigate. Choose a topic under "Topics Center."

Healthfinder

http://www.healthfinder.gov

This consumer-friendly site offers a free guide for consumer health and human services.

Heart Center

http://www.heartcenteronline.com

Click "Patients" on this consumer-friendly site. Cardiac procedures are described in plain language, and quizzes are provided.

How Stuff Works

http://www.howstuffworks.com

Click "Health Stuff."

Kidney

http://www.thekidney.com

This is an education site with links.

Knee

http://www.knee1.com

This site provides descriptions of various knee surgeries.

MayoClinic

http://www.mayoclinic.com

This site provides consumer-oriented information about illnesses.

Medicare's National CCI Edits

http://cms.hhs.gov/medlearn/ncci.asp

This site provides information about Medicare's National Correct Coding Initiative edits, questions and answers, and links to applicable program memoranda.

MedLearn

http://www.medlearn.com

MedLearn sells coding products, including a guide for interventional radiology coding.

MEDLINEplus

http://www.medlineplus.gov

Operated by the U.S. National Library of Medicine, MEDLINEplus includes encyclopedic background on all diseases, definitions of medical terms, and referrals to other organizations that deal with specific illnesses.

National Women's Health Information Center

http://www.4women.org

This site is sponsored by the U.S. Department of Health and Human Services. Focus is on women's health issues and offers links to resources such as dictionaries and journals.

Skin Lesions Morphology

http://www.skincancer.dermis.net/content

Different types of skin cancer and treatments are discussed on this site.

Society of Interventional Radiology

http://www.sirweb.org

The society sells coding products (for example, *Interventional Radiology Coding Users' Guide*).

Stanford Health Library

http://healthlibrary.stanford.edu/resources/internet/bodysys.html

This site offers links to many diseases/disorders and treatment.

Surgical Procedures

http://www.mic.ki.se/Diseases/e4.html

This site offers numerous links to surgical procedures.

WebMD

http://www.webmd.com

WebMD provides basic facts on any condition. The site guides you from general topics to more specific facts.

Appendix A

Evaluation and Management Documentation Guidelines

General Multisystem Examinations

Note: The following information was excerpted from the 1997 document developed by the CMS and the AMA. A complete copy of this document and up-to-date information on the status of revised guidelines can be found on the CMS Web site at www.cms.gov/medlearn/emdoc.asp.

To qualify for a given level of multisystem examination, the following content and documentation requirements should be met:

- A problem-focused examination should include performance and documentation of one to five elements identified by a bullet (•) in one or more organ system(s) or body area(s).

- An expanded problem-focused examination should include performance and documentation of at least six elements identified by a bullet (•) in one or more organ system(s) or body area(s).

- A detailed examination should include at least six organ systems or body areas. For each system/area selected, performance and documentation of at least two elements identified by a bullet (•) are expected. Alternatively, a detailed examination may include performance and documentation of at least twelve elements identified by a bullet (•) in two or more organ systems or body areas.

- A comprehensive examination should include at least nine organ systems or body areas. For each system/area selected, all elements of the examination identified by a bullet (•) should be performed, unless specific directions limit the content of the examination. For each area/system, documentation of at least two elements identified by a bullet is expected.

Examination Documentation Guidelines

- Specific abnormal and relevant negative findings of the examination of the affected or symptomatic body area(s) or organ system(s) should be documented. A notation of "abnormal" without elaboration is insufficient.

- Abnormal or unexpected findings of the examination of any asymptomatic body area(s) or organ system(s) should be described.

- A brief statement or notation indicating "negative" or "normal" is sufficient to document normal findings related to unaffected area(s) or asymptomatic organ system(s).

Content and Documentation Requirements

General Multisystem Examination

System/Body Area	Elements of Examination
Constitutional	• Measurement of **any three of the following seven vital signs:** (1) sitting or standing blood pressure; (2) supine blood pressure; (3) pulse rate and regularity; (4) respiration; (5) temperature; (6) height; and (7) weight (may be measured and recorded by ancillary staff) • General appearance of patient (e.g., development, nutrition, body habitus, deformities, attention to grooming)
Eyes	• Inspection of conjunctivae and lids • Examination of pupils and irises (e.g., reaction to light and accommodation, size, and symmetry) • Ophthalmoscopic examination of optic discs (e.g., size, C/D ratio, appearance) and posterior segments (e.g., vessel changes, exudates, hemorrhages)
Ears, Nose, Mouth, and Throat	• External inspection of ears and nose (e.g., overall appearance, scars, lesions, masses) • Otoscopic examination of external auditory canals and tympanic membranes • Assessment of hearing (e.g., whispered voice, finger rub, tuning fork) • Inspection of nasal mucosa, septum, and turbinates • Inspection of lips, teeth, and gums • Examination of oropharynx: oral mucosa, salivary glands, hard and soft palates, tongue, tonsils, and posterior pharynx
Neck	• Examination of neck (e.g., masses, overall appearance, symmetry, tracheal position, crepitus) • Examination of thyroid (e.g., enlargement, tenderness, mass)
Respiratory	• Assessment of respiratory effort (e.g., intercostal retractions, use of accessory muscles, diaphragmatic movement) • Percussion of chest (e.g., dullness, flatness, hyperresonance) • Palpation of chest (e.g., tactile fremitus) • Auscultation of lungs (e.g., breath sounds, adventitious sounds, rubs)
Cardiovascular	• Palpation of heart (e.g., location, size, thrills) • Auscultation of heart with notation of abnormal sounds and murmurs Examination of: • Carotid arteries (e.g., pulse amplitude, bruits) • Abdominal aorta (e.g., size, bruits) • Femoral arteries (e.g., pulse amplitude, bruits) • Pedal pulses (e.g., pulse amplitude) • Extremities for edema and/or varicosities
Chest (Breasts)	• Inspection of breasts (e.g., symmetry, nipple discharge) • Palpation of breasts and axillae (e.g., masses or lumps, tenderness)

System/Body Area	Elements of Examination
Gastrointestinal (Abdomen)	• Examination of abdomen with notation of presence of masses or tenderness • Examination of liver and spleen • Examination for presence or absence of hernia • Examination of anus, perineum, and rectum, including sphincter tone, presence of hemorrhoids, rectal masses • Obtain stool sample for occult blood test when indicated
Genitourinary	**Male:** • Examination of the scrotal contents (e.g., hydrocele, spermatocele, tenderness of cord, testicular mass) • Examination of the penis • Digital rectal examination of prostate gland (e.g., size, symmetry, nodularity, tenderness) **Female:** Pelvic examination (with or without specimen collection for smears and cultures), including: • Examination of the external genitalia (e.g., general appearance, hair distribution, lesions) and vagina (e.g., general appearance, estrogen effect, discharge, lesions, pelvic support, cystocele, rectocele) • Examination of urethra (e.g., masses, tenderness, scarring) • Examination of bladder (e.g., fullness, masses, tenderness) • Cervix (e.g., general appearance, lesions, discharge) • Uterus (e.g., size, contour, position, mobility, tenderness, consistency, descent, or support) • Adnexa/parametria (e.g., masses, tenderness, organomegaly, nodularity)
Lymphatic	Palpitation of lymph nodes in two or more areas: • Neck • Axillae • Groin • Other
Musculoskeletal	• Examination of gait and station • Inspection and/or palpation of digits and nails (e.g., clubbing, cyanosis, inflammatory conditions, petechiae, ischemia, infections, nodes) Examination of joints, bones, and muscles of **one or more of the following six areas:** (1) head and neck; (2) spine, ribs, and pelvis; (3) right upper extremity; (4) left upper extremity; (5) right lower extremity; and (6) left lower extremity. The examination of a given area includes: • Inspection and/or palpation with notation of presence of any misalignment, asymmetry, crepitation, defects, tenderness, masses, or effusions • Assessment of range of motion with notation of any pain, crepitation, or contracture • Assessment of stability with notation of any dislocation (luxation), subluxation, or laxity • Assessment of muscle strength and tone (e.g., flaccid, cog wheel, spastic) with notation of any atrophy or abnormal movements
Skin	• Inspection of skin and subcutaneous tissue (e.g., rashes, lesions, ulcers) • Palpation of skin and subcutaneous tissue (e.g., induration, subcutaneous nodules, tightening)

(Continued on next page)

System/Body Area	Elements of Examination
Neurologic	• Test cranial nerves with notation of any deficits • Examination of deep tendon reflexes with notation of pathological reflexes (e.g., Babinski) • Examination of sensation (e.g., touch, pin, vibration, proprioception)
Psychiatric	• Description of patient's judgment and insight Brief assessment of mental status, including: • Orientation to time, place, and person • Recent and remote memory • Mood and affect (e.g., depression, anxiety, agitation)

Content and Documentation Requirements

Level of Exam	Perform and Document:
Problem focused	**One to five** elements identified by a bullet
Expanded problem focused	**At least six** elements identified by a bullet
Detailed	**At least two** elements identified by a bullet **from each of six areas/ systems** *or* **at least twelve** elements identified by a bullet **in two or more areas/systems**
Comprehensive	Perform **all elements** identified by a bullet in **at least nine** organ systems or body areas and document **at least two** elements identified by a bullet **from each of nine areas/systems**

Appendix B

Additional Practice Exercises

The following surgical cases were performed in an ambulatory setting of Central Hospital. Determine the appropriate CPT code(s) for each case so that the hospital can receive the correct reimbursement. It is important to practice using the CPT index and to note how, in many instances, the codes may be found using more than one index entry. The appropriate modifiers should be assigned, when applicable, and the index entry(s) used to locate the code(s) should be noted.

If you wish to practice assigning codes by body system, the following reference will help.

Appendix B Practice Exercises
Indexed by Surgical Section

Integumentary System
Case #17
Case #25
Case #26
Case #27
Case #33
Case #39

Musculoskeletal System
Case # 4
Case #10
Case #12
Case #20

Respiratory System
Case # 6
Case #13 (also Digestive System)
Case # 18

Cardiovascular System
Case #15
Case #31

Hemic and Lymphatic Systems
Case # 38

Digestive System
Case # 1
Case # 3
Case #11
Case #13 (also Respiratory System)
Case #14
Case #19
Case #21
Case #22
Case #23
Case #24
Case #30
Case #32

Urinary System
Case # 2
Case # 9

Male/Female Genital System
Case # 7
Case # 8
Case #16
Case # 28
Case # 29
Case # 36

Nervous System
Case #35
Case #37

Eye and Ocular Adnexa
Case #5
Case #34
Case #40

Surgical Case #1

Operative Report

Procedure: Tonsillectomy

Diagnosis: Recurrent tonsillitis

Indications: This 10-year-old patient was found to have recurrent tonsillitis, and a tonsillectomy was planned.

Technique: The patient was placed in the supine position, and general endotracheal anesthesia was begun. The nasopharynx was inspected, revealing only a very small amount of adenoid, which was not removed. The tonsils were noted to be very large and obstructive, and were removed by dissection and snare technique. The bleeders were electrocoagulated. The inferior cuff was suture ligated with 2-0 plain catgut. The patient tolerated the procedure well and was brought to the recovery room in satisfactory condition.

1. Code(s): _____

   What index entries were used to find the code(s)?

   _____

   _____

Surgical Case #2

Operative Report

Procedure: Extracorporeal shock wave lithotripsy of right kidney stone

Diagnosis: Right kidney stone

Anesthesia: IV sedation

Technique: Under IV sedation, the patient was placed in the supine position. The stone in the upper right kidney was positioned at F2. The extracorporeal lithotripsy was started at 19 KV, which subsequently was increased to a maximum of 26 KV at 1,600 shocks. The stone was revisualized, and repositioning was done considering the transverse colon passing right anterior to the stone. Because the stone appeared to be in the same place after the repositioning, shocks were delivered. Apparent adequate fragmentation was obtained after a total of 2,400 shocks had been administered. The patient tolerated the procedure quite well.

1. Code(s): _____

   What index entries were used to find the code(s)?

   _____

   _____

Surgical Case #3

Operative Report

Procedure: Esophagogastroduodenoscopy with biopsy

Diagnosis: Gastritis and duodenitis

Technique: The patient was premedicated and brought to the endoscopy suite where his throat was anesthetized with Cetacaine spray. He then was placed in the left lateral position and given 2 mg Versed, IV.

The patient was premedicated and brought to the endoscopy suite where his throat was anesthetized with Cetacaine spray. He then was placed in the left lateral position and given 2 mg Versed, IV.

An Olympus gastroscope was advanced into the esophagus, which was well visualized with no significant segmental spasms. Subsequently, the scope was advanced into the distal esophagus, which was essentially normal. Then the scope was advanced into the stomach, which showed evidence of erythema and gastritis. The pylorus was intubated and the duodenal bulb visualized. The duodenal bulb showed severe erythema, suggestive of duodenitis. Multiple biopsies were taken. The scope was withdrawn, and the patient tolerated the procedure well.

1.   Code(s): _____

What index entries were used to find the code(s)?

_____

_____

Surgical Case #4

Emergency Department Record

Chief Complaint:	Right shoulder dislocation
History of Present Illness:	The patient is a 53-year-old male who has dislocated his right shoulder three previous episodes. Today, he was kayaking and dislocated his shoulder while paddling.
Past Medical History:	Previous right shoulder dislocation
Medications:	Vitamins
Allergies:	Sulfa
Physical Examination:	Alert, male in no acute distress
Right Upper Extremity:	He has obvious deformity with loss of the right shoulder prominence with a palpable anterior dislocation of the humeral head. He has good distal pulses with the remainder of his arm being nontender.
Emergency Department Course:	X ray of his right shoulder shows an anterior dislocation.
Procedure:	Reduction of the shoulder dislocation. The patient was placed on a monitor with continuous pulse oximetry. He was given Demerol and Phenergan IV for pain control. In-line traction and reduction was accomplished after three attempts. Reduction films showed good position of the shoulder. He had good distal neurovascular status after reduction. He tolerated the procedure well.
Diagnosis:	Anterior dislocation, right shoulder
Disposition and Plan:	Sling and swathe for two to three days. Vicodin #30. Follow up with Dr. Smith in one to two days or call for an orthopedic referral. The patient states he has been avoiding any potential surgery at this point and would prefer to avoid it. I explained to him that he should follow up with Dr. Smith or an orthopedist. He should not use the shoulder in the next several days until reevaluation.

1.   Code(s): _____

What index entries were used to find the code(s)?

_____

_____

Surgical Case #5

Operative Report

Procedure: Extracapsular cataract extraction with intraocular lens implantation, right eye

Diagnosis: Cataract of the right eye

Technique: The patient was given a retrobulbar injection of 2.5 to 3.0 cc of a mixture of equal parts of 2% lidocaine with epinephrine and 0.75% Marcaine with Wydase. The area about the right eye was infiltrated with an additional 6 to 7 cc of this mixture in a modified Van Lint technique. A self-maintaining pressure device was applied to the eye, and a short time later, the patient was taken to the OR.

The patient was properly positioned on the operating table, and the area around the right eye was prepped and draped in the usual fashion. A self-retaining eyelid speculum was positioned and 4-0 silk suture passed through the tendon of the superior rectus muscle, thereby deviating the eye inferiorly. A 160∫ fornix-based conjunctival flap was created followed by a 150∫ corneoscleral groove with a #64 Beaver blade. Hemostasis was maintained throughout with gentle cautery. A 6-0 silk suture was introduced to cross this groove at the 12 o'clock position and looped out of the operative field. The anterior chamber was then entered superiorly temporally, and after injecting Occucoat, an anterior capsulotomy was performed without difficulty. The nucleus was easily brought forward into the anterior chamber. The corneoscleral section was opened with scissors to the left and the nucleus delivered with irrigation and gentle lens loop manipulation. Interrupted 10-0 nylon sutures were placed at both the nasal and lateral extent of the incision. A manual irrigating aspirating setup then was used to remove remaining cortical material from both the anterior and posterior chambers.

At this point, a modified C-loop posterior chamber lens was removed from its package and irrigated and inspected. It then was positioned into the inferior capsular bag without difficulty, and the superior haptic was placed behind the iris at the 12 o'clock location. The lens was rotated to a horizontal orientation in an attempt to better enhance capsular fixation. Miochol was used to constrict the pupil, and a peripheral iridectomy was performed in the superior nasal quadrant. In addition, three or four interrupted 10-0 nylon sutures were used to close the corneal scleral section. The silk sutures were removed, and the conjunctiva advanced back into its normal location and was secured with cautery burns at the 3 and 9 o'clock positions. Approximately 20 to 30 mg of both Gentamicin and Kenalog were injected into the inferior cul-de-sac in a subconjunctival and sub-Tenon fashion. After instillation of 2% Pilocarpine and Maxitrol ophthalmic solution, the eyelid speculum was removed and the eye dressed in a sterile fashion. The patient was discharged to the recovery room in good condition.

1. Code(s): _____

   What index entries were used to find the code(s)?

   _____

   _____

Surgical Case #6

Operative Report

Procedure: Fiberoptic bronchoscopy

Diagnosis: Hemoptysis with easily bruisable mucosa and bronchiectasis

Technique: The patient was brought to the endoscopy suite and placed on a stretcher. Oxygen was given via nasal cannula at three liters per minute. Local anesthetic lidocaine was given to anesthetize the upper airway. Because the nostrils had considerable blockage secondary to trauma, the oral route was used for the bronchoscopy. Following placement of a bite block and application of Cetacaine to the posterior pharynx, the fiberoptic bronchoscope was placed without difficulty into the upper airway.

     The epiglottis appeared somewhat prominent, but normal. In addition, the vocal cords appeared normal. The bronchoscope was passed easily through the cords into the trachea, which also appeared normal, although somewhat easily bruisable. The carina appeared normal. The right side was entered first. The right upper lobe and its subsegments were seen very clearly, and there appeared to be bronchiectasis. The 6 mm bronchoscope would go very easily into the subsegments. No mass lesions were seen. The bronchus intermedius, right middle lobe, lower lobe, and its subsegments also were entered; and, again, bronchiectasis was noted. There appeared to be no abnormal mucosal lesions and no abnormal secretions; however, the bronchial tree was easily bruisable. The bronchoscope then was withdrawn to the carina and the left side entered.

     The left main bronchus, upper lobe, lower lobe, and its subsegments were seen. There appeared to be an extrinsic compression of a subsegment of the left lower lobe; however, no mucosal lesions were seen and this area appeared pulsatile, which suggested extrinsic compression from the descending aorta. Once again, easy bruisability of the mucosa was noted. The bronchoscope was withdrawn. There were no apparent complications.

1. Code(s): _____

     What index entries were used to find the code(s)?

     _____

     _____

Surgical Case #7

Operative Report

Procedure: Colposcopy

Diagnosis: Class II Pap; cervicitis

History of Present Illness: The patient is a 27-year-old female who had previously undergone a Pap smear showing class II Pap. She is admitted today for a colposcopy.

Technique: The patient was placed in the lithotomy position. Her vagina and cervix were examined and a speculum inserted; dying was done with acetic acid followed by gram iodine and methylene blue. Cervical biopsies were performed at indicated areas, with Monsel solution applied for cautery. There were no complications, and the patient tolerated the procedure well.

Plan: The patient is to call the office within one week for her biopsy report.

1. Code(s): _____

     What index entries were used to find the code(s)?

     _____

     _____

Surgical Case #8

Operative Report

Procedure: Laparoscopic tubal ligation with application of Falope rings; dilatation and curettage (D&C) and removal of intrauterine device

Diagnosis: Multiparity, voluntary sterilization; removal of retained intrauterine device

Anesthesia: General

Technique: Placed in the supine lithotomy position, the patient was prepped and draped in the usual manner for a laparoscopic and D&C procedure. A D&C was performed to gain access to a deeply embedded IUD. This was curetted up and eventually removed with some difficulty. Both the IUD and the curetted endometrial tissue were submitted to pathology.

A two-puncture laparoscopy was performed in the usual manner of insufflation through a Veress needle inserted infraumbilically. Through a first puncture, a trocar insertion infraumbilically was followed by the laparoscope and a second trocar insertion suprapubically in the midline was followed by, first, a probe and, then, a Falope ring applicator. Both tubes were ligated in their midsegment. On the right side, two rings were applied because of the round position of the Falope ring director. The left tube was ligated singly. The procedure was performed with no complications. After the operation, the trocar sites were closed with subcuticular sutures of 2-0 Vicryl and the patient was transferred to the recovery room in satisfactory condition.

1. Code(s): _____

What index entries were used to find the code(s)?

_____

_____

Surgical Case #9

Operative Report

Procedure: Transurethral resection of the prostate

Diagnosis: Bladder outlet obstruction; benign prostatic hypertrophy

Anesthesia: General

Technique: The patient was placed under general anesthesia and in the dorsolithotomy position. Two grams of Claforan parenterally were used. The Iglesias resectoscope was introduced through the obturator, and this was followed by the working element connected to the Olympus video camera. The obstructive prostatic tissue was appreciated mainly anteriorly and to the left lateral lobe. Resection was started at the bladder neck down to the level of the verumontanum and toward the capsule, as necessary, in all directions. Bleeders were fulgurated, with satisfactory patency with coagulation having been secured. Dissected tissues were removed using the Ellik evacuator. A size 24 three-way Foley catheter was retained with a 30 cc balloon inflation. Minimal blood loss was appreciated. The patient tolerated the procedure well and was transferred to the recovery room in stable condition.

1. Code(s): _____

What index entries were used to find the code(s)?

_____

_____

Surgical Case #10

Operative Report

Procedure: Open reduction of left zygomatic arch fracture

Diagnosis: Left zygomatic arch fracture

Anesthesia: General

Technique: The patient was placed on the operating table in the supine position and administered general endotracheal anesthesia. He was prepped and draped in the usual fashion. A small incision was made in the temporal scalp area and carried down through the superficial temporal fascia until the deep temporal fascia was identified. This was incised, and an elevator was passed beneath the deep fascia until it was below the zygomatic arch. The arch was reduced manually and elevated back into its anatomical position noted by palpation. The wound was irrigated, and hemostasis was obtained with cautery.

The superficial temporal fascia was reapproximated using interrupted 4-0 Monocryl sutures. The skin was closed with interrupted 4-0 nylon sutures, and a sterile dressing was applied along with a metal cup to protect the zygomatic arch. The patient was extubated and transferred to the recovery room in stable condition.

1. Code(s): _____

   What index entries were used to find the code(s)?

   _____

   _____

Surgical Case #11

Operative Report

Procedure: Lateral lobe parotidectomy with facial nerve preservation

Diagnosis: Warthin's tumor of the parotid gland

Anesthesia: General

Findings: The patient has a long history of a right parotid mass that apparently has grown and fluctuated in size. An office examination revealed the nose, nasopharynx, larynx, and neck to be normal. She is status post thyroidectomy with a well-healed thyroidectomy incision. The parotid mass is overlying the mandible approximately 2 to $2^1/_2 \times 3$ cm in diameter, and there is a possibility of another mass or lymphadenopathy in the lower aspect of the parotid gland. Facial nerve functions are normal.

Technique: Placed in the supine position, the patient was given general endotracheal anesthesia. Her neck was positioned, and the whole right side of her face and neck was prepped and draped in the usual manner.

The modified Blair type of incision was made in the preauricular area vertically, and then curved behind and below the earlobe and extended as a curved submandibular incision. The bleeders were electrocoagulated and the dissection deepened in the lower part to the platysma. The dissection and front of the tragus were done by both sharp and blunt dissection until the external ear canal cartilage was identified and palpated. The dissection was pushed through this and inferiorly, identifying the anterior border of the sternocleidomastoid muscle, mastoid process, and, subsequently, the main trunk of the facial nerve, which was preserved from trauma. The major lower and inferior subdivisions were followed, identifying the cervical, mandibular, and buccal branches, as well as the upper division.

The cystic mass was bluish in color. The lateral lobe of the parotid gland was removed and given for frozen section, and this was reported as a benign cystic mass. No lobe was encountered with suspicion of malignancy, and no other masses were in the deep lobe. Hemostasis was obtained by electrocautery on the superficial oozing points and ligature of the small vessels. The wound was washed, and afterward the main trunk and subdivisions of the facial nerve again were identified and verified to be intact.

The lower Hemovac drain was placed. The wound was closed with 3-0 chromic catgut interrupted involving both the subcutaneous tissue and the platysma muscle with continuous and interrupted mattress sutures using 5-0 silk. The wound was cleaned, Bacitracin ointment was applied, and a dry sterile occlusive dressing was placed over it. After the procedure was terminated, the patient was extubated and brought to the recovery room in good condition.

1. Code(s): _____

    What index entries were used to find the code(s)?

    _____

    _____

Surgical Case #12

Operative Report

Procedure: Arthroscopic partial medial meniscectomy

Diagnosis: Torn left medial meniscus

Anesthesia: General

Technique: After induction with general anesthesia, a standard three-portal approach of the knee was evaluated. Mild synovitic changes were noted in the suprapatellar pouch. No chondromalacia changes were noted in all three compartments. The anterior cruciate ligament was intact, as was the lateral meniscus; and there were only slight synovitic changes in the anterior compartment. The anterior portion of the medial meniscus had a flap tear, which was debrided with an aggressive resector.

After all instruments were withdrawn, 4-0 nylon horizontal mattress stitches were used to close the wound and pressure dressings were applied. The patient was awakened and removed to the recovery room in good condition.

1.   Code(s): _____

What index entries were used to find the code(s)?

_____

_____

Surgical Case #13

Operative Report

Preoperative Diagnosis: Bilateral vocal cord neoplasm

Postoperative Diagnosis: The same with right postprocedural pharyngeal bleed

Procedures: 1.   Laryngoscopy with bilateral vocal cord stripping with   use of operating microscope
    2.   Control of oral pharyngeal hemorrhage, less than 20 cc

Indications for Surgery: This 65-year-old female presented to the ENT Service with a two-year history of hoarseness. Upon evaluation, she was noted to have bilateral vocal cord neoplasms. The patient also has a history of smoking. A decision for the above-stated procedure was made for definitive diagnosis.

Procedure: The patient was brought to the Operating Suite, given a general anesthetic, and properly prepped and draped. It was noted that her teeth were not in good repair and that the lateral incisor was already loose on the right side. However, teeth guards were put into place. The Jako laryngoscope was carefully introduced into the oral cavity with attention not to injure the lips, gums, or teeth. The base of the tongue, vallecula, epiglottis, paraform sinuses, and false and true vocal cords were all visualized. The laryngoscope was fixed into place with microsuspension. The vocal cords were well visualized. There were polypoid-type neoplasms bilaterally. These were grasped anteriorly, stripped to the posterior bilaterally, and sent to Pathology. Hemostasis was obtained with an adrenaline cotton ball and silver nitrate. After good hemostasis was obtained, the scope was removed. However, upon removal, she was noted to have a pooling of blood in the posterior pharynx and that the blood was coming from the right tonsillar fossa. Apparently, this had been abraded with the laryngoscope upon insertion. Therefore, a self-retaining mouth gag was carefully introduced into the oral cavity. The patient did not have good extension of the mandible, but after this was visualized, the right pharyngeal wall was noted to have oozing and some irritation. This was controlled with the help of silver nitrate and suction cautery. After good hemostasis was obtained, the oral cavity was irrigated with a saline solution. When the patient exhibited good hemostasis, she was taken out of anesthetic and transferred to the Recovery Room in stable condition.

1.   Code(s): _____

What index entries were used to find the code(s)?

_____

_____

Surgical Case #14

Operative Report

Procedure: Percutaneous endoscopic gastrostomy (PEG) tube placement

Diagnosis: Old cerebrovascular accident with inanition and need for supplemental nutritional support with no contraindication to enteral access

Technique: After anesthetization of the gag reflex, the gastroscope was introduced. There was no abnormality of the esophagus, stomach, pylorus, or duodenum. The abdomen had been prepped and draped as a sterile field. The light was found to transilluminate in the left upper quadrant. The skin was anesthetized with 1% Xylocaine. A blunt needle was used to access the stomach percutaneously and a guide wire inserted. The guide wire was grasped with a snare and brought through the mouth, along with the gastroscope. The feeding tube was threaded over the guide wire and brought through the abdominal wall with a small stab incision made along the guide wire. The gastroscope was reinserted and the PEG tube photo documented. There was no evidence of bleeding or undue tension as a result of tube placement. Air was suctioned from the stomach, and the gastroscope was removed with no other findings. The Silastic fastener was placed on the PEG tube near the skin entrance. The PEG tube then was connected to dependent drainage. The patient tolerated the procedure well and was taken to the recovery area with stable vital signs.

1. Code(s): _____

    What index entries were used to find the code(s)?

    _____

    _____

Surgical Case #15

Operative Report

Procedure: Right carotid thromboendarterectomy and vein patch angioplasty

Diagnosis: Right carotid artery stenosis with hemorrhagic plaque

Anesthesia: General

Technique: Under general anesthesia, the right side of the patient's neck was prepped and draped in a sterile fashion. An incision was made along the sternocleidomastoid muscle, and a sharp dissection was carried down to expose the common internal and external carotid arteries. Care was taken to avoid injury to the hypoglossal, vagus, and ansa cervicalis nerves. The vessels were inserted with elastic tapes. The patient was heparinized, and an arteriotomy was made. A very high-grade stenosis estimated at 1.5 mm opening was present at the origin of the internal carotid artery, and there was evidence of significant hemorrhage and degeneration in the plaque. A shunt was placed for cerebral perfusion, and then the endarterectomy was done in the usual fashion. The vessel was picked free of any debris or other plaque and then closed with a patch angioplasty using saphenous vein from the left groin. This was sutured in place with 6-0 Prolene. Flow was first directed into the external carotid to allow any possible air or debris to escape and then restored to the internal carotid. The wound was packed open until the end of the procedure and after the heparin was reversed. Then the wound was closed with 3-0 Vicryl in the subcutaneous and platysma muscle and 4-0 Vicryl for a subcuticular skin closure. The patient left the operating room in satisfactory condition.

1. Code(s): _____

    What index entries were used to find the code(s)?

    _____

    _____

Surgical Case #16

Operative Report

Procedure: McDonald's cerclage placement

Diagnosis: Intrauterine pregnancy at 12 weeks, history of cervical incompetence

Anesthesia: Epidural

History: The patient is a 36-year-old gravida 3 para 2 with a last menstrual period (LMP) on January 28. Positive HCG was noted on March 1. Intrauterine pregnancy was determined to be at 12 weeks by last LMP and at first trimester by ultrasound. She has a history of cervical incompetence in a previous pregnancy that was brought to term with a cerclage. She also has a history of diethylstilbestrol (DES) exposure and of cerclage placement times 2, D&C times 2, and umbilical herniorrhaphy.

Findings and Technique: Preoperatively, her internal os was approximately 1 cm dilated. The posterior cervix was approximately 2 cm long, and the interior cervix was approximately 1 cm long. At the end of the procedure, the knot could be felt at the 12 o'clock position and the internal os was closed to digital examination.

The patient was in the dorsal lithotomy position. She had internal and external perineal preps and was draped for the procedure. A Mersilene band on two needles was used with one needle placed in at the 6 o'clock position and brought out at 3 o'clock, and replaced at the same position and brought out at 12 o'clock. The other needle was taken in at 3 o'clock and brought out at 9 o'clock, and then replaced and brought out at 12 o'clock. The Mersilene band then was tied at the 12 o'clock position until the internal os was closed. It was palpable at the end of the procedure, and the two ends were cut long. The patient received perioperative antibiotics, and her heart tones were Dopplerable before the procedure. The procedure was without complications, and the patient was taken to the recovery room in stable condition.

1. Code(s): _____

What index entries were used to find the code(s)?

_____

_____

Surgical Case #17

Operative Report

Procedure: Modified radical mastectomy

Diagnosis: Infiltrating ductal carcinoma, left breast

Indications: The patient is a 79-year-old female who recently noticed a left breast mass. A subsequent mammogram revealed a spiculated suspicious lesion. On examination, she had a 2.5 to 3 cm palpable mass with no obvious axillary adenopathy. After an outpatient breast biopsy performed a week ago showed the mass was positive for carcinoma, she was admitted for a mastectomy.

Technique: Under general anesthesia, the patient's left breast was prepped. A transverse elliptical incision, including the nipple, areolar complex, and the previous biopsy site were utilized. Flaps were elevated medially to the sternum, superiorly to the clavicle, laterally to the latissimus, and inferiorly to the rectus. The depressed and anteropectoral fascia were dissected from medial to lateral with cautery dissection. The axilla was entered and the axillary vein identified. The venous tributaries were clipped inferiorly and divided. The long thoracic and thoracodorsal nerves were identified and traced to their insertions; and the axillary contents were swept inferiorly and laterally out with the breast specimen.

Hemostasis was obtained with a Bovie in addition to clips and sutures. Two Jackson Pratt drains were placed. The subcutaneous tissue was reapproximated with interrupted 3-0 Vicryl, and the skin was closed with clips. Some of the skin flaps were trimmed to make the closure more acceptable cosmetically. The patient tolerated the procedure well and was returned to the recovery area in satisfactory condition.

1. Code(s): _____

What index entries were used to find the code(s)?

_____

_____

Surgical Case #18

Operative Report

Procedure: Direct microlaryngoscopy under general anesthesia

Diagnosis: Dysphonia

Technique: A 40-year-old patient was taken to the OR where, under general anesthesia, the Jako laryngoscope was inserted with the operating microscope to perform a laryngoscopy. The vocal cords were found to be totally normal on both sides with no evidence of nodules or granuloma formation. The entire endolarynx was well visualized. Moreover, there was no evidence of subglottic stenosis; and as the patient was awakening, vocal cord mobility appeared to be normal. The procedure was terminated, and the patient awakened and taken to the recovery room in good condition with stable vital signs.

Recommendation: Speech therapy

1. Code(s): _____

What index entries were used to find the code(s)?

_____

_____

Surgical Case #19

Operative Report

Procedure: Colonoscopy

History and Indications: The patient is a 30-year-old female who has had complaints of abdominal pain, altered bowel habits, and a 2- to 3-gram documented decline in her hemoglobin. Her stools have been heme negative, but there is significant suspicion that she may have pathology in the colon.

Technique: The patient was sedated with 1.5 mg Versed and received antibiotics prior to the procedure per the recommendations of the cardiology service. She is status post heart transplant with significant cardiac complications.

In the endoscopy suite with appropriate monitoring of pulse, oxygenation, temperature, blood pressure, and other vital signs, a digital rectal examination was performed. Following the exam, the Pentax video colonoscope was inserted through the anus and advanced to the cecum. There was no evidence of malignancy. The scope was withdrawn.

1. Code(s): _____

What index entries were used to find the code(s)?

_____

_____

Surgical Case #20

Operative Report

Preoperative Diagnosis: Sebaceous cyst, right posterior neck

Postoperative Diagnosis: Lipomatous lesion, approximately 1.5 cm, right posterior neck, intramuscular

Procedure: Excision of lipoma, right posterior neck

Technique: The patient was brought to the operating suite and was placed in the prone position on the operating table. The patient's right neck was then prepped and draped in a sterile fashion. At this point, we suspected the patient to have a cyst. We subsequently decided to do a circumferential incision around what was thought to be the puncta. The incision was marked, and the area was prepped and draped with a local anesthetic. A skin incision was made. The incision was carried down to the subcutaneous tissue. At this point, we realized that it was not a cyst but, rather, a lipoma, which was actually deep into the muscle area. We excised the skin, dissected down through the capsule of the lipoma, and then were able to harvest this from its capsule within the muscle fibers. This was done with sharp dissection. Bleeding was controlled with cautery. The wound was closed with 3-0 Vicryl subcutaneous sutures, and a 4-0 Vicryl subcuticular stitch was placed. The wound edges were painted with Benzoin and Steri-Strips applied. The patient tolerated the procedure well and was taken to the recovery area in stable condition.

1. Code(s): _____

What index entries were used to find the code(s)?

_____

_____

Surgical Case #21

Operative Report

Procedure:	Colonoscopy
Indications for Procedure:	This is a 65-year-old female with a family history of colonic malignancy who is being evaluated for altered bowel function.
	When evaluated in my office prior to the procedure, her vital signs, cardiac status, pulmonary status, and mental status were stable and adequate for conscious sedation.
Description of Procedure:	The patient was given Demerol 50 mg IV and Versed 3 mg IV, and the CF100I video colonoscope was inserted and passed without difficulty to the cecum. Its position was confirmed by the ileocecal valve. Diverticulosis was observed in the left colon. A 5 to 7 mm circular, semipedunculated polyp was observed in the cecal area. It was secured with the snare and recovered. The patient tolerated the procedure well.
Impression:	She has a small cecal polyp, which has been removed. She has diverticulosis and will need reevaluation in three years.
Clinical Diagnosis:	Polyp, cecum
Pathological Diagnosis:	Polyp, cecum: Villotubular adenoma

1. Code(s): _____

   What index entries were used to find the code(s)?

   _____

   _____

Surgical Case #22

Operative Report

Preoperative Diagnosis:	Cholecystitis with cholelithiasis
Postoperative Diagnosis:	Cholecystitis with cholelithiasis
Procedure Performed:	Laparoscopic cholecystectomy with operative cholangiogram
Anesthesia:	General
Bleeding:	None
Complications:	None

Description of procedure: The patient was brought to the OR, placed in the supine position, and given general anesthesia. The skin over the abdomen was prepped with Duraprep and draped in the sterile fashion. A 1 cm incision was made above the umbilicus, and the Veress needle was introduced into the abdomen cavity obtaining pneumoperitoneum. A 10 mm trocar was inserted and a laparoscope introduced. The patient had significant cholecystitis. Direct exploration of the abdomen was normal. Other trocars were inserted into subcostal space under direct vision. Lysis of adhesions was performed. Exposure to the gallbladder bed was obtained, and the cystic artery and the cystic duct were isolated. The common duct was of normal size. The cystic duct was ligated distally and proximally and was opened. We inserted the biliary catheter and obtained a cholangiogram that showed a normal biliary tree. The catheter was removed and the cystic duct double-ligated with hemoclips and divided. The gallbladder was removed through the upper trocar and dissected with electrocautery. The area was irrigated with saline solution. The trocars were removed under vision and pneumoperitoneum decompressed. The skin was closed with subcuticular #4-0 Vicryl, and a sterile dressing was applied. The patient tolerated the procedure well.

1. Code(s): _____

   What index entries were used to find the code(s)?

   _____

   _____

Surgical Case #23

Operative Report

Procedure: Endoscopy

Preoperative Diagnosis: Abdominal pain, possible peptic ulcer disease.
Patient has upper abdominal pain, unresponsive to H2 blockers.

Postoperative Diagnosis: 1.   Hiatal hernia
                          2.   Moderate reflux esophagitis
                          3.   Healing prepyloric gastric ulcer
                          4.   Normal sigmoidoscopy

Findings: Endoscopy was performed with the Olympus video panendoscope, which was easily introduced into the esophagus. This was normal to the proximal midportion of the esophagus, but at the GE junction, there was evidence of a moderate degree of reflux esophagitis with several small superficial erosions at the location and also isolated erosions several centimeters above. The endoscope was advanced into the stomach and turned in a retrograde direction. The cardiac and fundic areas were examined and found to be otherwise normal. The antrum showed normal peristalsis and mucosa. In the immediate prepyloric area, a small defect was thought to represent scarring from a previous ulcer, which was still healing. Biopsies were obtained. The duodenum, including the second portion, was normal. Subsequently, the endoscope was withdrawn and the patient turned onto his left side. Flexible sigmoidoscopy then was carried out to the lower descending colon. A biopsy of the sigmoid was obtained. Patient tolerated the procedure well.

1.   Code(s): _____

    What index entries were used to find the code(s)?

    _____

    _____

Surgical Case #24

Operative Report

Procedure: Esophagogastroduodenoscopy

Instrument Used: Olympus GIF-100

Premedication: The patient was premedicated with a total of Fentanyl, 50 mcg, and Versed, 4 mg, intravenously.

Indications: The patient has presented with recurrent dysphagia. She has a history of a Schatzki's ring, which has been dilated in the past.

Procedure: The endoscope was inserted into the esophagus without difficulty. The esophageal mucosa was normal. A reformed Schatzki's ring was located at the Z line, which was at approximately 29 cm. The endoscope could be inserted through this area with no resistance. The ring was located above a 3 cm hiatal hernia. The stomach, duodenal bulb, and descending duodenum were all normal. After the endoscope was withdrawn, a #60 French Maloney dilator was passed with very mild resistance. The patient tolerated the procedure well, and there were no immediate complications.

Impression: 1.   A reformed Schatzki's ring, which was dilated
                        2.   A 3 cm hiatal hernia

1.   Code(s): _____

    What index entries were used to find the code(s)?

    _____

    _____

Surgical Case #25

Emergency Department Report

Chief Complaint: Lacerations, left face

History of Present Illness: Patient is a 26-year-old male who was driving a car with the window down when another car moving in the opposite direction hit his mirror. Glass from the broken mirror flew into his face, and he sustained two small lacerations. There were no other injuries.

Past Medical History: Unremarkable

Medications: None

Allergies: None

Physical Examination:

General: Alert male in no acute distress

Head, Ears, Eyes, Nose, and Throat: Pupils are equal and reactive to light. Extraocular muscles intact. Nose is clear. Oropharynx negative. Two lacerations are on left cheek region. The uppermost laceration is about 2 cm below the eye laterally and is about 3/4 cm in length. Full-skin thickness. The second laceration is about 1.5 cm below the first and is 1-1/4 cm in length. Full-skin thickness. No palpable foreign bodies.

Procedure: Local injection with a total of 3 cc 1% lidocaine with epinephrine. Prepped and routine exploration performed. The upper laceration is only about 5 mm deep. No foreign bodies noted. No neurovascular injuries. It was closed with three 6-0 Nylon sutures. The lower laceration was approximately 12 to 15 mm deep. I could not palpate any foreign bodies. There are no obvious neurovascular injuries. Closed in single layer with five 6-0 nylon sutures. Polysporin ointment was applied.

Laboratory Data: X ray to rule out foreign body negative

Diagnosis: 1. Simple facial laceration, $1^1/_4$ cm
2. Simple facial laceration, $^3/_4$ cm

Disposition and Plan: Wound care instructions given; sutures out in 5 to 7 days

1. Code(s): _____

What index entries were used to find the code(s)?

_____

_____

Surgical Case #26

Operative Report

Preoperative Diagnosis: Dermal cyst of right breast

Postoperative Diagnosis: Dermal cyst of right breast

Procedure Performed: Excision of dermal cyst of right breast

Description of Procedure: Erythematous dermal cystic area of the right breast was marked out with an elliptical incision, anesthetized with local anesthesia, and prepped and draped sterilely.

Incision was made elliptically, including the whole cyst down through the fatty tissue. On palpation afterward no abnormalities were noted. Then the area had hemostasis obtained with electrocautery. The incision was closed with interrupted 3-0 Vicryl sutures.

The skin was closed with interrupted 5-0 nylon sutures. Steri-Strips and a sterile dressing were applied over it. The patient tolerated the procedure well and was sent to the recovery room with instructions to be discharged home with follow-up appointment given.

1. Code(s): _____

What index entries were used to find the code(s)?

_____

_____

Surgical Case #27

Operative Report

Preoperative Diagnosis: Right arm lipoma

Postoperative Diagnosis: Same

Procedure Performed: Excision of right arm lipoma

Anesthesia: Local

Indications for Procedure: The patient is a 48-year-old female who presents with a 4.0 cm mass on her right arm. She has had the mass for several months, and it is getting larger. She now presents for an excisional biopsy.

Description of Procedure: The patient was brought to the OR and placed on the operating table in the supine position. Her right arm was prepped and draped in the usual sterile fashion, and anesthetized with 1% lidocaine with bicarbonate. A longitudinal incision was made measuring 3 cm and carried down through the skin and subcutaneous tissues, and the underlying lipoma was dissected away from the surrounding tissues and removed. Parts of the lipoma were intermingled with surrounding tissues, requiring these areas to be pulled out. Hemostasis then was assured and the wound closed with layered Vicryl, followed by Benzoin, Steri-Strips, and a Tegaderm dressing. The patient tolerated the procedure well and was taken to the recovery room in stable condition.

Pathological Diagnosis: Forearm, right: lipoma

Gross: The specimen consists of nine pieces of soft, predominantly fatty yellow tissue ranging from 0.9 cm to 3 cm in greatest diameter; representative sections submitted in one cassette.

1. Code(s): _____

    What index entries were used to find the code(s)?

    _____

    _____

Surgical Case #28

Operative Report

Preoperative Diagnosis: Elevated PSA of 16.6 and bladder outlet obstruction

Postoperative Diagnosis: Same

Procedure: Cystoscopy and transrectal needle biopsy of the prostate

Anesthesia: General

Procedure: This man was taken to the Operative Suite, placed in the dorsolithotomy position after being administered anesthesia, and sterilely prepped and draped in the normal fashion. A needle was used to take multiple transrectal biopsies of his prostate. After this, a cystoscopy was performed and bladder outlet obstruction and BPH were noted. The urethra was normal, and the bladder was moderately trabeculated. There was no evidence of neoplasm, infection, or calculus; and the ureters were normal in position, effluxing clear urine. The bladder was emptied, and the patient was sent to the Recovery Room in satisfactory condition.

1. Code(s): _____

    What index entries were used to find the code(s)?

    _____

    _____

Surgical Case #29

Operative Report

Preoperative Diagnosis: Incomplete abortion

Postoperative Diagnosis: Same

Operation: Dilatation & curettage

History: This 22-year-old female, Gravida IV, Para II, AB I, comes in today because of abdominal pain and passing fetus on the sidewalk just outside the hospital. Apparently, her last menstrual period was two months ago. She had been doing well, and this problem just started today.

Procedure: The patient was placed on the operating table in the lithotomy position, and prepped and draped in the usual manner. Under satisfactory intravenous sedation, the cervix was visualized by means of a weighted speculum and grasped in the anterior lip with a sponge forceps. Cord was prolapsed through the cervix and vagina, and a considerable amount of placental tissue was in the vagina and cervix. This was removed. A sharp curet was used to explore the endometrial cavity, and a minimal amount of curettings was obtained. The patient tolerated the procedure well.

1.   Code(s): _____

    What index entries were used to find the code(s)?

    _____

    _____

Surgical Case #30

Procedure: Sigmoidoscopy

Indications for procedure: The patient is 75 years old. She has had an alteration in her bowel pattern and is being evaluated with a sigmoidoscopy.

Description of procedure: She was given Fleet's enema preparation. She required no sedation. The CF100L video colonoscope was inserted and passed without difficulty to 50 cm. The mucosa was normal. No diverticulosis was observed. Some scybalous stool was present, but this was minimal. The patient tolerated the procedure well.

1.   Code(s): _____

    What index entries were used to find the code(s)?

    _____

    _____

Surgical Case #31

Diagnosis: Hodgkin's disease, nonsclerosing type

Operation: Placement of right subclavian Hickman catheter

Indications: The patient is a 35-year-old female with the diagnosis of Hodgkin's disease. Her indication for a Hickman catheter was chemotherapy infusion.

Procedure: The patient was taken to the operating room and placed in the supine position. The right chest and subclavian area, neck, and shoulder were prepped and draped in routine manner. A total of 48 cc of 1% Carbocaine without epinephrine was used for anesthesia. The subcutaneous area below the right clavicle was numbed with the Lidocaine down to the periosteum. The subclavian vein was stuck with the needle. Good blood flow was returned. The guide wire was passed. At this time, a 2-cm incision was made below the clavicle at the middle aspect. The Hickman catheter was then placed over the guide wire into the superior vena cava. This was documented with fluoroscopy. A second incision was made 3 cm below the first distance of 2 cm transverse. The area between the two incisions was then tunneled with a curved six. The distal aspect of the catheter was brought out through the second inferior incision. The teflon Hickman catheter was trimmed to the appropriate length with Teflon coating at the skin incision. The superior skin incision was closed with interrupted #3-0 nylon, as was the inferior skin incision. The patient tolerated the procedure well.

1. Code(s): _____

    What index entries were used to find the code(s)?

    _____

    _____

Surgical Case #32

Preoperative Diagnosis:	Ventral hernia
Postoperative Diagnosis:	Ventral hernia
Operation Performed:	Laparoscopic repair of ventral hernia
Anesthesia:	General

Details of Procedure: The patient was taken to the operating room, placed in the supine position. The abdomen was prepped and draped in the usual sterile fashion. A Veress needle was then inserted in the left lateral abdominal wall. The abdomen was insufflated with CO_2 gas. A 10 mm Surgiport was then placed. The laparoscopic camera was then inserted. Additional 5 mm Surgiports were placed under direct vision, one in the left lower quadrant of the abdomen, the other in the left upper quadrant of the abdomen.

The 5 mm harmonic scalpel was used along with the dissecting forceps to take down the adhesions from within and around the hernia sac. There were a number of adhesions, primarily involving the omentum. These were all removed.

Two hernia defects were noted, one just above the umbilicus, perhaps 3 to 4 cm in diameter, and another toward the upper aspect of the midline incision, that had not been previously recognized.

It was elected to place an 18 x 24 cm segment of Gore-Tex dual mesh. #1 Prolene was sewn at each of the corners of this as well as in between, at the midpoint of each of the sides. Suitable locations were chosen for tying the anchoring sutures. The patch then was rolled around a grasper and inserted into the abdominal cavity through the 10 mm port. The patch was then unrolled and the orientation placed with the smooth side down against the bowel. An endo-close device was used to grasp each of the sutures and bring out through the previously placed incisions for the anchoring sutures. The patch was anchored at each of the six locations as noted above. Then, an auto suture protac was placed around the periphery of the patch. Additional staples were placed within the inner aspect of the patch using an Ethicon tacking stapler. The patch was noted to be quite taut and applied closely to the abdominal wall to prevent any movement of the patch. The abdomen was then desufflated and the ports withdrawn. Each of the skin incisions was closed with 4-0 clear PDS subcuticular suture and Steri-Strips. Tegaderm dressings were then applied. The patient tolerated the procedure well with no apparent difficulty. She was then taken to the postanesthesia recovery room for further postoperative care.

1. Code(s): _____

    What index entries were used to find the code(s)?

    _____

    _____

Surgical Case #33

Preoperative Diagnosis: Right breast mammographic abnormality

Postoperative Diagnosis: Same

Indications: This is a 53-year-old woman who presented with a nonpalpable right breast mammographic abnormality. A stereotatic biopsy showed columnar cell hyperplastia without evidence of obvious malignancy; however, excision was recommended. Possible perioperative risks and complications and alternatives were discussed with her prior to surgery.

Details of Procedure: After informed consent was obtained from the patient, she was taken to the OR and placed on the table in the supine position. The right breast was noted to contain a localization wire. The films were reviewed. The breast was prepped with Betadine solution and draped sterilely. Sedation was administered by anesthesia. Local anesthesia was achieved with 1% lidocaine and 0.5% Marcaine with epinephrine. An incision was made over the course of the localization needle, and the underlying core of tissue surrounding the localization needle was excised using electrocautery. This was forwarded to radiology, which confirmed the presence of the previously marked mammographic abnormality within the specimen. It was then forwarded to pathology.

Wound was inspected for hemostasis, which was excellent. The deep tissues were approximated with interrupted 3-0 Vicryl, and a running 4-0 Monocryl subcuticular stitch was used to approximate the skin edges. Benzoin, Steri-Strips, and dry sterile dressing were applied.

The patient was then awakened from anesthesia and returned to the recovery room in stable condition.

Radiologist already billed for localization wire.

1. Code(s): _____ 19125-RT

    What index entries were used to find the code(s)?

    breast, excision, lesion — 19120 - 19126

    by needle local 19125, 19126

Surgical Case #34

Preoperative Diagnosis: Chalazion, left lower lid

Postoperative Diagnosis: Same

Operation: Excision of mass, left lower lid

Procedure: Under adequate topical anesthesia and block anesthesia, the eye was prepared and draped in the usual manner. Chalazion speculum was applied. The left lower lid was everted and a vertical incision made. Excision of the mass was performed using curet, and a biopsy of the capsule of this 9 mm mass was made, as requested. Patient tolerated the procedure well and left the operating room in good condition after application of Cortisporin Ointment and pressure patch.

1. Code(s): _____

    What index entries were used to find the code(s)?

    _____

    _____

Surgical Case #35

Preoperative Diagnosis: Carpal tunnel compression, left, severe

Postoperative Diagnosis: Same

Operation: Release, left carpal tunnel

Technique: After successful axillary block was placed, the patient's left arm was prepared and draped in the usual sterile manner. Tourniquet inflated. A curvilinear hypothenar incision was made and the palmaris retracted radially. The carpal tunnel and the transverse carpal ligament were then opened and completely freed in the proximal directions. It was noted to be severely tight in the palm with flattening and swelling of the median nerve. The carpal tunnel was opened distally in the hand and noted to be clear, out to the transverse palmar crease. The wound was then closed with 4-0 Dexon in subcuticular tissues. Sterile bulky dressing was applied, and the patient was awakened and taken to the recovery room in satisfactory condition.

1. Code(s): _____

    What index entries were used to find the code(s)?

    _____

    _____

Surgical Case #36

Preoperative Diagnosis: Keratosis of glans penis

Postoperative Diagnosis: Same

Procedure: The penis was prepared and draped in the usual manner. Along the distal portion of the penis on the right side and adjoining the urinary meatus was a well-defined, firm area suggesting a keratosis. The entire lesion was excised and submitted for pathological examination. The pathologist confirmed the diagnosis of keratosis. The glan penis was then approximated with black silk. The patient returned to the recovery room in satisfactory condition.

1. Code(s): _____

    What index entries were used to find the code(s)?

    _____

    _____

Surgical Case #37

Preoperative diagnosis: Herniated disc at L4-5, L5-S1; good relief with previous two epidural blocks

Postoperative diagnosis: Same

Procedure: Therapeutic epidural block

The patient is kept on the left lateral side. The back is prepped with Betadine solution, and 1% Xylocaine is infiltrated at the L5-S1 interspace. Deep infiltration is carried out with a 22-gauge needle, and a 17-gauge Touhy needle is taken and an epidural is performed. After careful aspiration, which was negative for blood as well as for cerebral spinal fluid, about 80 mg of Depo-Medrol then were injected along with 5 cc of 0.25% Marcaine and 1 cc of 50 mcg of Fentanyl. The injection was done in a fractionated dose in a slow fashion. The patient was examined and evaluated following the block and found to have excellent relief of pain. The patient is advised to continue physical therapy and to come back in a month for further evaluation.

1.   Code(s): _____

    What index entries were used to find the code(s)?

    _____

    _____

Surgical Case #38

Procedure: Excision of left axillary lymph nodes

Indications for Procedure: This female patient had a lumpectomy for a breast lesion approximately two and a half years ago. She presents with palpable adenopathy in the left axilla.

Description of Procedure: The patient was brought into the operating room and placed upon the OR table in the supine position. The left axilla was prepped and draped in the usual sterile fashion. After an adequate level of general anesthesia had been achieved, a knife with a #10 blade was used to make a curvilinear incision in the skin overlying the adenopathy.

This incision was carried down deep through the subcutaneous tissue using a Bovie knife. Babcock forceps were used to grasp the area of tissue surrounding the lymph node and there were carefully dissected from the surrounding tissues using a Bovie knife and scissors. All vessels encountered were either Bovied or clipped.

The wound was irrigated and carefully examined for bleeders. The subcutaneous tissue was closed using a Vicryl suture placed in interrupted fashion, and the skin was reapproximated using staples. Drainage was achieved with a Jackson-Pratt drain brought out through a separate wound. Sterile dressings were applied, and the patient was taken to the Recovery Room in a stable postoperative condition

1.   Code(s): _____

    What index entries were used to find the code(s)?

    _____

    _____

Surgical Case #39

Preoperative Diagnosis: Subepidermal nodular 1.5 cm lesion of the left side of the nose

Operation: Excision, lesion of nose

Procedure: Under local anesthesia, we excised the 1.5 cm lesion with .5 cm margins on all sides of the defect. The lesion was excised in fragments and submitted to pathology along with an ellipse of skin margins. Bleeding is controlled with electrocautery, and the wound is closed with four vertical mattress sutures of 5-0 nylon. Polysporin and dressing were applied.

Pathological Diagnosis: Well-organized basal cell carcinoma with no significant increase in activity or dysplasia of the cells.

1.   Code(s): _____

    What index entries were used to find the code(s)?

_____

_____

Surgical Case #40

Emergency Department Physician Report

Chief Complaint: Left eye, foreign body x 2 days

History of Present Illness: The patient is a 29-year-old male who presents to the emergency room after having a piece of metal fly into his left eye yesterday. Since that time, he still continues to have the metal present. He denies any major disturbance in vision, although he states that his vision is slightly more blurry and irritated. He does complain of some pain.

Past Medical History: Hypertension

Allergies: None   Immunizations: Unknown for tetanus.

Social and Family History: Noncontributory.

Physical Exam of Eyes: Reveals the left eye to have some periorbital erythema, but minimal swelling of the lids. PERRLA: No papilledema. EOMs intact. Vision intact. Inspection of the left eye shows a foreign body that resembles a piece of metal at 6 o'clock. At this time, Tetracaine was applied. The foreign body was successfully removed with the bevel of a 22-gauge needle. Two more drops of Tetracaine were applied, followed by Homatropine and Polysporin Ophthalmic ointment.

Assessment: Foreign body of left eye, removed

The patient understood all instructions and agreed with the plan at which time he was discharged.

1.   Code(s): _____

    What index entries were used to find the code(s)?

_____

_____

Glossary

Abstracting: The process of extracting information from a document to create a brief summary of a patient's illness, treatment, and outcome; also, the process of extracting elements of data from a source document or database and entering them into an automated system

Ambulatory care: Preventive or corrective healthcare services provided on a nonresident basis in a provider's office, clinic setting, or hospital outpatient setting

Ambulatory payment classification (APC) system: The prospective payment system used since 2000 for reimbursement of hospitals for outpatient services provided to Medicare and Medicaid beneficiaries

Ambulatory payment classification (APC) relative weight: A number reflecting the expected resource consumption of cases associated with each APC, relative to the average of all APCs, that is used to determine payment for hospital outpatient services provided to Medicare and Medicaid beneficiaries

Ambulatory surgery: An elective surgical procedure performed on a patient who is classified as an outpatient and who is usually released from the surgical facility on the day of surgery

Ambulatory surgery center: A freestanding or hospital-based facility that provides outpatient surgical services

Ambulatory surgical center (ASC): Under Medicare, an outpatient surgical facility having its own national identifier; existing as a separate entity with respect to its licensure, accreditation, governance, professional supervision, administrative functions, clinical services, record keeping, and financial and accounting systems; having as its sole purpose the provision of services in connection with surgical procedures that do not require inpatient hospitalization; and meeting the conditions and requirements set forth in all subparts of this part

Ambulatory surgical center (ASC) list: The list of surgical procedures that the Centers for Medicare and Medicaid Services considers safe and appropriate in an outpatient setting and for which Medicare pays a prospectively determined ASC facility fee

Ambulatory surgical center (ASC) services: Services that a Medicare-approved ambulatory surgical center provides in connection with procedures on the ASC list

American Health Information Management Association (AHIMA): The professional membership organization for managers of health record services and healthcare information systems as well as coding services; provides accreditation, certification, and educational services

American Hospital Association (AHA): The national organization that represents and serves all types of hospitals, healthcare networks, and patients and communities; the publisher of *Coding Clinic*

American Medical Association (AMA): The national professional membership organization for physicians that distributes scientific information to its members and the public, informs members of legislation related to health and medicine, and represents the medical profession s interests in national legislative matters

Ancillary services: Tests and procedures ordered by a physician to provide information for use in patient diagnosis or treatment

Attending physician: The physician primarily responsible for the care and treatment of a patient

Balanced Budget Act (BBA) of 1997: Public Law 105-33 enacted by Congress on August 5, 1997, that mandated a number of additions, deletions, and revisions to the original Medicare and Medicaid legislation; the legislation that added penalties for healthcare fraud and abuse to the Medicare and Medicaid programs

Bundled: The grouping of CPT codes related to a procedure when submitting a claim

Carrier, Medicare: An organization under contract with the Centers for Medicare and Medicaid Services to serve as the financial agent that works with providers and the federal government to administer Medicare eligibility and Part B payments on the local level

Category I codes: Procedures or services identified by a five-digit CPT code and organized within the six sections

Category II codes: Codes located in the CPT codebook that represent performance measurement tracking; use is optional

Category III codes: Temporary emerging technology codes located within the CPT codebook

Centers for Medicare and Medicaid Services (CMS): The division of the Department of Health and Human Services that is responsible for developing healthcare policy in the United States and for administering the Medicare program and the federal portion of the Medicaid program; called the Health Care Financing Administration (HCFA) prior to 2001

Certified coding associate (CCA): An AHIMA credential awarded to entry-level coders who have demonstrated skill in classifying medical data by passing a certification exam

Certified coding specialist (CCS): An AHIMA credential awarded to individuals who have demonstrated skill in classifying medical data from patient records, generally in the hospital setting, by passing a certification examination

Certified coding specialist—physician based (CCS–P): An AHIMA credential awarded to individuals who have demonstrated coding expertise in physician-based settings, such as group practices, by passing a certification examination

Charge code: The numerical identification of a service or supply that links the item to a particular department within the charge description master

Chargemaster: A financial management form that contains information about the organization's charges for the healthcare services it provides to patients; also called the charge description master (CDM)

Chief complaint: The principal problem a patient reports to a healthcare provider

Claim: A billing statement submitted to a third-party payer by a healthcare provider to describe the services that were provided to a patient

Claims processing: The process of accumulating claims for services, submitting claims for reimbursement, and ensuring that claims are satisfied

Classification system: A system for grouping similar diseases and procedures and organizing related information for easy retrieval; also, a system for assigning numeric or alphanumeric code numbers to represent specific diseases and/or procedures

Clean claim: A claim that has all the billing and coding information correct and can be paid by the payer the first time it is submitted

Clinic: An outpatient facility providing a limited range of healthcare services and assuming overall healthcare responsibility for patients

Clinical abstract: A computerized file that summarizes patient demographics and other information, including reason for admission, diagnoses, procedures, physician information, and any additional information deemed pertinent by the facility

Clinical coding: The process of assigning numeric or alphanumeric classifications to diagnostic and procedural statements

Clinical data: Data captured during the process of diagnosis and treatment

CMS-1500:   A Medicare claim form used to bill third-party payers for provider services, for example, physician office visits; previously called HCFA-1500

CMS-1450:   A Medicare form used for standardized uniform billing; often called UB-92

Code: In information systems, software instructions that direct computers to perform a specified action; in healthcare, an alphanumeric representation of the terms in a clinical classification or vocabulary

Code editor: Software that evaluates the clinical consistency and completeness of health record information and identifies potential errors that could affect accurate prospective payment group assignment

Code of Federal Regulations (CFR):   The official collection of legislative and regulatory guidelines mandated by final rules published in the *Federal Register*

Coded data: Data that are translated into a standard nomenclature of classification so that they may be aggregated, analyzed, and compared

Coder: A person assigned solely to the function of coding

Coder/biller: A person in an ambulatory care or a physician office setting who is generally responsible for processing the superbill

Coding: The process of assigning numeric representations to clinical documentation

Coding Clinic: A publication issued quarterly by the American Hospital Association and approved by the Centers for Medicare and Medicaid Services to give coding advice and direction

Coding specialist: The healthcare worker responsible for assigning numeric or alphanumeric codes to diagnostic or procedural statements

Community of Practice (CoP): A Web-based electronic network for communication among members of the American Health Information Management Association

Consolidation: The process by which the ambulatory patient group classification system determines whether separate payment is appropriate when a patient is assigned multiple significant procedure groups

Consultation: The response by one healthcare professional to another healthcare professional's request to provide recommendations and/or opinions regarding the care of a particular patient/resident

Conversion factor: A monetary multiplier that converts relative value units into payments

Correct Coding Initiative (CCI): A national initiative designed to improve the accuracy of claims processed by Medicare carriers; also called the National Correct Coding Initiative (NCCI)

CPT Assistant: The official publication of American Medical Association that addresses CPT coding issues

CPT-5 Project: The initiative to improve CPT to address the needs of hospitals, managed care organizations, and long-term care facilities

Current Procedural Terminology, Fourth Edition (CPT-4): The comprehensive, descriptive list of terms and numeric codes used for reporting diagnostic and therapeutic procedures and other medical services performed by physicians; published and updated annually by the American Medical Association

Denial: The circumstance when a bill has been accepted, but payment has been denied for any of several reasons (for example, sending the bill to the wrong insurance company, patient not having current coverage, inaccurate coding, lack of medical necessity, and so on)

Department of Health and Human Services (HHS): The cabinet-level federal agency that oversees all of the health- and human services–related activities of the federal government and administers federal regulations

Diagnosis: A word or phrase used by a physician to identify a disease from which an individual patient suffers or a condition for which the patient needs, seeks, or receives medical care

Diagnosis chiefly responsible for services provided (outpatient): The diagnosis, condition, problem, or reason for an encounter/visit that is chiefly responsible for the services provided

Diagnostic codes: Numeric or alphanumeric characters used to classify and report diseases, conditions, and injuries

Diagnostic services: All diagnostic services of any type, including history, physical examination, laboratory, X ray or radiography, and others that are performed or ordered pertinent to the patient's reasons for the encounter

Discharge diagnosis: Any one of the diagnoses recorded after all the data accumulated during the course of a patient's hospitalization or other circumscribed episode of medical care have been studied

Discharge status: The disposition of the patient at discharge (that is, left against medical advice, discharged to home, transferred to skilled nursing facility, or died)

Documentation: The recording of pertinent healthcare findings, interventions, and responses to treatment as a business record and form of communication among caregivers

Durable medical equipment (DME):   Medical equipment designed for long-term use in the home, including eyeglasses, hearing aids, surgical appliances and supplies, orthotics and prostheses, and bulk and cylinder oxygen; also known as home medical equipment (HME)

Durable medical equipment regional carrier (DMERC):   A fiscal intermediary designated to process claims for durable medical equipment

Edit: A condition that must be satisfied before a computer system can accept data

E/M coding: *See* Evaluation and management codes

Emergency: A situation in which a patient requires immediate medical intervention as a result of severe, life-threatening, or potentially disabling conditions

Emergency patient: A patient admitted to the emergency services department of a hospital for the diagnosis and treatment of a condition that requires immediate medical, dental, or allied health services in order to sustain life or to prevent critical consequences

Emergency services: Immediate evaluation and therapy rendered in urgent clinical conditions and sustained until the patient can be referred to his or her personal practitioner for further care

Encoder: Specialty software used to facilitate the assignment of diagnostic and procedural codes according to the rules of the coding system

Encounter: The direct personal contact between a patient and a physician or other person authorized by state licensure law and, if applicable, by medical staff bylaws to order or furnish healthcare services for the diagnosis or treatment of the patient

Episode of care: A period of relatively continuous medical care performed by healthcare professionals in relation to a particular clinical problem or situation

Established patient: A patient who has received professional services from the physician or another physician of the same specialty in the same practice group within the past three years

Evaluation and management (E/M) codes: CPT codes that describe patient encounters with healthcare professionals for assessment counseling and other routine healthcare services

Facilities, health: Buildings, including physical plant, equipment, and supplies, necessary in the provision of health services (for example, hospitals, nursing homes, and ambulatory care centers)

Federal Register: The daily publication of the U.S. Government Printing Office that reports all changes in regulations and federally mandated standards, including HCPCS and ICD-9-CM codes

Fee schedule: A list of healthcare services and procedures (usually CPT/HCPCS codes) and the charges associated with them developed by a third-party payer to represent the approved payment levels for a given insurance plan; also called table of allowances

Fee-for-service (FFS) basis: A method of reimbursement through which providers receive payment based on either billed charges for services provided or on annually updated fee schedules

Fiscal intermediary (FI):   An organization that contracts with the Centers for Medicare and Medicaid Services to serve as the financial agent between providers and the federal government in the local administration of Medicare Part A claims

Fraud-and-abuse legislation: Federal laws that address the intentional and unintentional misrepresentation of reimbursement claims submitted to government-sponsored health programs

Freestanding facility: In Medicare terminology, an entity that furnishes healthcare services to beneficiaries and is not integrated with any other entity as a main provider, a department of a provider, or a provider-based entity

Geographic adjustment factor (GAF): Adjustment to the national standardized Medicare fee schedule relative value components used to account for differences in the cost of practicing medicine in different geographic areas of the country

Geographic practice cost index (GPCI): An index developed by the Centers for Medicare and Medicaid Services to measure the differences in resource costs among fee schedule areas compared to the national average in the three components of the relative value unit: physician work, practice expenses, and malpractice coverage

Global payment: A form of reimbursement used for radiological and other procedures that combines the professional and technical components of the procedures and disperses payments as lump sums to be distributed between the physician and the healthcare facility

Global surgery package: A CPT code denoting a normal surgical procedure with no complications that includes all of the elements needed to perform the procedure

Group practice: An organization of physicians who share office space and administrative support services to achieve economies of scale, often a clinic or ambulatory care center

Grouper software: A computer software program that automatically assigns prospective payment groups on the basis of clinical codes

Grouping: A system for assigning patients to a classification scheme via a computer software program

Hard code: A code applied through a healthcare organization's chargemaster

Hard coding: The process of attaching a Healthcare Common Procedural Coding System code to a procedure so that the code will automatically be included on the patient's bill

HCFA-1500: Previous name for CMS-1500

HCFA-1450: *See* CMS-1450

HCFA Common Procedural Coding System (HCPCS): Previous name for the Healthcare Common Procedural Coding System

Health Care Financing Administration (HCFA): Previous name of the Centers for Medicare and Medicaid Services

Health Insurance Portability and Accountability Act of 1996 (HIPAA): The federal legislation enacted to provide continuity of health coverage, control fraud and abuse in healthcare, reduce healthcare costs, and guarantee the security and privacy of health information

Health record: A paper- or computer-based tool for collecting and storing information about the healthcare services provided to a patient in a single healthcare facility; also called a patient record, medical record, resident record, or client record, depending on the healthcare setting

Healthcare Common Procedural Coding System (HCPCS): A classification system composed of three levels: I, CPT codes; II, codes for equipment, supplies, and services not covered by CPT codes as well as modifiers that can be used with all levels of codes; and III, local codes developed by regional Medicare Part B carriers (eliminated in 2003)

Healthcare provider: A provider of diagnostic, medical, and surgical care as well as the services or supplies related to the health of an individual and any other person or organization that issues reimbursement claims or is paid for healthcare in the normal course of business (hospitals, physicians, and so on)

HIPAA: *See* Health Insurance Portability and Accountability Act of 1996

History: The pertinent information about a patient, including chief complaint, past and present illnesses, family history, social history, and review of body systems

Hospital: A healthcare entity that has an organized medical staff and permanent facilities that include inpatient beds and continuous medical/nursing services and that provides diagnostic and therapeutic services for patients as well as overnight accommodations and nutritional services

Hospital ambulatory care: All hospital-directed preventive, therapeutic, and rehabilitative services provided by physicians and their surrogates to patients who are not hospital inpatients

Hospital outpatient: A hospital patient who receives services in one or more of the hospital's facilities when he or she is not currently an inpatient or a home care patient

Hospital outpatient care unit: An organized unit of a hospital that provides facilities and medical services exclusively or primarily to patients who are generally ambulatory and who do not currently require or are not currently receiving services as an inpatient of the hospital

Hospital-based ambulatory care center: An organized hospital facility that provides non-emergency medical or dental services to patients who are not assigned to a bed as inpatients during the time services are rendered (an emergency department in which services are provided to nonemergency patients is not considered an ambulatory care center)

Hospital-based ambulatory surgery center: A department of an inpatient facility that provides same-day surgical services using the facility's equipment, staff, and support services

Hospital-based outpatient care: A subset of ambulatory care that utilizes a hospital's staff, equipment, and resources to render preventive and/or corrective healthcare services

Hospitalization insurance (Medicare Part A): A federal program that covers the costs associated with inpatient hospitalization as well as other healthcare services provided to Medicare beneficiaries (hospice and some home health care services)

Individual provider: A health professional who delivers, or is professionally responsible for delivering, services to a patient; exercises independent judgment in the care of the patient, and is not under the immediate supervision of another healthcare professional

International Classification of Diseases, Ninth Revision, Clinical Modification (ICD-9-CM): A classification system used in the United States to report morbidity and mortality information

International Classification of Diseases, Tenth Revision (ICD-10): The newest revision of the disease classification system developed and used by the World Health Organization to track morbidity and mortality information worldwide (not yet adopted by the United States)

Item description: An explanation of a service or supply listed in the chargemaster

Level of service: The relative intensity of services given when a physician provides one-on-one services for a patient (such as minimal, brief, limited, or intermediate); also, the relative intensity of services provided by a healthcare facility (for example, tertiary care)

Line item: A service- or item-specific detail of a reimbursement claim

Local medical review policies (LMRPs): Documents that define Medicare coverage of outpatient services via lists of diagnoses defined as medically reasonable and necessary for the services provided

Managed care: A generic term for reimbursement and delivery systems that integrate the financing and provision of healthcare services by means of entering contractual agreements with selected providers to furnish comprehensive healthcare services and developing explicit criteria for the selection of healthcare providers, formal programs of ongoing quality improvement and utilization review, and significant financial incentives for members to use those providers associated with the plan

Managed fee-for-service plan: A type of prepaid healthcare plan that uses traditional fee-for-service reimbursement methods and controls costs by controlling utilization of services (that is, by conducting prospective and retrospective reviews of medical necessity)

Medicaid: An entitlement program that oversees medical assistance for individuals and families with low incomes and limited resources; jointly funded between state and federal governments

Medical care unit: An assemblage of inpatient beds (or newborn bassinets), related facilities, and assigned personnel that provide service to a defined and limited class of patients according to their particular medical care needs

Medical consultation: *See* Consultation

Medical history: A record of the information provided by a patient to his or her physician to explain the patient's chief complaint, present and past illnesses, and personal and family medical problems; includes a description of the physician's review of systems

Medical nomenclature: A recognized system of preferred terminology for naming disease processes

Medical record: *See* Health record

Medicare: A federally funded health program established in 1965 to assist with the medical care costs of Americans sixty-five years of age and older as well as other individuals entitled to Social Security benefits owing to their disabilities

Medicare economic index (MEI): An index used by the Medicare program to update physician fee levels in relation to annual changes in the general economy for inflation, productivity, and changes in specific health sector expense factors including malpractice, personnel costs, rent, and other expenses

Medicare fee schedule (MFS): A feature of the resource-based relative value system that includes a complete list of the payments Medicare makes to physicians and other providers

Medicare Part A: A program that reimburses institutional providers for inpatient, hospice, and some home health care services

Medicare Part B: A program that reimburses noninstitutional healthcare providers for outpatient services

Medicare prospective payment system: *See* Acute care prospective payment system; Home health prospective payment system; Outpatient prospective payment system; Skilled nursing facility prospective payment system

National Codes: (Level II): Five-digit alphanumeric codes for procedures, services, and supplies that are not classified in CPT; often called HCPCS codes

National Correct Coding Initiative (NCCI):   A series of code edits on Medicare claims

New patient: An individual who has not received professional services from the physician or any other physician of the same specialty in the same practice group within the past three years

Nomenclature: A recognized system of terms used in a science or art that follows preestablished naming conventions

Observation patient: A patient who presents with a medical condition with a significant degree of instability and disability and who needs to be monitored, evaluated, and assessed to determine whether he or she should be admitted for inpatient care or discharged for care in another setting

Omnibus Budget Reconciliation Act (OBRA) of 1989:   The federal legislation that mandated important changes in the payment rules for Medicare physicians; specifically, the legislation that requires nursing facilities to conduct regular patient assessments for Medicare and Medicaid beneficiaries

Operating room (OR) procedure: A predefined procedure that usually requires the use of an operating room

Operation: *See* Surgical operation

Operative report: A formal document that describes the events surrounding a surgical procedure or operation and identifies the principal participants in the surgery

Other diagnoses: All conditions (recorded to the highest documented level of specificity) that coexist at the time of admission, develop subsequently, or affect the treatment received and/or length of stay

Outpatient: A patient who receives ambulatory care services in a hospital-based clinic or department

Outpatient Code Editor (OCE):   A software program linked to the Correct Coding Initiative that applies a set of logical rules to determine whether various combinations of codes are correct and appropriately represent the services provided

Outpatient coder: An individual responsible for assigning ICD-9-CM and CPT/HCPCS codes to ambulatory surgery or emergency department cases

Outpatient prospective payment system (OPPS):   The Medicare prospective payment system used for hospital-based outpatient services and procedures that is predicated on the assignment of ambulatory payment classifications

Outpatient unit: A hospital-based ambulatory care facility organized into sections (clinics) whose number depends on the size and degree of departmentalization of the medical or clinic staff, available facilities, type of service needed in the community, and the needs of the patients for whom it accepts responsibility

Outpatient visit: A patient's visit to one or more units located in the ambulatory services area (clinic or physician's office) of an acute care hospital

Packaging: A payment under the Medicare outpatient prospective payment system that includes items such as anesthesia, supplies, certain drugs, and the use of recovery and observation rooms

Partial hospitalization: A term that refers to a limited patient stay in the hospital setting, typically as part of a transitional program to a less intense level of service (for example, psychiatric and drug and alcohol treatment facilities that offer services to help patients reenter the community, return to work, and assume family responsibilities)

Patient: A living or deceased individual who is receiving or has received healthcare services

Patient health record: *See* Health record

Physical examination report: Documentation of a physician's assessment of a patient's body systems

Primary care physician (PCP):   The physician who makes the initial diagnosis of a patient's medical condition and who manages referrals to other healthcare providers and utilization of healthcare services both inside and outside a managed care plan

Primary diagnosis: The most significant condition for which services and/or procedures are provided (entered first in block 21 of the CMS-1500 claim form)

Principal diagnosis: The disease or condition that was present on admission, was the principal reason for admission, and received treatment or evaluation during the hospital stay or visit; also called most significant diagnosis

Principal procedure: The procedure performed for the definitive treatment of a condition (as opposed to a procedure performed for diagnostic or exploratory purposes) or for care of a complication

Procedural codes: The numeric or alphanumeric characters used to classify and report the medical procedures and services performed for patients

Procedures and services (outpatient):   All medical procedures and services of any type (including history, physical examination, laboratory, X ray or radiograph, and others) that are performed pertinent to the patient's reasons for the encounter, all therapeutic services performed at the time of the encounter, and all preventive services and procedures performed at the time of the encounter

Professional component (PC):   The portion of a healthcare procedure performed by a physician; also, a term generally used in reference to the elements of radiological procedures performed by a physician

Prospective payment system (PPS):   A type of reimbursement system that is based on preset payment levels rather than actual charges billed after the service has been provided; specifically, one of several Medicare reimbursement systems based on predetermined payment rates or periods and linked to the anticipated intensity of services delivered as well as the beneficiary's condition

Provider: A generic term that refers to an individual clinical practitioner or organization that delivers healthcare services

Referral: A request by a provider for a patient under the provider s care to be evaluated and/or treated by another provider

Referred outpatient: An outpatient who is provided special diagnostic or therapeutic services by a hospital on an ambulatory basis, but whose medical care remains the responsibility of the referring physician

Reimbursement: A payment for services provided

Rejection: The process of having a submitted bill not accepted by the payer, although corrections can be made and the claim resubmitted

Relative value unit (RVU): A measurement that represents the value of the work involved in providing a specific professional medical service in relation to the value of the work involved in providing other medical services; consists of these components: physician work, practice expense, and malpractice expense

Resource-based relative value scale (RBRVS): A payment system that reimburses physicians' practice expenses based on relative value for the following components: physician work, practice expense and malpractice insurance expense

Retrospective payment system: A reimbursement system based on charges calculated after the delivery of healthcare services

Revenue code: A three- or four-digit number in the chargemaster that totals all items and their charges for printing on the form used for Medicare billing

Significant procedure: A procedure that is surgical in nature or carries a procedural or an anesthetic risk or requires specialized training

Significant procedure (ambulatory payment classification): A procedure status code that constitutes the reason for the visit, dominates the time and resources rendered during the visit, and is not subject to payment reduction/discounting

Special care unit: A medical care unit in which there is appropriate equipment and a concentration of physicians, nurses, and others who have special skills and experience to provide optimal medical care for critically ill patients or continuous care for patients in special diagnostic categories

Superbill: The office form used for physician office billing that is initiated by the physician and states the diagnoses and other information for each patient encounter; often referred to as an encounter form

Supplemental medical insurance (SMI) (Medicare Part B): A voluntary medical insurance program that helps pay for physicians' services, medical services, and supplies not covered by Medicare Part A

Surgery: An umbrella term referring to the procedures of incision, excision, amputation, introduction, endoscopy, suture, and manipulation

Surgical operation: One or more surgical procedures performed at one time for one patient via a common approach or for a common purpose

Surgical procedure: Any single, separate, systematic process upon or within the body that can be complete in itself; is normally performed by a physician, dentist, or other licensed practitioner; can be performed with or without instruments; and is performed to restore disunited or deficient parts, remove diseased or injured tissues, extract foreign matter, assist in obstetrical delivery, or aid in diagnosis

Tax Equity and Fiscal Responsibility Act of 1982 (TEFRA): The federal legislation that modified Medicare's retrospective reimbursement system for inpatient hospital stays by requiring implementation of diagnosis-related groups and the acute care prospective payment system

Technical component (TC): The portion of radiological and other procedures that is facility based or nonphysician based (for example, radiology films, equipment, overhead, endoscopic suites, and so on)

Third-party payer: An insurance company (for example, Blue Cross/Blue Shield) or health-care program (for example, Medicare) that reimburses healthcare providers and/or patients for the delivery of medical services

UB-92: *See* CMS-1450

Unbundling: The practice of using multiple codes to describe the individual steps in a single procedure rather than the appropriate single code that describes all the steps of a comprehensive procedure

Undercoding: A form of incomplete documentation that results when diagnoses or procedures are missing that should be coded

Uniform Bill-92 (UB-92): *See* CMS-1450

Unlisted procedure: A CPT procedure code assigned when the provider performs a procedure or service for which there is no CPT code

Upcoding: The practice of assigning diagnostic or procedural codes that represent higher payment rates than the codes that actually reflect the services provided to patients

Usual, customary, and reasonable (UCR) charges: Charges a health plan pays a provider for a particular service or procedure, based on what is considered reasonable for that service or procedure in a community

Visit: A single encounter with a healthcare professional that includes all of the services supplied during the encounter

World Health Organization (WHO): The international organization responsible for publishing the *International Classification of Diseases, Ninth Revision, Clinical Modification* (ICD-9-CM)

Index